First Edition, 2022

Published by Savory Words Publishing
www.savorywords.com

ISBN 978-1-7377117-1-1
Printed in the United States of America

*Cover photo by Theodore C. Miller, taken with an iPhone 12 Pro Max
at Peralta Trails State Trust Land near Gold Canyon, Arizona*

OUR FIRST Discovery

MARVIN T. MILLER

TABLE OF CONTENTS

Disclaimer: The advice in this book from the Discovery Owners group and other sources are not to be taken as expert advice. Readers should seek their own professional advice or consultation.

DEDICATION

Dedicated to our beloved cats, Chicago and Nauvoo.

Chicago, who passed away on July 5, 2017, was an amazing cat, along with his sister Nauvoo, who continued to live and travel with me until her passing on September 27, 2021. The names came about because my children's mother, Jen, and I were sealed for time and eternity in the Church of Jesus Christ of Latter-day Saints in Chicago. We also toured the Nauvoo, Illinois temple. As is customary, we wore white clothing in the temples—just like our cats.

My family adopted both cats at a rescue shelter in Sioux Falls, South Dakota when the kids were toddlers. The kids, at their young ages often played roughshod with the cats, and Chicago always purred happily at this; Nauvoo, not so much.

In honor of our cat, we named the Discovery *Chicago*. I intend to dedicate the next motorcoach to Nauvoo.

Chicago and Nauvoo, we miss you terribly. Thank you for all the memories.

Chapter 1
LOVE AT FIRST SIGHT

The customer falls in love with the idea of owning a motorhome and the dream of traveling the country, and in their rush to become an owner, they become emotionally married to the idea and fail to do a proper inspection.

BILL H. MYERS,
BUYING A USED MOTORHOME, PAGE 101

There she was.

She was beautiful. A pearly white exterior with slightly faded gray swirls gracing the seventeen-year-old Fleetwood Discovery. She retailed for $155,000 brand-new, an amount out of my reach given my fixed income as a graduate student, an income occasionally supplemented by teaching Deafhood classes and workshops across the country.

The Discovery represented my soon-to-be-realized dream of pulling up my roots to travel across the country in style and relative comfort. This Discovery had it all, and I knew it after several months of hopping on and off over fifty Class A diesel pushers on used RV lots. She had beautiful hardwood flooring, a leather loveseat, a leather sofa, and a dining table with chairs.

I planned to replace one of the dining room chairs with an expensive office chair that I had gotten for a bargain at the Haworth company store for employees—my uncle Scott used to

The Discovery, parked at the Robert F. Panara Theater at the Rochester Institute of Technology in New York in May 2018.

work at the factory in Holland, Michigan. That table, with the ergonomic office chair, would serve as my writer's desk.

Not only did the Discovery have hardwood flooring—in actuality, a resilient, heavy floating laminate—she also had a new queen-sized mattress, a large wardrobe closet, a comfortable and airy shower stall, and a toilet. There was also a Corian™ kitchen countertop, double sink, extendable kitchen faucet, and a double-door refrigerator that could run on either electric or liquid propane gas (LP). That meant I could live off-grid, or boondocking as it was commonly known in the RV world, with ease. She even had an oven along with a stovetop and a convection microwave.

Plus, she smelled clean. The RV was nothing like some other Class A diesel pushers I had seen that smelled like fish, mildew, or mold, or had a stuffy weird smell that I couldn't shake. And get this... she had a Splendide 2000 washer and dryer combined unit. Basically, she had everything I wanted in a diesel pusher. She measured nearly thirty-eight feet long, and drove like a dream riding over air bags typically available only on diesel pushers. She also had a few amenities installed by the seller, including side-by-side video cameras, updated window valances and blinds, and so forth.

Theo, my oldest son, came with me to see the Discovery for sale in the Sterling, Virginia area. It was only an hour's drive from Gallaudet University where I was attending graduate school. I had been looking quite a while for a 1999 to 2002 Fleetwood Discovery for less than $35,000. Some earlier models had a liquid propane (LP) generator that I did not want. I wanted a diesel Onan 7500-watt generator, which limited my search. But I knew exactly what I wanted.

The first RV I test-drove was in December 2017 in Dillsburg, Pennsylvania: a 1999 Discovery 36T that looked to be in great condition and cost $24,900. I just couldn't finance a motorhome that old. Most lenders required motorhomes to be 2007 or newer, which meant $80,000 and an over-$1,000 monthly payment. No, thanks.

One lender did finance older models but not for full-timers, a term to describe people without a permanent home who lived in their RVs. So I couldn't buy the Discovery 36T that December. I was disappointed but kept on looking. In the ensuing five months, it was rare to find a Discovery so close to its NADA Blue Book value. Most were easily tens of thousands higher. Several that looked good were sold within a day or two, and most were from places across the country like Colorado, New Mexico, and Texas, which would have created logistical headaches for me. It was much easier to buy from a local dealer, but their asking prices were usually higher than I was willing to pay.

I had done a lot of homework. I read Bill H. Myers' *Buying a Used Motorhome* on my Kindle and I pored through several other books, including Heath and Alyssa Padgett's *A Beginner's Guide to Living* in an RV. I even copied and pasted the purchase checklist from Myers' book so I could print it out and bring it along when we inspected a motorhome in person.

One day, I saw an ad and quickly noticed that the RV was within an hour's drive. I immediately emailed the seller and set up a time to check it the same day. It was a 2001.5 Fleetwood Discovery, a mid-year model update with a major change in its engine. The update swapped out the fuel-efficient Cummins ISB 275 hp engine for the more powerful—and pricey to maintain—Caterpillar 330 hp. I did not realize the significance of this change until much later. For starters, the Caterpillar 330 hp meant it would get an average of seven and a half miles per gallon, as opposed to the 275 hp Cummins at ten to twelve miles per gallon. I later learned that Caterpillar engines are also more expensive to maintain when compared to Cummins. Caterpillar was out of the RV engine business by 2007, and Fleetwood has used only Cummins since then.

We drove up to the seller's house. There she was, sitting on the street, looking white and clean. We were smitten. I looked at Theo and said, "Wow… she looks good." Theo nodded slowly, a slow grin crawling across his face.

We walked around her and noticed that the rear tires had dry cracks on the sidewalls—a sign that we would need to replace them soon. The newer front tires were in better shape. When we went inside, the power steps extended automatically when the front door opened, adding a sense of magic to the moment. We immediately loved the hardwood flooring, clean interior, updated blinds, and how everything smelled inside— clean. The floors were sturdy. The walls were solidly in place. There was no major leak damage except for the shower ceiling.

"Oh, that… a tree fell on the Discovery, a branch went through the skylight. This happened before I bought it and the previous owner did an interesting fix on it," Steve, the seller, said. The previous owner had glued a piece of plexiglass on top of the cracked dome hole. "You can find a new replacement dome for about seventy-five dollars if you want to. For me, that fix did the trick, so it wasn't a priority."

The Discovery had a cracked skylight with a homemade fix.

I wasn't a fan of this cheap fix, so I told Theo we would replace this as soon as we could. Theo was the handy one, but I required special help when doing repairs. Yet today, more than three years later, that cheap fix is still there.

We continued our walk through the inside, oohing and aahing at the cleanliness. The space was perfect. The floor plan was brilliant. We were overwhelmed, but excited.

The inspection checklist I printed out from Bill Myers' book fell by the wayside because there was too much to look at. The microwave seemed to work fine, and the refrigerator was running cold. I was eager to test-drive this baby, and we went outside and looked underneath and into the cargo bays.

There, we found the first sign of serious concern.

Chapter 2
THE FIRST SIGN
OF RUST

[The coach needs to have] no rust—rust can be a serious problem...
If a motorhome has visible rust, it most likely has more rust that you
can't see. Just walk away from it.

BILL H. MYERS,
BUYING A USED MOTORHOME, PAGE 54

O n the passenger side, the cargo bays looked to be in excellent condition. The wiring and the fiberglass lining all looked good. As we worked our way around to the driver's side, we saw the first signs of significant rust, particularly on the left side cargo and battery bays. The rust was evident everywhere, including the slide-out compartments.

I was concerned, but Theo looked confident, nodding knowingly as he said, "We can grind these down and repaint if we need to. I think it's doable."

I told him that Myers's advice was to walk away if we saw rust. The question became: how much rust was acceptable? What kind of rust was manageable and what wasn't? I didn't know.

We looked at the air cleaner unit right above the exhaust pipe in the rearmost bay, and it didn't look good even to our untrained eyes. Even so, Theo and I didn't know the significance of a rusted air cleaner unit until it was too late.

We agreed to hire a qualified RV inspector to help us decide whether the rust was acceptable, on top of checking out the engine, transmission, the drivetrain, and everything else.

Evidence of rust was everywhere on the driver's side.

The air cleaner unit casing looked rough, and the house frame showed evidence of rust too.

As we continued our amateur inspection, Steve showed us how to maintain the house batteries through interconnected water tubes. I'm terrible with watering plants, which always die under my care. I wasn't confident about this kind of task.

After we finished the walk-around, we got inside the Discovery. Steve pulled in the slides and pulled up the hydraulic leveling jacks. He pointed out that the leveling jacks buttons didn't work properly so after the jacks were back in their place, we had to hit the power button off and back on to see if the "jacks down" light went off.

It did, so off we went. Steve drove first. Theo and I were grinning in a big way as she started up and pulled away from Steve's home, gliding over the road.

I had always wanted a diesel pusher. I looked on and off for years at MCI conversion buses because I grew up riding on an Indian Trails bus from Flint to Kalamazoo, Michigan. I sat in the front seat every chance I had, observing how bus drivers drove the forty-five-foot MCI coaches through the 150-mile journey. My grandmother Della Smith would pick me up with a huge smile and a hug at Kalamazoo bus terminal as I got off the bus. I had memorized each bus name—Indian Trails named each bus after Indian tribal chiefs, and I can still rattle off their names today: Chief Ontawa. Chief Pokagon. Chief Chebainse. Chief White Pigeon.

Being Deaf had a lot to do with riding Indian Trails buses because the state's residential school for Deaf people was in Flint, Michigan, and Aunt Laura and my grandparents lived on a sixty-eight-acre rolling hills farm near Marcellus, Michigan—a good three-hour drive one way.

My children and I come from a multi-generational Deaf family, and we are proud of our heritage and of being Deaf, with our rich signed languages and cultures. My grandparents were the first Deaf generation in my family, and they went on to have my mother, Lisa. She was born hearing and became Deaf at eight months old when an errant softball bounced and hit her head during a Deaf softball tournament in South Bend, Indiana.

She married my father, Michael, right out of high school; they met at the Michigan School for the Deaf (MSD) in Flint. My father was the first in his family born Deaf, although he had

Here, I am 10 years old, and about to ride an Indian Trails motor coach to MSD. Grandma Della is signing to me.

a younger brother who was Deaf; his other four siblings were hearing.

I became the third generation to be born Deaf and grew up as an only child. I went on to marry a Deaf woman, and we had five children together. The first, Paige Chelsea, lived only seventeen days because of a heart-wrenching, rare form of brain tumor. Our next four babies were also Deaf: Theodore, Stefania, Alexander, and Warrick.

When I was an elementary student at MSD, Aunt Laura, a senior at the same school, rode the bus from Kalamazoo to Flint each week where she stayed in the dorm. I joined her sometimes when my mother worked overtime as a master electrician at the massive General Motors factory complex in downtown Flint. So, family-owned and family-operated Indian Trails was a big part of our lives back then.

I remember an antique Chief Minnow, one of the oldest MCI Crusader buses I rode on, with a manual transmission and an enormous, springy driver's seat. Grandma Della had driven Aunt Laura and me to the Kalamazoo bus terminal. At the terminal, I saw Chief Minnow pull up and was immediately enamored with the unique, old-school look—a curved top, reminiscent of early Scenicruisers.

"Grandma, I want to ride the Chief Minnow," I said excitedly. Aunt Laura looked at the old bus with revulsion, and said, "No way! I want that new bus!"

Grandma Della pointed out we would have to get off the new bus in East Lansing and wait for the Chief Minnow, so it didn't make a difference. I grinned. The only child always gets what he wants.

But I soon regretted it. Well, sort of.

It was an experience I never wanted to repeat. Chief Minnow rode with fits and starts as the result of its manual transmission. I realized then I much preferred newer buses that rode smoother. I loved the vibration, the road feel of these buses, gliding over highways and scenic routes through the state of Michigan. With this love, it was much later when I was buying my diesel pusher that I learned the secret ingredient to the smooth riding experience of these buses: air bags. No, not the kind that protect you in accidents, but the suspension system that rides over large rubber air bags for a smoother and softer ride.

The Discovery Theo and I were looking at had a smaller version of the airbags, so the ride exhibited a similar floating, gliding characteristic that I so appreciated.

If you are looking for a high-end diesel pusher at a great price, look for a six- to eight-year-old Fleetwood Discovery with low miles and expect to find one for under $40,000. The Fleetwood Discovery is a top-of-the-line luxury diesel pusher, perfect for a family traveling long distance or full timers.

BILL H. MYERS
BUYING A USED MOTORHOME, PAGE 129

One of the reasons I did not hunt for a converted MCI coach was the limited space. Most of the conversion buses in the price range I was looking for didn't have slide-outs. I didn't want to feel cramped when my four children visited me. Fleetwood Discovery was the first one on RV expert Bill Myers's list, along with the Winnebago Journey.

This was the first time the Fleetwood Discovery appeared on my radar, and I scoured the Internet. Sure enough, I found a 1999 Discovery 36T for $24,500 on CentralPARV.com in Dillsburg, Pennsylvania, an easy two-hour drive from Washington, DC. This was the first time I drove a diesel pusher in my life, and I was over the moon. I handled the Discovery with ease out of the lot onto the state highway and back, heads over heels in love.

When I found out I couldn't finance the Discovery, despite several weeks of trying to line up personal loans and credit lines, I was dejected. But I quickly learned that finding a six- to eight-year-old Discovery for under $40,000 was next to impossible. I'd have better luck finding a pinstriped unicorn. It also was clear that Myers wrote his book not long after the 2008 stock market crash, despite his book being published in 2017. A quick search on RVT.com of 2010-2012 Discovery models turned up a range of $98,000 to $180,000. Used RV prices had more than tripled in the past few years. Many models were beautiful, and some of them even had full wall slides on the drivers' side, making a huge difference in interior space. I would have loved one of those, but my target price was $35,000 to $50,000.

In the subsequent months from December 2017 until April 2018, I went on RV hunting sprees, going to Commonwealth RV sales in Ashland, Virginia where used Class A motorhomes were all jammed in a small lot, making it so much easier for me to jump inside and check out the floor plans.

My heart sank each time as I kept smelling disgusting, fishy odors, feeling ominous creaks in the weakened floorboards, and seeing visible wall damage. None could compare to the clean condition of the first Discovery I saw, and the floor plans were mostly unacceptable. I leaned towards a 2004 Winnebago

Vectra but it didn't have a built-in washer and dryer, and there seemed to be black mold in the bathroom vent. They were asking $57,000 for her.

I hopped on and off over fifty diesel pushers, with prices going from $15,000 to $275,000. I did not like the Tiffins and Monacos. I thought they were too garish, which was also true for newer Discovery models—shiny marble tiles, everything too bright, and I worried our kids would slip on the floor after coming in from a swim. I didn't look at Newmar models; they had excellent floor plans and were well-built, yet most models I saw were out of my reach because of cost.

One thing that Myers did not mention was something I find to be a valuable resource. The Discovery Owners Association (discoveryowners.com) is an active and helpful support group with tons of valuable advice and tips; most of my questions were answered within twenty-four hours, if not within a few minutes.

I was now driving my second Discovery, and boy, she felt great. The bigger CAT 330 hp engine made a difference in speeding up and merging onto busy highways. She felt perky. In fact, she wasn't happy if I went too light on the accelerator. She would shift up strongly, and the only way to avoid that was to be more assertive in accelerating so the shifting became smoother and easier.

By the time we got back, Theo and I were ecstatic. She drove well. She smelled clean. She looked great from inside. She had no weird or unexplained vibrations. Still, we fretted about the rust. I told the seller Steve we needed to find a company to finance an RV this old. As I told him that, my stomach tightened at the prospect of losing this Discovery.

Steve nodded, saying, "No worries. I financed this through Mountain America Credit Union, and they can finance RVs this old on a case-by-case basis. You can contact them. No sweat."

The possibility floored me. Now I had the Discovery I wanted, and I seemed to have the financing lined up. I immediately called Mountain America Credit Union, and they confirmed that they could indeed finance the Discovery. I applied, eagerly anticipating the outcome. After a week of back-and-forth calls and emails, I was approved. I had to get some documents, including my driver's license, notarized because the bank was in Salt Lake City and I was in DC but officially an Indiana resident buying a motorhome in Virginia. This made things far more complicated than necessary.

I told Steve that I wouldn't be able to get a temporary license plate unless I brought the Discovery to Indiana for an in-person visual inspection of the VIN. Steve assured me he would lend me his license plates for a month or two.

I still had to jump through more hoops. The credit union approved my loan for twelve years at 8.49 percent interest. I had to come up with a large down payment that also covered the cost of the Indiana sales tax of 6 percent, which amounted to about $2,200 alone. That almost tempted me to consider trying the Montana LLC route, a loophole allowing buyers to form an LLC in Montana so they can finance and register their RVs and avoid sales taxes in their home states. However, many states have cracked down on this practice, which was a bit dishonest, anyway. I also had already been approved for the loan, so I discarded that thought quickly.

While working on the financing, I searched for a qualified RV inspector and came up with LemonSquad, which could do an inspection for $299. This paled in comparison to local certified inspectors in Maryland who quoted between $600 to $800. LemonSquad wasn't available for two more weeks, and I wanted to have the inspection done quickly. I also wasn't convinced that LemonSquad would do a good job for that price so I continued my search. I came across an RV inspection company that listed a "qualified RV mechanic" for $450, including a thorough inspection and riding along during the test drive. They didn't do a fluid analysis, which was expensive and time-consuming (about two to three weeks after drawing oil samples).

Danielle from that RV inspection company said in an email, "Also, we check the fluid levels but we found that the fluid analysis weren't cost-effective for our customers; they take several weeks to get the results back and they didn't provide much value."

Hmm. Okay, then.

The best part was they had someone available to look at the Discovery within a couple of days. The inspector, John, went to look at the Discovery, although I couldn't be there in person given the traffic and my classes.

I was getting excited. The financing was mostly in place. I had found a qualified RV inspector within a week. Steve said he had another interested buyer, but I told him to hold off the other person. I was feeling a little pressure because I had seen several Discovery units snapped up within days, if not hours, so I knew I couldn't just sit back and take my time. Theo and I waited with such excitement and anticipation for the inspection report.

Caveat emptor. Buyer beware.

AN OLD LATIN SAYING

The report finally came. "The rust was not severe. It is from a salt state. That is to be expected. Everything else looks good," John, the inspector, texted me.

The salt state comment made sense because this Discovery was first sold in Vermont, then later in New York and Virginia. She had around 109,000 miles and 1,440 hours on her, which meant the previous owners used her regularly—a good thing. Well-maintained diesel pushers are known to last half a million to a million miles before needing an engine rebuild. Bruce Plumb informed me just before this book went to press that our "medium duty" diesel engines have a B50 life (half will fail by then) of around 400,000 miles, not a million.

I was elated and couldn't wait for my copy of the inspection report. It arrived the next day via email. Theo and I immediately pored through the report, and there were no red flags other than a nonfunctional bathroom vent and washer and dryer.

I contacted Steve, and he replied, "I'm puzzled about the bathroom vent because it works fine. All you have to do is to switch on the bathroom wall, and it will go. As for the washer and dryer, yeah, the unit itself works fine if connected to shore power. I suspect there is a problem in a junction box somewhere. I can show it to you."

I thought to myself, *Well… my mother is a retired master electrician, and she can help me fix this.* This would give me some leverage if I offered to take care of the electrical issue and replace the four rear tires. The asking price for the RV was $38,000, so I offered $31,000, and he countered with $32,000 plus taxes. I took it, and Steve agreed to install the remaining flooring in the bedroom floor engine cover and repair the eighty-gallon freshwater tank drain. I knew I would have to buy four new tires for the rear axle as soon as possible, and they were not cheap. To stick with the original Michelin tires—a rather large tire, so four of them would have cost $2,880 mounted and balanced. Yikes!

Steve suggested that I check out simpletire.com and order cheap Chinese-made tires, but I wasn't willing to do that. Later, I found a good deal on four Yokohoma 270/80/r22.5 tires for $1,250 shipped to Rice Tire, a commercial truck tire place nearby. They installed, balanced, and disposed of the old tires for $275.

Looking back on this, I went too easy on Steve. I should have asked him to spring for new tires and fix the washer and dryer. I did foresee some expenses that would come with buying a seventeen-year-old motorhome and working to mitigate the rust in several areas. But that didn't even scratch the surface of what was to come.

The inspector also noted that the belts and hoses were "old but good," so I did not give this another thought until we picked her up and brought her home.

Chapter 3
BRINGING HER HOME

APRIL 9, 2018

- Inspection report: **$450.00**
- Down payment on $34,000 loan
  (with Indiana sales tax): **$4,000.00**
- Loan: **$30,000** for 12 years at 8.47%
- Monthly payment: **$341.00**
- Credit score: **715**

The day finally came after two weeks of constant miscommunication with Mountain America Credit Union and repeated visits to the notary public. I had to cancel my camping reservations at Assateague National Seashore because of the constant delays, and the sites filled up as the month of May pulled closer. I wanted to see the Discovery parked by the oceanfront and watch the wild horses roam. Not just yet, it seemed.

Steve and I agreed that we would meet at the Reston Metro station so Theo and I could easily ride the subway there and then drive the Discovery back to Gallaudet.

On Wednesday, April 11, 2018, I was filled with happy anticipation as I awakened. My first diesel pusher, my first motorhome! I looked forward to driving her all over the good ole U.S. of A., seeing the sights and giving presentations and workshops on Deafhood, positive aspects of being Deaf, and promoting healing within our Deaf communities across the country. This is critical because nearly 80 percent of Deaf children are mainstreamed and are the only Deaf kid in their entire school. Many of them grow up without ever seeing Deaf adults as their role models, and a good number of them believe that they will become hearing when they graduate, or worse, die, simply because they've never seen Deaf adults. This is an epidemic of psychological, social, spiritual and emotional damage that we continue to see across the country, all under the guise of inclusion and equality.

This oppression is something that drives me with a passion, and I wanted the Discovery to be an essential part of what I would call the Deafhood Discovery Tour of the United States, Canada, and Central America.

Theo and I got on the Gallaudet University shuttle bus to Union Station and hopped on the red line to Metro Center before swapping to the silver line to Reston. We came out of the station to a beautiful, sunny day. Steve pulled up in the Discovery, and we were thrilled to see her and take over the wheel. We climbed into the RV, and Steve brought us to an empty parking lot. He took us through the final run-through of things such as battery maintenance, battery readouts , and where the LP gas connector, the inverter reset buttons, and the LP, black, gray and freshwater tanks were.

Steve handed me the keys and shook my hand. The Discovery was now ours. With a signed agreement for the use of his license plates until I got Indiana license plates, we were all good to go. I pulled the RV out of the parking lot and started driving back. I was slightly nervous about driving such a huge rig into a busy city with its infamously horrible roads. But I told myself if there were hundreds of city buses and intercity buses traversing through DC easily, I could do it.

The trip back was easy and smooth. We stopped at Pupatella, our favorite Neapolitan pizza place, in North Arlington,

My family with the 2001 Fleetwood Discovery by the front steps of the iconic Gallaudet University Tower Clock. L-R: Alec (17), Stefania (19), me, Theo (20), and Warrick (14).

Virginia. We couldn't stop grinning. Theo said, "I can't believe how good this feels. Steve told me that this RV was in bad shape before he bought it… and this looks good."

I paused. "What do you mean?"

"He did a lot of good work on the RV… it was in bad shape before," Theo said.

At this moment, being overwhelmed by so many moving parts of a large diesel pusher, I had forgotten one crucial detail as advised by Bill Myers: ask for detailed maintenance records. This was a mistake on my part. *Stupid*, I muttered to myself.

When you buy a used motorhome, insist on having complete (or near complete) maintenance records showing that oil, fluids, lubrication, parts and others have been replaced regularly. If you can't get that, WALK THE @#$% AWAY.

Again: do not skip this step. Ask for maintenance records. If there is none, *walk away*.

I gamely nodded to Theo, "You're right. Steve did pretty good work here, making her beautiful… the flooring, the blinds and valances and nice add-ons such as side-by-side cameras, Fantastic Vent fans, a new queen mattress."

We pulled up to the main entrance of Gallaudet University, and I was filled with excited pride. My kids were eagerly awaiting us—a welcoming committee of sorts. We took a victory lap around the campus, stopping in front of Tower Clock and taking family photos.

My daughter Stefania looked around inside and declared that she loved the Discovery. She suggested that we redo the walls and repaint the cabinetry to something brighter. She didn't like the china blue-on-white pattern of the living area valances. I responded that the decor wasn't a priority for me; I wanted to spend money on solar panels, better batteries, and other stuff so I could boondock for longer periods of time without relying on the generator.

Ah, the generator. We brought her home on a slightly more than a one-fourth full tank of diesel fuel. She had a ninety-gallon tank capacity, so she easily had over 250 miles in her.

No worries.

With permission from the campus police, we parked the Discovery in front of Kendall Demonstration Elementary School in a space reserved for school team buses. We backed her in gently and got the slides out so we could show it to our friends. Both slides came out easily, but I realized I had forgotten to level the RV first. We leveled her while the slides were already out, which wasn't a very good idea. We also forgot to lower the air bags before leveling her.

BANG!

We were startled, having no idea where this noise came from. Being Deaf, we were keenly sensitive to vibrations, but we had a hard time locating them. We took a walk around and looked for signs of problems. The level jacks were on ground, and they were fine. But whoa! The rear left tires were clear off the ground.

There she is, parked in front of our fifth-floor apartment overlooking the rooftop of Kendall Demonstration Elementary School.

These leveling jacks are powerful. They can easily lift a 26,000-pound RV off the ground. We had to redo the leveling, letting out the airbags this time before we closed the slides. Theo was in the back of the coach, monitoring how the leveling jacks were coming down—slowly. We didn't know if this was normal until later. We finally got her level.

Suddenly, Theo ran to the front and signed frantically, "I smell something burning in the back!" Alarmed, I followed him out to the back, and he was right. Something was burning.

Did we blow the hydraulic fluid in the jacks? We decided to shut her down for the night. It was too dark to see anything. We sat inside our RV, appreciating the interior and discussing improvements. We started the Onan 7500-watt diesel generator, and she ran smoothly for the next half hour. We called it a night.

It was a thrill seeing the Discovery from our apartment. I beamed with such pride, but also was worried we might have blown something serious.

The next day, in broad daylight, I was eager to take another look. Theo and I immediately went under her and found that engine oil had burst all over the engine, dripping onto the pavement. I was devastated that there was yet another setback. We checked her engine oil levels, which looked fine. We tried to figure out what happened, and decided to take up the floors in the bedroom and closet to look at the engine.

It was a mess. Oil burst patterns were all over the floor underside, so we carefully wiped them down with paper towels. We both decided we needed help, so I texted our friend Troy Stevenson, who worked for the Gallaudet facilities department. He graciously agreed to come over during his break. He pointed out that the air compressor intake hose had been broken for a long time—not a recent break—and pointed to a specific oil hose that was leaking.

"You have to replace that hose, and have that intake hose reattached," he said. Apparently, it was a high-pressure oil line, and someone installed the wrong kind of hose. I called around for mechanic shops and I talked with Johnson Freightliner in DC. When I said I had a Caterpillar engine in my RV, they said, "What? You have a CAT engine in an RV? Wow. I thought they all ran on Cummins engines. Sorry, but we can't look at it for another two weeks."

Ugh. I called Alban CAT Power and spoke with the service manager Bob Miller. He said they could look at it the next day, as long as the hose wasn't producing a huge stream of oil. We tried to tape the hose with high pressure tape, and it held. With that done, we ran through the RV checking for other issues.

We tried to start her generator. She struggled to start up before giving up. Now the generator wasn't starting?! I texted Steve, who said it was because the fuel tank was too low at a quarter full. *Oh.*

I took her out and filled her up at a nearby gas station to the tune of nearly two hundred dollars and brought her back home. We leveled her again, but the generator still struggled to start before it quit again. I was aghast.

Theo and Alec worked together on the generator, priming it and starting it several times. I was fuming by now, so I had to take a breather. After some time, Theo came over with good news: the generator was now running smoothly. I asked him what he did, and he said he just kept priming and starting the generator with ample time in between.

Apparently, the fuel line for the diesel generator went into the same diesel tank as the Discovery's CAT engine, and the factory set fuel lines higher so the running generator wouldn't accidentally empty the tank, stranding the Discovery in the middle of nowhere, a safety feature.

After the fix was in place, we drove her around the campus with Theo in the back to make sure it wasn't leaking too much. Theo came up to the front and said she was fine to drive and then put the floor back in place. Theo saw his friend while I was driving, so I told the friend to hop on the RV and join us for the short ride around the campus. As the friend tried to get onboard, the front door lock jammed. We were stuck inside. I had to circle back and park her again, and I was beyond frustrated. Oil hose, generator, and now this? What the hell did we get ourselves into? Just moments later, we also noticed that our microwave's touchpad was on the fritz.

I took a deep sigh. This wasn't good.

Chapter 4
THE FIRST
REPAIR BILL

drove the Discovery to Elkridge, Maryland, approximately forty-five minutes from Washington, DC, as Theo followed me in our 1997 Honda Civic. Theo observed that the RV engine exhaust had produced minimal smoke, but she mostly ran cleanly. There was no loss of power while driving her, and she was peppy in her acceleration and could pass other cars on the road. I still drove conservatively, mindful of the oil hose leak. I prayed that we would make it all the way there.

We pulled into the huge lot of Alban CAT Power and parked her by the service bay door. Bob Miller said they would look at her and let me know what they found. We went back home, with Theo driving. I also learned that there were no free estimates in the world of diesel engine maintenance; the labor rate was $115 an hour.

Oof. I was hoping the cost of replacing the oil hose would be a few hundred dollars. How hard could it be, right? Just take out the old hose and replace it, and fix the air compressor intake hose… an hour or two of work, right? *Right?!*

I also asked that the engine oil be changed. Meanwhile, I emailed the RV inspection company.

Danielle,

I hate to ask but I am asking for some kind of compensation—the inspector didn't catch that a hose connecting to the air compressor had been cut off for quite a while (months). We discovered that when the high-pressure oil hose burst a leak when we ran leveling jacks on the first night we took delivery. The inspector said the hoses were "old, but good" so he gets a pass on that… but to miss a broken hose connection to the air compressor? Ouch. The RV is now at Alban CAT Power service in Elkridge, MD and they have quoted us $1,315 repair costs ($431 in parts for the oil hose and air compressor hose plus $800+ for labor). They will steam clean the engine and clean up some rust, then test for further leaks anywhere else before doing the oil change which we have to do so since the oil loss… so I will pay $350 on top of this.

I could have known of this and negotiated a lower price with the seller. :-(

Marvin

Danielle replied quickly:

Marvin,

Thank you for bringing this to my attention. I never want my customers to be unhappy of their inspections, so I took the liberty in seeking an answer from the inspector's supervisor. She said she's assuming you are speaking of the hose connecting to the air compressor for the hydraulic leveling jacks, and depending on the RV, there can be multiple air hoses/line connections to its compressor, most of which are not completely visible unless unit is placed on a special lift or some tear down. However, the leveling jacks were operated during the inspection, so if it's a single air hose connection to the compressor, then it had to be connected, otherwise the jack(s) would not have operated (pix of jacks up and down on report). If the hose connection you are referring to is not what she assumed, please let me know so we can get this straightened out.

Warmest Regards,
Danielle

I wasn't sure what the air compressor was for until I learned later that it had nothing to do with the leveling systems and everything to do with air brakes and air bags on the chassis. A few days later, Bob Miller called and emailed me a picture of the front left wheel seal leaking. I sent another email to Danielle.

April 16, 2018

Hi,

The service has replaced both hoses, and I'm waiting for them to come back and

The seal was clearly broken, the leaking fluids visible from the outside. How did the inspector not catch this?

explain what the hose connection to inflow valve of the air compressor—what it does. Once I know, I will get back to you.

And there's one more thing they found—after replacing the hoses, inspecting other belts and hoses and all looks good—is that the left front wheel is leaking. Here's a photo. They're telling me it would take them two hours at $115 an hour labor to take it apart just to give me an estimate. They will do that tomorrow. I don't know how much this repair will set me back on top of an approximately $1,400 repair (not including the oil change).

Here's the picture. I believe the inspector should have caught this. I'm really disappointed.

Marvin

A quick reply came back from Danielle, claiming that some seepage was normal.

Hi Marvin,

Thank you for bringing this to my attention; the picture does not display a leak, but what appears to be normal seepage. This is on the inside of the wheel which is not visible without the RV being placed on a lift, raised, and a creeper used. There was no wheel bearing or axle noise experienced during the test drive. This is not something that would be visible during an inspection.

Warmly,
Danielle

I came back to do some title paperwork, and I got a Howard County police officer to fill out the VIN inspection for the Indiana Bureau of Motor Vehicles title application. I spoke with the mechanic, Matt, and he showed me how bad the leak was. They already had taken off the brake drums and pads, and he showed me the drum lining, which was all cracked because of a broken seal, allowing oil to seep inside.

I told Matt that the inspection company claimed that some seepage was normal, and he laughed in my face, saying, "No

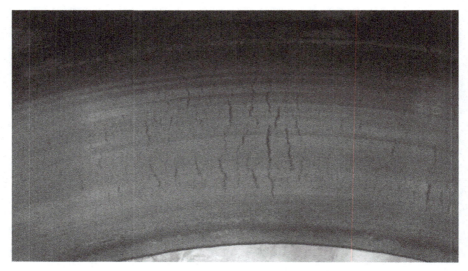

Cracks were visible in the brake drum lining from a broken seal, allowing oil to seep inside.

way. If your RV was a commercial Department of Transportation truck, I would never allow you to leave with that broken seal."

So, $655.33 for the front left brake drum and pad replacement along with new seals since the ball bearings were still good. But seriously, $655.33 just for one set of brake drums and pads? I was used to paying less than that for the entire set of front brakes on my van.

While at the shop, I asked Matt for his opinion on the condition of my CAT 330 hp engine. "I think the engine is running good and strong. I don't feel that there's any issue with that. Gaskets are leaking because it's a seventeen-year-old engine so maybe it's time to replace them," he said. In their steam cleaning of the engine, they had found several oil leaks in various places. They told me they would give me an estimate to replace all the gaskets.

The total repair bill in replacing both oil hose and air compressor intake hose, along with the left front wheel seal and brake was $2,464.51. That was my first bill, and I felt like I had been punched in the gut. I knew I had to buy new rear tires, so that alone was expensive. But now this?

Even so, that gut punch was nothing compared to what was to come.

A few days later, after picking up my Discovery, Alban CAT Power sent me an estimate for replacing all the gaskets and taking out my radiator for a deep cleaning.

The estimate was $13,042.15.

Chapter 5
A NIGHT OF
COLD SWEATS

APRIL 19-22, 2018

- Previous total: **$4,450**
- Alban CAT Power for brakes, oil hose, and air compressor intake hose: **$2,464.51**
- Current total: **$6,914.51**
- Credit score: **705**

Over thirteen thousand dollars? I was flabbergasted. I texted my dad with the estimate, with only one line: "This is a joke."

"Ouch," he replied.

That night, I woke up in the middle of the night in a cold sweat, wondering what I had gotten myself into. I knew I couldn't just sell the RV because the engine condition was questionable with oil leaks everywhere. I was stressed.

Why didn't the inspector catch the leaky front wheel? Why didn't he see any clues about leaking oil gaskets everywhere? The inspection report showed he took pictures of the engine underside, and it was dry at that time.

I even called the national CAT RV support line and spoke with Grant about the leaky gaskets all over the engine. Could this have been a result of overfilling the oil tank when Alban CAT changed out the oil? Especially after I caught on the invoice that they put in twenty-six quarts of oil when the Discovery took only twenty-two quarts (and it turns out the tank really takes about nineteen quarts, I learned much later). I was quite upset.

Grant replied, "No, that isn't even likely. The worst it could do is make a mess in the slobber tube where excess oil would be sent out onto pavement. What's more likely is that your seller steam-cleaned the engine before inspection."

I was taken aback. I did not think Steve would do that. Then I became outraged and ran through my options. A lawsuit against the inspector or the inspection company? Perhaps small claims court, which maxed out at $5,000 in Maryland and Virginia, while in California where the RV inspection company was located, it maxed out at $10,000. Could I try the same case in Maryland and California and get a combined $15,000 in damages?

My friend, Kelby Brick, an attorney who serves as the executive director of the Maryland Office of Deaf and Hard of Hearing, wasn't so sure I could do this. Neither did the owners on the Discovery Owners Association email list. Kelby came to my home every Tuesday evening after teaching his class at Gallaudet, and we shared a beer or two, discussed our families, our lives, and our dreams and plans.

The Tuesdays with Kelby—I know how I'm totally aping Mitch Albom here—was one of the best things I had in a long time. I asked Kelby, "So, you are telling me that the inspector can produce a fictional document and get away with it?"

He grimaced, feeling my pain. I was pissed.

I wanted to find another way to fix these gasket leaks, preferably by working with a lower labor rate—maybe an independent truck shop somewhere in the Midwest. I found later that we could clean the radiator and charged air cooler (CAC), a smaller radiator that cools turbo diesel, that sit side-by-side facing the rear by hosing Simple Green and water mixture through the radiator fan while the engine was on high idle. I got the instruction sheet from the Discovery Owners Association group email list; this list came in handy later.

I wasn't sure about the exact mechanics of doing this, and there wasn't a faucet and hose available anywhere on campus. So this had to wait. But I finally had the Discovery back, and we could go out camping for the first time… a shakedown cruise of sorts, going through each function as we slept as a family of four (Alec decided not to go with us this time). We went to Bethany Beach, Delaware and got a site at Delaware Seashore State Park—basically, a little more than a glorified parking lot—but it was so close to the inlet and the ocean that the trip was well worth our time.

Chapter 6
OUR FIRST FAMILY CAMPING TRIP

With the new brakes and hoses in place, my kids and I were raring to go camping. I ordered a four-bike hitch from etrailer.com to hold our three Sondors electric bikes, which came to $564.60. Our bikes—both thin and fat—fit the hitch perfectly and securely. We even brought our seventeen-year-old white cat, Nauvoo, named after a picturesque Mormon town along the Mississippi River in Illinois. As we loaded our refrigerator, we noticed it was struggling to stay cool. Another potential issue, even though the inspection had showed that the refrigerator was fine.

I knew we had to keep the RV as level as possible so the gas absorption refrigerator would continue to work properly, and I worried that we might have screwed things up by allowing the refrigerator to operate while she wasn't level. But the refrigerator ran fine while the coach was in motion because the fluids were moving around constantly. Okay, good. We crossed our fingers and headed to cross the long Chesapeake Bay Bridge. I stopped by Target to shop for additional food items and camping chairs.

Theo and I took turns driving, and he was proving to be an excellent driver. He loved driving the Discovery and we often talked about how great she felt while driving. We had to adjust our driving habits, making acceleration more assertive than we usually did to make the transmission shift smoother. Later, my friend Ric Marcus wisely remarked, "Lose a few dollars in fuel

In front of the Indian River bridge at Delaware Seashore State Park, Theo and Warrick set things up.

mileage or cause more problems with the transmission—what's the repair bill for that?"

Good point.

We drove through Delaware in the dark, and the Discovery's new LED headlights, a selling point by Steve, turned out to be one of the best features. The lights made everything more visible, even better than high beam lights.

When we arrived at the Delaware Seashore state park, we didn't really know what to do. There was nobody at the office. After a quick reading of signs, we pulled an envelope from a box on the entrance office for payment and picked out a site without a reservation sticker. We leveled the RV and moved the slides out before hooking her up to a 50-amp outlet and water. We decided to hook up the sewer later.

Right before we left, we had added a good amount of bleach into the fresh water tank and ran all the faucets and toilet until we smelled bleach. We then let the forces of driving slosh the liquid around in the plumbing system. The next day, we ran

All set for our first night!

the water and drained everything. She was clean and ready to go.

We jackknifed the sofa into a flattened position easily along with the loveseat. The front passenger seat swiveled around and was level with the loveseat, making

Warrick and me in front of the Indian River bridge in Delaware.

it easier for the taller kids to sleep in. We added a twin-sized air mattress for Theo in the middle of the kitchen and living room area. We were comfortable.

I took my first shower, and it was amazing. As a six-foot guy, I had plenty of room and hot water, and it was easy to move around in the bathroom and bedroom. I had seriously considered removing the shower stall, the sink, and the dividing wall to put in a tub along with a movable sink right above it.

Warrick and Theo chat on the road.

I can't emphasize enough how I love taking long baths, reading on my Kindle. I drooled when I saw that Foretravel was selling a new model of their IH-45 Class A Diesel pushers, the Luxury Villa Spa.

There was a jacuzzi complete with HDTV and awesome ambience. I absolutely loved that. The only catch? The price. Even at 32 percent off the sale price, it was $839,999. A tad bit out of my reach, methinks. Perhaps one day. Always good to set life goals, you know?

Although my kids and I had discussed the feasibility of installing a bathtub, the first set of repair bills gave us a harsh reality check. I hadn't even gotten to upgrading the batteries or an inverter and adding solar panels. I was mulling all of that while taking my first hot shower in the Discovery, and the sunrise was beautiful. We went for a ride on our electric bikes, and the ocean breeze

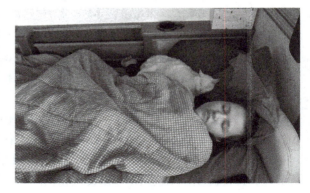

Nauvoo sleeps with Stefania on our first night in the Discovery.

Nauvoo enjoys the beach, a rare treat for our beloved family cat.

along with the pristine beach was a perfect introduction to the RV life.

The kids and I went out for a walk with our cat, Nauvoo, who walked freely and slowly. She seemed terrified of the crashing ocean waves, quickly making her way back inland. We were just happy to walk with her, freely roaming. She was an indoors cat almost all her life, along with her late brother, Chicago, who delighted us with his playfulness. It was gratifying to see her outside and sniffing her heart out.

Nauvoo seemed to adjust to the RV life with ease, but she still wouldn't sit or lay down on the expansive front dash area. She was scared of other vehicles seemingly coming at her.

Chapter 7
OFF TO ROCHESTER, NY

Alec and me in front of one of the Finger Lakes in upstate New York.

After the beautiful weekend at Delaware Seashore State park, we got back home without any trouble. We loved the brief taste of RV life and wanted more. I was scheduled to give Deafhood presentations at the Rochester School for the Deaf in New York on April 26. Initially, I had planned to go up there by myself for some me time. Yet I wanted Alec to experience RV life since he couldn't join us the previous weekend, so I asked him to join me. I was glad when he agreed. I wanted some father-and-son bonding time, and what a better way to do that than to be in the Discovery and seeing sights?

Alec and I discussed possible stops, including going to the National Technical Institute of the Deaf's performance of *Oz* on

Friday night; the college is one of nine at the Rochester Institute of Technology. We considered visiting the Knoebels Family Park in Elysburg, Pennsylvania on the way back down, and I wanted to drive through the Finger Lakes area.

We left for Rochester, making our way through Baltimore and Erie, Pennsylvania. We paused at a truck stop to make sure the tires were correctly inflated. Truck stops don't really have stand-alone air inflators for trucks—not that I could find, anyway—and the ones at regular gas stations only go up to 75 psi. My Discovery tires needed 95 to 110 psi. We went back on the road and stopped at a rest area for the night.

It was at this moment that I realized we might need a tire pressure monitoring system, costing anywhere from $300 to $600, depending on the brand and features. This is yet another often-overlooked cost to consider when buying a diesel pusher for the first time. But I was tired and wanted to sleep on it. Fortunately, as Deaf people, sounds don't bother us, so we slept like babies that night, especially in the very dark RV. This was true for any place we parked, even Walmart parking lots.

As we were driving to Rochester School for the Deaf (RSD) located downtown, my contact at RSD informed me that I could not park the RV at the school. *Damn.* I pulled over at a scenic lookout area and checked for nearby parking or even a Walmart where someone could pick us up. The Google ratings for that Walmart had us concerned about our safety, so I told my contact we would find on-street parking next to the campus. But I was told the area wasn't safe, either.

"I don't really have much of a choice," I replied.

"Hold on," my contact texted.

All right. We drove straight to the school, and they let us park on campus with permission. *Whew!* I realized at that moment that I needed to be more prepared for visiting Deaf schools across the country and parking overnight, especially with background check requirements for us to be near students and parking issues. Safety first, after all.

As we drove through downtown, we had to make several detours due to low bridge clearances. The Discovery measured twelve feet and one inch tall, and the bridges were eleven feet and six inches, so we had to work our way around. I felt adrenaline rush through my body each time I encountered a bridge, scanning for signs with clearance measurements. Some weren't posted clearly, and that created some heart-pounding moments as I slowly drove under overpasses. And there were quite a few of them in Rochester, unlike in the DC area.

We arrived and parked. We met with the school director, and were led inside where I gave three presentations that day—first to the middle and high school students with some staff and teachers, second to the teachers and staff, and then finally to the RSD community. It was the first time Alec saw my Deafhood presentation, and I was pleased. He was ready to go back to the RV after the first presentation, though. Guess he didn't like reruns.

We headed out to look for a place to park overnight. The nearby campgrounds weren't open for the season yet, so we found a Wegman's grocery store, and we asked the manager for permission to park. She told us where to park, and we picked up some food. We set up for the night, and even had the slides out as well. Some say you shouldn't have your slides out if you are overnighting at a parking lot, and I tend to agree. This was an exception, though.

We got comfortable and slept well that night.

The next day, we drove around looking for places to park so we could take a bike ride. We found a spot overlooking Lake Ontario, but unfortunately, it was quite cold outside and we didn't have proper outerwear. Instead, we walked around for a bit, and headed to REI to buy some gloves and hats. But first, we

The Discovery at National Technical Institute of the Deaf; Alec is walking towards me.

went to the Ontario Beach state park and biked a little bit and had a bit of sushi nearby.

At this point, we did a walk-around of our RV to make sure the tires were in good shape. As we unloaded our bikes off the rack, we noticed how grimy the vehicle was, covered in a fine layer of engine oil that apparently was leaking. I also noticed that the same layer of oil was all over the back.

I said to Alec, "Damn it. This means I really need to address the oil leaks. This can't be good for the engine in the long run, and it's messy to deal with."

Alec agreed. "But does that mean you will have to spend $13,000 to get this done?"

I groaned. "There has to be another way. There has to be."

We wiped down our bikes with paper towels, and off we went to the pier It was a simple, enjoyable, and relaxing afternoon—just what the doctor ordered.

It was getting late, and it was nearly time to make our way to the NTID Robert F. Panara Theater for the performance of *Oz*. We stopped by Costco to get some diesel, and again, the price tag was massive. We then went to REI next door and bought the gloves and caps we needed.

As we drove onto campus, we felt a certain amount of pride driving the RV. We easily found a parking spot, and we went to watch the play. *Oz* was incredible. The cast was excellent, especially *Deaf Life* publisher Matthew S. Moore as the Wicked Witch and Miss Gulch; he absolutely nailed that character. Alec and I looked at each other in amazement as Alec said, "Wow, he's good." Patrick Graybill, the legendary actor and translator, also was terrific in his role.

At Seneca Lake along Route 14 in upstate New York.

The stage was beautifully designed by Rochester native Ethan Sinnott, a professor in the theater department at Gallaudet University. He sat in the audience right next to us, and I told him he did a fantastic job. We saw a few friends who were surprised by our appearance. We explained that we had kept our trip a bit low-profile so I could focus on the necessities of preparing the vehicle; we were still in our shakedown cruise mode.

We spent the night in a rest area just before the exit that took us through one of the renowned Finger Lakes, passing through Geneva, New York. We had an incredible view of Seneca Lake on our left side as we drove all the way down on Route 14.

I stopped at a local brewery, Starkey's Lookout, and tried a flight of their beers as well as an appetizer while Alec napped in the Discovery. He was happy to just lounge around. I felt pretty good knowing that I could explore while he was comfortable in our "home." This was one of the many advantages of owning a motorhome: we were never far from home, even though we hadn't really moved in yet. Our refrigerator wasn't working properly. The microwave was on the fritz with a faulty touchscreen. Oil was still dripping slowly, and we added about one quart of oil for every five hundred miles driven.

We continued our way down through the winding state highway appreciating the beautiful views, and the large windshield and windows on the Discovery made these views extra special. We eventually arrived at Knoebels Family Campground. We pulled up next to a water-filling station and filled her up while I checked ourselves in. We got a campsite way back, the furthest possible point away from the amusement park. I wasn't thrilled about that, but the campground looked full. Alec and I were excited; this felt like a real camping experience to us. Woodsy, hilly, rustic, and we could easily see the amusement park, which also looked family-oriented, not like those kind-of-sterile wide-open spaces in the well-run Cedar Fair parks. I turned to Alec and said, "This is amazing. I've never seen an amusement park like this—so much character."

We drove up the hills then down the narrow road to our first campsite, and a truck was parked in our spot. The RV next door claimed that space for themselves, and I noticed that the site wasn't really level. We tried another site nearby, where we backed in and set the leveling jacks down. The jacks went through the soft ground. We returned to the office and asked for a different, more level site. They gave us one down the road, and as we went there, we drove past a large Forest River Georgetown motorhome that was leveled completely clear off her front wheels by a foot and a half, easily.

I stared at the Georgetown RV, slack-jawed. Alec looked at me, "Are they for real?" I found myself hoping we would never be in such an extreme situation. Fortunately, our new site was just perfect. We backed her in and leveled her—with wooden boards this time to prevent the jacks from going through the

Alec building a campfire at Knoebels RV Park in Elysburg, Pennsylvania.

soft ground—and it worked like a charm. We set up the awning, chairs, and everything. And even better, we started our very first campfire.

But before we started the campfire, we ran to the amusement park and checked things out. We found out we didn't need to pay for admission. We just had to pay for the rides, so we got a sheet of tickets for a few rides before the park closed for the day. We enjoyed ourselves, and the next day, Knoebels ran a buy-one, get-one half-off deal so it was even better. This was probably why the campground was nearly full.

Upon return to our site, we built a campfire according to the Upside-Down fire method[1] popularized by Tim Ferriss, author of *The Four-Hour Body*. He shared how to build a trouble-free and maintenance-free fire that would last a long time and reduce itself to mere ashes at the end. We enjoyed the toasty warm, colorful campfire.

On Monday morning, after agreeing that the site was a must-return, we cleaned up and checked out before making

[1] http://www.tim.blog/2009/02/02/how-to-build-an-upside-down-fire

our way home. We ran into heavy winds, and it was my first time driving a large coach through fourteen-miles-per-hour crosswinds. This took a lot of effort.

Chapter 8
TIRES AND
VIRGINIA BEACH

MAY 1, 2018

- Previous total: **$6,914.51**
- Four Yokohoma tires from simpletire.com: **$1,286.92**
- Refund for delayed shipping: **$-128.69**
- Balance, mount, and dispose of tires at Rice Tire: **$275.00**
- Current total: **$8,426.74**
- Credit score: **700**

Just before our trip to Rochester, I had found four Yokohoma tires through simpletire.com for $1,286.92, a steal compared to what four original equipment Michelin XRV tires would have cost (around $2,700). I had the tires shipped to a nearby Rice Tire shop and brought my Discovery there after the New York trip. They balanced and mounted the tires and disposed of the old ones for $275.

I later realized I forgot to check the manufacturing date on all four tires. The tires were mounted with their DOT labels facing each other on the inside, making it next to impossible to find out how new (or old) these tires were. They did look new and fresh, but I didn't want tires that had been sitting on the warehouse floor for a long time.

While waiting at Rice Tire, two MCI buses pulled up to have their tires changed. I took the liberty of looking at their tires, and theirs were much bigger than mine. I also took a look at the underside of MCI, and their air bags were easily twice the size of my Discovery along with the tag axle, making this bus a much smoother and softer ride. Driving an MCI bus one day is on my bucket list, for sure.

Two peas in a pod: Theo and the CAT 330 hp 3126B diesel engine.

When we came back to Gallaudet, Theo and I wanted to look at the engine and see if we could see how bad the oil leaks were. It wasn't pretty. We also wanted to see if we should replace the air cleaner unit. After the inspection, we determined that, yes, it was time to replace the unit even though the air cleaner gauge was showing as not dirty. We didn't have any record of when the unit was replaced. I called Johnston Freightliner in DC to order an air cleaner, and I had to make two trips because they didn't have it in stock as promised on phone.

I was ready to bite someone's head off there, but on my second trip, I picked up a large cardboard box containing the filter. I also picked up black rubber gloves so we could keep our hands clean. But we couldn't work on the air filter until after our Virginia Beach trip. I was also wrapping up my first semester internship teaching Deafhood at Gallaudet University. So the air filter replacement had to wait just a bit.

My friend Ric Marcus flew in from Grand Rapids, Michigan to join me on the drive south to Virginia Beach for a Deafhood 101 class. The course is a twenty-hour workshop for Deaf adults, a consciousness-raising seminar that examines the oppression we experience as Deaf people and why, and some of the first steps in healing ourselves and our peoples. The course typically runs on Thursday and Friday nights from 5:30 to 9:30 p.m. then all day on Saturday and Sunday. Ric had wanted to take the class for years, so I was thrilled to have him.

I had a reservation at the Virginia Beach KOA, only a mile away from the beach, so we also brought my electric bikes. It was going to be a wonderful time. We made our way down on Thursday early afternoon, and I had to be sure we left on time because I-95 would literally be a parking lot for hours. Upon arrival at the KOA site, we were guided to our drive-through site. The sites were set up quite close to each other, unlike the state park campgrounds, so it felt like we were in a city of sorts with very little space. At least this place had a fire pit. The Thursday night class went smoothly.

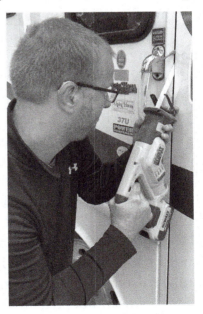

On Friday, disaster struck. The door lock broke again. We couldn't even open the door. We couldn't get inside. The windows were all sealed up.

"Crap," I said to Ric. I thought the lock had been fixed. It seemed like things kept breaking down one after another. I wanted a trouble-free trip just for once.

After some discussion on what we could do, Ric suggested

Within ten minutes, Ric powered through cutting the striker bolt that held the jammed door lock in place.

that we ask the KOA staff for a reciprocating saw to cut through the door latch. They sent a maintenance employee who told us that he couldn't do it for us due to liability issues. No problem. We would do it ourselves. Ric stepped up, but it took us a while to finally saw through that striker bolt, damaging the rubber seals. It wasn't pretty but we could get inside. All weekend, we had to rely on the deadbolt to keep the door latched.

I ordered a new door latch kit from Fleetwood REV Parts, and it wasn't cheap. Ric and I went out for a bike ride that night to the beach, and the sight of ocean waves helped soothe my troubled spirit. We had a few beers as we relaxed and caught up.

I asked Ric, "What the hell do you think I should do? I can't sell her right now because of the leaky engine. That would kill my asking price. Yet the problems seem to keep on coming."

Ric looked at me. "Man, I don't know. You really wanted to do this thing, so giving up at this point seems a bit premature."

I agreed. I didn't want to give up, not by a long shot. But I had to fix the major issues before I could even consider selling her, and I wasn't sure if I could live with myself by knowingly passing the buck to someone else. I always saw myself as a person with integrity. I tried to live my life with honesty. Even if I did not always succeed, I always kept on trying. But I couldn't justify the lower price the conditions would bring were I to sell her, so I figured I had to get her fixed one way or other. Discovery Owners Group member Stephen Thorner had mentioned a small two-man RV repair shop in Union Bridge, Maryland that did good work for ninety dollars an hour. I thought maybe I could try that shop when I had time. I was starting my final summer semester as a graduate student and the first four weeks in May was online, which was intense. Lots of homework to do.

It was a nice weekend regardless of the setback, and hey, the broken door did force us outside for a bit longer.

Chapter 9
BYE-BYE, JACKS...
AND AIR CLEANER SHOCK

We returned to Gallaudet safely and Ric flew back home. Theo had asked me earlier if he could take the Discovery to camp with his date Brianna. I was thrilled. Theo was comfortable with the motorhome and he knew how to drive it well. He proved himself to be handy in fixing things, even better than me.

The day after I returned, Theo and Brianna took her out to the Bull Run State park campground in Virginia for two nights. As any parent would do, I worried... a bit. Just a teeny bit. I mean, after all, this was DC. Traffic and road conditions were nasty. They got there without any issues, and Theo said everything went well until the hydraulic leveling jacks stopped working.

Theo was leveling her, and the jacks went down for a moment before retracting and becoming nonoperational. Theo called me on FaceTime and we both guessed a fuse tripped somewhere. Theo worked on it, looking for fuses under the dashboard and other places. But everything looked good. No broken fuses.

Damn.

I called the Fleetwood and Lippert PowerGear support groups and one possibility mentioned was that the 300-amp fuse had tripped. Theo looked for that fuse but couldn't find it. In fact, we couldn't find it for months to come. Someone in the Discovery Owners group pointed out that if the 300-amp fuse was tripped, a lot of things inside the RV wouldn't be working at all. So it likely wasn't the fuse then.

Nevertheless, Theo and Brianna had a great time. They even baked a pizza in the oven that baked quickly and nicely. After two days, they came home. Theo and I talked about what to do with the leveling jacks, and we decided much later to order a replacement solenoid. That took Theo two long hours of labor. It was messy work, and the unit was covered with oil and grime and a bit of rust. It was nasty.

Yet that didn't work, either.

It was also time to replace the air cleaner unit. Theo and I watched YouTube videos and each video kept saying how we had to be careful not to allow any kind of debris inside the hoses while replacing the unit. The debris would get sucked through the diesel turbo unit and damage the engine.

That made me nervous. We got clean towels ready and made sure we cleared up the area under the unit for optimal cleanliness. I opened the cardboard box containing the new unit, and immediately my heart dropped through the floor.

The air cleaner unit came with its own metal casing. It wasn't just a paper filter that we could take out of the old case and put the new one inside. The whole thing would be replaced. This meant... the piece of crap, rusted, beaten up air cleaner unit currently in the Discovery had been there for a long, *long* time.

What the unholy hell was this?

"Shit. We definitely will be seeing a very dirty filter," I said.

Theo nodded grimly as he went to work disassembling the unit. As soon as he got the intake accordion hose off the filter, we were dumbstruck. The bent filter was beyond filthy. Theo had to work the unit back and forth to pull it out of the outtake steel pipe going to the turbo. It took some doing, but the unit finally came out.

Oh. My. Gosh.

The air filter had blown out, shooting huge chunks of the paper into the turbo diesel. Theo looked at me in disbelief.

"Dad, this is really bad."

Stunned, I could only stare at the

And this? So much rust everywhere.

destruction. I had no words. Theo turned around and focused on the steel pipe connecting to the turbo and suddenly waved at me. "You got to look at this."

Rust. There was rust everywhere inside, flaking out. All I could think of were the warnings from YouTubers saying to be careful of any tiny speck of dirt or debris.

Well, we were clearly way past that concern.

Unbelievable. I was so angry. Why couldn't the inspector have red-flagged this damn unit when he inspected the RV? It was clear from the outside that the unit was badly overdue for replacement. The only reason I didn't catch this was that I had absolutely no idea that the air cleaners came as a complete unit, unlike the cars and vans I've driven all my life. The so-called "qualified RV mechanic" should have known better and protected me from this heartbreaking purchase.

The differences between the air cleaner units were staggering. Replace yours on a regular basis.

And the rust was fricking everywhere! Why the hell did the inspector say the rust wasn't severe?! I couldn't believe this at all. Then I started to blame myself. Why didn't I see this myself? Why didn't I crawl underside and see these things for myself? I had to admit that I honestly wouldn't have known the difference at the time.

I immediately took pictures and emailed the Discovery Owners group:

May 9, 2018

Please tell me we are still able to drive around with this engine for a long time to come, considering what we found on the old air filter.

I did not know that Freightliner air filters came with metal casings. If I had known, this would have been a huge red flag given the condition of case itself. I, for the life of me, cannot understand how the inspector did not red flag this!?!

The seller said he didn't bother to replace the filter ... because the air filter gauge was at good levels. No way that's possible given the condition of the filter shown. Clearly, we need to replace the gauge and hose as well. Do we need to replace the air filter intake hose as well? Or what's that called?

Did my intent to bring the inspection company to small claims court based on the missed leaky front left wheel seal and broken intake air compressor hose just get upgraded to a full-scale court trial?

Marvin Miller
2001.5 Discovery 37U
CAT 330 HP
4-bike hitch with 3 Sondors electric bikes

One member quickly responded with one word: "Sorry." Another chimed in:

I hate to say it but:

1. The inspector does not remove the air filter to check it so I would not look in that direction. I don't see much of a case there.
2. That is the reason that the paper filter with housing is supposed to be changed periodically. They disintegrate otherwise. Never actually seen it before but there it is. I would suspect several years of not being changed not just one. The gauge is probably correct, there is no interference to the air flow like that.
2a. The tubing between the filter and the rubber intake should probably be replaced and you should look around the corner all the way to the turbo intake to insure that there are no filter pieces that have not gone through the turbo yet.
3. The condition of the housing/straps is consistent with the coach as you described it although you are right, the filter housing/filter is replaced complete as one part.
4. Chances are good that the turbo (intake side) is damaged by the debris (although mostly paper) and beyond that the CAC could well be clogged up internally (not the outside cooling

fins but the internal tubes for the charged air). Possibly there could be some damage in the engine due to debris but hard to say. Certainly did not get any clean air with the filter in that condition. Add dusty roads, etc. and who knows?

5. I don't think anyone here can give you much help as to whether you can drive it "for a long time to come" or not. No idea other than to say that the condition of the rest probably won't be a whole lot different than the air filter and the CAT is sensitive to poor maintenance (for example lack of oil changes, etc., can seriously damage the fuel injection).

Sorry but I don't see what else to say.

Al & Karin 99 34Q
Cummins ISB 5.9 275

Another jumped in, wisely using my situation as a teaching moment for everyone else in the group:

This is exactly why Cummins and Freightliner says that air filters need to be changed every two years. The glue that is part of putting the filters together degrades over time and these pictures that Marvin's shows is what happens when the glue goes bad. Also not paying attention to how dirty the filter is, the engine, when the filter gets blocked will suck the filter apart and suck the element pieces into the turbo. When it does, hold your wallet.

When you buy an air filter it will have a manufacture date on it, respect the date.

Thanks,
Peter

Theo continued removing the piping, rubber elbow housing, and other things so we could get it sanded and cleaned up. The replacement parts had to be shipped in from Freightliner's Memphis center, and we had to go out of town with the Discovery. There wasn't much time, so Stefania pitched

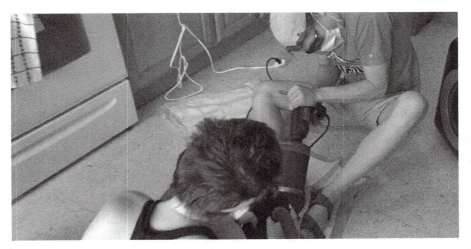

Stefania pitched in and helped Theo wire-brush the inside of rusted pipe. It came out smoother so we could reuse this pipe temporarily. It didn't get replaced until almost a year later.

in and worked with Theo wire-brushing the rusted pipe interior and lightly oiling the interior.

With the pipe taken care of, Theo turned his attention to the turbo unit. He took a picture and what we saw wasn't pretty. I emailed the photo to Bob Miller of Alban CAT Power asking him for his opinion on

The turbo diesel intake fan clearly showed signs of sandblasting by the look of the fan edges. It had been ingesting debris for quite some time.

whether the fins showed signs of "sandblasting," which meant debris had been going through the turbo for some time. Bob emailed back:

> Marvin, Unfortunately, yes, it does and appears to been ingesting debris for awhile (not a recent failure). This explains a lot. This is why you have so many engine oil leaks, as the engine takes in

this debris it wears the internal engine components. The engine shows all the signs of needing to be overhauled... Sorry for the bad news...

I was dismayed, as were my children—although Theo remained steadfastly optimistic. He felt since the Discovery drove well, the engine ran well, and he got a lot of paper material out of the sides of turbo, there was a reason to hope. He said, "I think we got lucky here. Most of the air filter material didn't go through. It got stuck to the sides and I had to dig a lot out."

Theo eventually cleaned out the mess in the turbo and put everything back together, including the brand-new air cleaner unit. The Discovery started up and was ready for travel again despite a weak refrigerator, a faulty microwave, non-functioning leveling jacks, and a non-functioning washer and dryer.

Chapter 10
YET SHE KEEPS
ON TRUCKIN'...

A rainbow shining over our Discovery, which to me always is a sign that everything will work out in the end.

The gut punch we felt that day reverberated for a long time to come. I was livid. I wanted to sue the inspector, even if I knew I probably wouldn't succeed.

May 10, 2018

A quick update:

I called the CAT RV group and spoke with Grant. He said after the air filter damage, the first thing to check immediately is the turbo unit. He said the CAC may possibly be affected, but the turbo is the priority. So, I called Alban CAT Power and spoke with Bob Miller. He agreed that the first unit to be affected is the turbo unit—there may be a sandblasting effect from intake of dirty air, especially if the RV spent a lot of time in dusty areas or near beaches/oceans. This theoretically could affect the engine cylinders, in the worst case.

However, Bob said they saw no concern with the turbo or the engine when they had my RV in the shop—the air filter damage is fairly old, the tear is not recent. There is absolutely no loss of power—which I would definitely notice while driving so this means turbo unit is okay. We may have lucked out here.

Marvin

Luck or not, this wasn't a good feeling at all. She was still dripping oil. And it was time for us to get ready to head to Cedar Point's Lighthouse Point RV Park so we could get in some rides on our favorite roller coasters. We also had to drive the RV to Indiana to get license plates; the Indiana Bureau of Motor Vehicles kept sending back the paperwork to Mountain America Credit Union because there wasn't a VIN inspection form attached. I had a Howard County police officer come over to inspect the VIN number and fill out the form, but that wasn't accepted, either. It had been over a month, and I still didn't have license plates for the RV. I knew the trip to Indiana would cost me a pretty cent, approximately $480 round-trip for fuel alone.

I tried to get Mountain America Credit Union to reimburse me for a portion of the trip cost due to their repeated screw-ups and delays, but no luck there. The fear and panic subsided a little bit the next couple days, and since the RV was running strong, maybe there was a reason to hope after all.

My family and I love roller coasters to the point of near-obsession. But we're also roller coaster snobs. We avoid those that are uncomfortable, head-banging, and vertigo-inducing. Being roller coaster connoisseurs meant going to the parks for only a select number of coasters. For instance, Kings Dominion in Virginia had three or four coasters out of maybe ten that our family approved of. Carowinds, located on the border of North and South Carolinas, had only three of ten. Cedar Point, about half of the coasters. Kings Island near Cincinnati is the golden nugget park for us—just right and not too big (Cedar Point) or too small (Carowinds).

The criteria for the coasters making into the rarefied list of Miller family favorites: the coaster must be smooth, exhilarating, easy on the body thus making it a great marathon ride, easily rode many times in a day, and so forth. We absolutely loved the free-floating sensation the Bolliger & Mabillard hypercoasters offered, such as Diamondback at Kings Island, Intimidator at Carowinds, and Behemoth at Canada's Wonderland. These were by far some of the best.

Theo, Warrick, Stefania and I rode on Cedar Point's venerable Magnum XL-200, the first hypercoaster by Arrow Dynamics. Not the smoothest ride, but if you sit in the middle row of any car and strap the belt on tight, you can enjoy the ride.

We are also crazy about gigacoasters. Over three hundred feet tall and at speeds over 90 mph, they are crazy smooth and incredibly exhilarating. There are only five gigacoasters in the world. The first two designed and built by Intamin were Millennium Force in Cedar Point and Intimidator 305 at Kings Dominion. Kings Island added the fifth giga with Orion in 2020. The Intimidator 305 is far more aggressive and has more restrictive restraints, making it less marathon-able for us. We still love it but riding it more than five times in one day is simply asking for trouble.

The third one was built at Canada's Wonderland, Leviathan, designed and built by Bolliger & Mabillard, our number-one favorite coaster company. The restraints are so liberating, so freeing. Their seat design, I swear, is almost like riding a recliner—incredibly comfortable. Intamin, by contrast, makes uncomfortable seats and restraints that aren't as reliable as B&M ones.

The fourth one—ooh, the absolute best in the world is a doozy: the Fury 325 at Carowinds. Pure speed with incredible comfort, the coaster screams—smoothly, mind you—throughout the course, swaying your body like a suave dance move. The ride doesn't even let up until way past the second half and stays great until the finish. My personal best on Fury 325? Twenty-one times in one day, and I was definitely feeling it at the end of the day. But my highest number of rides in one day anywhere still is on the Diamondback with Theo. He rode twenty-seven times and I went twenty-six times; my second-best was twenty times in one day on the Diamondback.

You think I'm crazy? Well, I'm not Gary Coleman of Monfort Heights, Ohio. He's a retired minister who has ridden the Diamondback over 15,800 times. His personal best in one day is 117 times. And he's older than I am. I was fortunate enough to ride the Diamondback with Gary in 2019.

My brush with fame: Riding with record-holder Gary Coleman (15,800 rides) on the Diamondback.

I made a four-night reservation at Cedar Point's RV Park, the Lighthouse Point, which was pricey at about ninety dollars a night. Yet the location could not be beat: right next to Lake Erie, walking distance to the historic Hotel Breakers, the Lake Erie beach, the boardwalk, and restaurants—even sushi!—and an easy walk into the amusement park. We also got early-admission tickets for the park.

Theo drove the Discovery on I-70 past Frederick, home to the Maryland School for the Deaf, and the hills became more challenging—steeper and higher, which was when we noticed the first sign of trouble. The radiator overheating light came on. Theo and I panicked, and we noticed that the temperature was climbing into the dangerous zone.

"Crap! That's what Bob Miller warned us about, the reason for cleaning the radiator. That's why they wanted $13,000, to remove the radiator and charge the air cooler," I said.

Theo looked at me. "Right. What should we do?"

We slowed down, turned on the blinkers, and pulled over onto the shoulder as we crept along at 15 mph until the temperature slowly returned to normal. Once we went over the hill, we were in the clear.

Whew.

As we turned towards Breezewood, Pennsylvania the hill again ascended sharply, the engine threatening to overheat again. The radiator temperature climbed steadily and hit the overheat indicator again. We again pulled to the shoulder and crept along carefully until the temperatures were back to normal before we proceeded carefully to a truck stop in Breezewood.

"Remember the instructions on radiator cleaning. We gotta use SimpleGreen and spray on the radiator as a stop gap measure," Theo suggested.

I agreed. We couldn't wash her down completely, according to one guide put out by a Discovery Owners member. We were supposed to open up the floor, run the engine, and spray a hose filled with SimpleGreen to force the liquids through the CAC and the radiator. We couldn't do that because we didn't have access to a garden hose or water so we instead walked around to the back and opened up the radiator grill. We sprayed Simple Green all over inside the radiator and waited for an hour. The weather took a turn from hot, sunny, and humid to dark clouds that brought rain and cooler temperatures.

"We have to do the radiator wash when we get to Indianapolis," I said. Theo nodded.

We napped in the Discovery and then finally left for the Pennsylvania Turnpike, knowing that the route brought more challenging hills. I doubt our spraying Simple Green into the radiator helped. It was more likely the cooler and rainy weather, or perhaps a combination of both, but we never saw the temperatures rise above the halfway point again. This brought us enormous relief, and I asked around on how to best clean the radiator before our return to DC.

We made it to Cedar Point and headed to the Lighthouse Point RV Park. We were so excited. This was our first time together as a family in this RV park. I had been there a year earlier with my father Mike and stepmother Sonja's thirty-two-foot Forest River Class C motorhome. They had graciously agreed to let me borrow their RV for two weeks, and that was when I was seriously bitten by the RV bug.

Theo works on the slide-out floor wood trim as Nauvoo looks on.

I must tell you: I am not an outdoors person. In fact, I am a mosquito magnet to the nth degree; if you and I were walking side by side, you probably would get bitten two or three times and I would easily have fifty bites. In a way, getting an RV for someone like me didn't quite make sense if I couldn't really enjoy the outdoors much due to these vampires, er, mosquitoes.

Luckily, Cedar Point in May was still fairly chilly, so no bugs were around. We brought our cat Nauvoo with us, and we made sure the RV was set at a comfortable temperature for her.

As we set up, we did some small projects such as gluing the floor trim onto the slide-out portion. Eventually, I decided to do away with the trim because I didn't want to walk over what felt like an astronomically large bump; instead, I went with brown duct tape to seal the edge for the time being.

My mother, Lisa, a retired master electrician of thirty-three years at General Motors, came to visit us along with my children's mother, Jen, as we stayed at the park. I had hoped to make good use of my mom's electric skills while she was here. But she was stumped by the wiring and layout of the RV, and we didn't have the electrical blueprints with us, either. I wanted to wait on this for another time.

Before when the jacks were functional, the Discovery felt much sturdier with several of us inside walking around. Without the jacks, we could feel her wobble a little bit, but it wasn't too bad. We had to fold away the sofas, blankets and pillows and set up each night for kids to sleep in. There weren't bunk beds or cab-over beds, which would have helped a lot. My father eventually traded his Class C Forest River for a 2017 Fleetwood Flair with a cab-over bed that dropped down, something I wished the Discovery had.

At Cedar Point, we managed to get on the newest and outstanding ride, Steel Vengeance, even though only one train ran at a time, making lines ridiculously long even with the light crowd. When all was said and done, we were ready to head home to Indiana, where we could finally get our license plates.

When we pulled up at Aunt Laura's home in the Irvington area of Indianapolis, I wanted to tackle the license plate issue before the radiator cleaning. We took the Discovery to the Bureau of Motor Vehicles on Emerson Road. It took the lady with a co-worker a few minutes, armed with a stepladder, to climb up and peer through the window to verify the VIN.

I don't know why government agencies don't make it easier for people to buy from private sellers out of state. The process was ridiculously painstaking. After what seemed like forever, I received my own temporary license plate, and I was finally able to mail the seller's plate back to him. That felt good. This meant this Discovery was officially ours, for better or for worse.

I brought her back to my aunt's home, and we began the process of cleaning the radiator. We took off both the bedroom and closet floors so we could see the engine, radiator, and fan. We fed the hose using a garden weeder attachment filled with

Simple Green fluid and started her up at 1500 rpm. She usually idled at 500 rpm, and we hosed the mixture through the spinning fan, before we ran out of the first portion of the fluid. We shut her down and I took a nap inside my aunt's house, because we had to wait an hour to let the mixture work its magic. After an hour, we went back and hosed straight water through the radiator. Again, with the mixture at high idle, we waited and rinsed and repeated.

By the third cleaning, the radiator was nearly full of bubbling soapy water, showing the process had worked—a huge relief to see. There were still some dead spots, and these represented maybe 20 percent of the cooling capacity. Clearly, the radiator and charged air cooler likely would have to be replaced one day.

When you buy a diesel pusher, check that the radiator is in good shape—no bent or missing fins anywhere. Be sure to start her up and run her at high idle at around 1,000 to 1,500 rpm. You can lock in that idle speed by setting the cruise control, then going around back and feeling the air moving through the radiator. You should feel air coming out every part of the radiator. If you don't, then you will need to weigh that; maybe it needs a simple cleaning, or maybe it needs to be replaced. And this isn't cheap. Replacing a radiator can cost around $4,000, including parts and labor and a few days. There are diesel pushers with the radiators on the side, not rear-facing ones like ours, that might be better at avoiding this problem.

With that taken care of, we were ready to head back to DC for my final semester of intensive face-to-face classes. We intended to bring the Discovery to the East Coast Repair shop once we got back to address the oil leaks and nonfunctional leveling jacks.

For a long time, the trucking industry wouldn't let Deaf people drive semi-trucks. This was despite several Deaf people successfully making livings as truck drivers. In fact, statistics have long shown that Deaf people are safer drivers than the general population. We are more visually oriented, less distracted by "other" stuff such as music, radio talk shows, and so forth. Yet, at the federal level, the Deaf community had no luck in convincing the Department of Transportation (DOT) to revise regulations to allow Deaf drivers.

One of the biggest reasons cited for not allowing Deaf people to drive trucks was the assumption that one had to hear to drive a big rig safely. Another cited reason was air brakes.

Most trucks, if not all, run on air brakes operated by air compressors built onto diesel engines. Without air pressure, the brakes will lock into place and the driver cannot move the vehicle at all. The air brakes make noises when they operate, and it was assumed you had to hear them in order to ensure safe operation. No, not really.

In 2013, after a long, intensive lobbying effort by the National Association of the Deaf (NAD), the DOT finally agreed to make exemptions for Deaf drivers to obtain commercial driving (CDL) A and B licenses, except for passenger motor coaches.

NAD says on its website at www.nad.org:

> For decades, the DOT has maintained a hearing standard that has excluded safe and skilled deaf drivers from a career in commercial trucking. The DOT hearing standard...requires that a CDL applicant be able to hear a forced whisper in the better ear at not less than five feet, or that an applicant does not have an average hearing loss in the better ear greater than 40 decibels at 500 Hz, 1,000 Hz, and 2,000 Hz with or without a hearing aid. The NAD has long argued that this standard has no relevance to safe operation of commercial motor vehicles and has insisted that the DOT rescind this standard.

Today, there are over 1,000 members of the national Deaf Truck Drivers organization[2].

---

[2] http://www.deaftruckersunited.com

Stefania washes the RV windows. Truck stops have longer windshield cleaners, which is a bonus, but the gas prices are usually higher.

The exemption application process is lengthy. I applied a few years ago, just for the heck of it. I wanted to maybe drive trucks for a while; it was something to do, something different. I was rejected based on one six-point infraction levied by an overzealous park ranger who was hiding in a spot behind Devils Lake State Park in Wisconsin that even had a sign welcoming people—albeit walkers, hikers and bicyclists, or so they claimed. I made the mistake of missing the "DO NOT ENTER" sign because it was in an obscure place. I got ticketed, and later learned I wasn't the only one. I drove back to the county courthouse there and contested this ticket. I made their lawyer nervous because I was cross-examining the park ranger, and they kept objecting to almost all my questions, including, "How many others have you ticketed in the same spot?" Their objections were sustained.

I lost. And I forgot to ask the judge to waive the points and let me pay the $300-something fine. I tried the next day, but the clerk pointedly said the case was closed and it was too late to do anything about that.

So that bogus six-point marred my otherwise near-perfect record. I have never had an accident while I was driving in the thirty-plus years I've driven. Too bad. There's a labor shortage in the trucking industry, and we could make a difference.

Truck stops have longer windshield cleaners, which is a bonus, but the gas prices are usually higher.

As we pulled out of Aunt Laura's home's driveway down a slight decline, I braked carefully to ease the RV out onto the street. Laura, who could hear a little, remarked that there was a loud screech. She wasn't sure what it meant or where it came from. I thought to myself, "Hmm. Maybe I need to get this looked at. But gosh, I hope this won't be expensive."

We made our way to St. Clairsville, Ohio where we stopped to fill up. By now it was nighttime. We wanted to use the truck stop's long windshield cleaner usually unavailable at regular gas stations. After washing the bug splatter off the windshield, I started to drive her out but I couldn't. She wouldn't move. The LOW AIR light went on. We struggled to increase the air pressure so the brakes could be released. After we ran it at high idle, we were able to move her. We drove on the highway for a while, but the air pressure kept dropping slowly. I turned to my kids and lamented, "We got to stop at the rest area coming up. We need to take her into a shop." When we set up for the night at the next rest area, I called around for shops to take us at the last minute.

Western Branch Diesel said they could take a look at it later in the day. After we slept the night, we carefully made our way after stopping at a fast-food restaurant. We were lucky that there was enough air pressure to move her, but it was clear that she was in trouble. We pulled into Western Branch Diesel and waited in the lounge area until they were able to look at her. A mechanic started her up, ran her at high idle, hit the brakes repeatedly, and turned her off. He then went under and took a brief look.

Theo observes Western Branch Diesel mechanics doing their stuff in St. Clairsville, Ohio.

Dan Greer, the manager and diesel mechanic for fifteen years, came to us with the total cost. The parts were $11.43 and $39.95. With labor, the total came to $522.29.

Sigh. They worked on it for quite a while, and as lunchtime came around, we realized there wasn't anything within walking distance for lunch. Dan graciously took all of us in his pickup truck to a nearby Subway. At that point, I told Dan my sob story about the blown air filter, leaky engine gaskets everywhere, and sandblasted turbo fins. I told him that we were told that the engine needed to be rebuilt, something we couldn't afford.

"Ooh, I am so sorry, man," he grimaced. "But I got to tell you, the engine is running pretty good. I see that kind of sandblasting in the turbo fins all the time. I think she may be okay. Let us look at her and see what we find."

Awesome. His mechanic found that the engine oil cooler unit was leaking, which he suggested that we take care of soon. The mechanic also found that engine coolant hose was leaking badly. We would be stranded on the road if this hose wasn't immediately replaced, with potentially serious consequences to the engine. I told him to go ahead with the hose replacement.

But they had to special order it and they weren't sure when it would get in.

It was getting late in the day, and Theo and I tried to unscrew the sawed-off striker bolt for the door lock. We just couldn't get it off. It was so tight, and Dan sent a younger mechanic to help us. No luck there. We couldn't get any traction on it either. After about a half hour, I told the mechanic to forget it.

Dan came up and told us that the part wouldn't arrive until tomorrow, so we had to spend another night in the area. His front desk guy suggested nearby Barkcamp State Park. The Discovery was drivable since the air brakes were fixed. The park was beautiful, and we got in and got ourselves comfortable. This was the second time we built a campfire.

We set up the awning, got our four lawn chairs, and we had a nice fire going. Nauvoo came out and enjoyed the outdoors along with us. We were preparing to cook hamburgers and hot dogs. We even had s'mores ready to be assembled. All the makings of a perfect evening.

What else could go wrong, right?

Chapter 11
CLANK!

With the campfire going, we sat around and had drinks, feeling great. Stefania was preparing the food, and the others pitched in by chopping veggies and preparing the hamburgers. Since I am a vegetarian, I had portobello mushrooms marinated and ready to be grilled. Actually, I always joke and say I am a vegan wanna-be. I don't eat red meat, chicken, or pork. But I love sushi. I can't resist good spicy tuna or spicy salmon rolls. I also love eggs, and some gourmet cheeses. So... a vegetarian-pescarian.

A few reasons I changed my diet was due to *The China Study* by T. Colin Campbell. That book really opened my eyes to healthy eating, and I lost about forty pounds. I still love me lots of sugar and chocolate, and for convenience while in graduate school, I relied heavily on processed foods. But I'm still eating healthier than I did in the past.

As we got closer to dinner time, menacing dark clouds came into view. We wanted to cook on the campfire grill, but the rain started to come down lightly. We ran outside and brought the lawn chairs under our awning.

Theo looked outside and said, "Dad, I think we need to bring in the awning."

"Nah. I checked the weather app and we are expecting three-miles-an-hour wind. The awning will be fine. I googled this up earlier, and the forums say to retract the awning if we expects winds higher than 12-15 mph."

"Dad, I think we gotta retract the awning. The clouds look foreboding," he insisted.

I didn't want to go to the trouble. Also, I was FaceTiming with my dad, who shared Theo's concern. He suggested, "At least bring down one corner of the awning so the water can run off easily."

I didn't listen. I just didn't want to go outside, and come on… the awning should be designed to handle a little rain and some wind, right?

Right. The skies opened, and it poured while the wind gusts kicked in, much stronger than predicted. We had to cook our dinner inside on our LP stove. This is what makes RV living so appealing—you are out in nature, yet you are also sheltered from the elements as well. Dry, comfortable, and we still could eat a good dinner.

"This is really nice… we are nice and dry inside, and this food is really good. Even though it's raining hard outside," I happily said to the kids.

As if right on cue, the Discovery shook hard. There was a loud bang, and we all were startled.

"Wow, was that lighting?" I asked. We looked at each other, processing what had just happened. Suddenly, Theo jumped up and said, "I told you! The awning broke in half!" He frantically gestured to the limp awning shade that was now blocking the view of our large window.

I was gobsmacked. My dad and Theo were right. The total weight on the awning was just too much, and it was bent in half, damaging the support struts.

First the oil burst, with the oil leaking into six gaskets, the left wheel seal and brake, the door lock breaking, a jittery microwave touchpad, the nonfunctional hydraulic leveling jacks, the air brake repair, and now this?! All in the span of a month and half.

This one was completely on me, though. A mixture of rookie arrogance and laziness of not wanting to go out in the rain and do the work had given us a broken awning and no way to put it back together, especially in this weather.

I sat there, angry and defeated. I turned to my kids and sighed. "We have to go out and cut out the awning fabric and discard the awning equipment into the dumpster."

Theo sat there for a while, not saying anything, deep in his thought. I was just too busy feeling pissed at myself and at this Discovery. Why couldn't anything go right for a nice stretch of time? I mean, we were pummeled with so many issues in such a short time, and the inspector caught none of these issues? Come on. There was still one repair to come the next day, and I knew it wouldn't be cheap. Nothing comes cheap in the world of diesel maintenance.

I've read up on the pros and cons of buying a diesel pusher RV, and many people say they can't get by on anything less than $2,500 per year in regular maintenance—so I was expecting that.

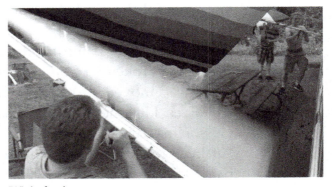

Wait for it...

But not this! I glared at the broken awning.

Theo looked at us. "We can save the awning and fix it later. Come on. Let's go outside and follow my lead."

I wasn't convinced, but I trusted him wholeheartedly. The skies were clearing up with only a drizzle coming down. Theo inspected the damage and told me to go

Stefania had her phone out and caught everything on video. Ouch! The universe clearly had a message for my skepticism.

ahead and bring the support post down slightly. He would carefully bend the roller back into its original shape and position, then we would all roll it back to the top.

Well, okay. I was still skeptical. And then the universe sent me a message.

Needless to say, that was painful. I didn't realize that the upper support rod had broken off from the roof, and it fell right on my head as soon as I moved the bottom frame. Everyone had a good laugh, and yes, I laughed… after I was done cussing.

With that lesson from the universe learned, Theo hammered the portions of bent roll tube repeatedly until it was nearly straight. Theo and I, along with Warrick's help, managed to roll the awning slowly back into position. I was amazed. It looked as if it wasn't broken at all. I took a step back and admired Theo's confidence and handiwork. I really didn't think this was possible. But there it was, looking good.

Theo was able to pull this off within minutes. For me, this was a lesson in confidence and

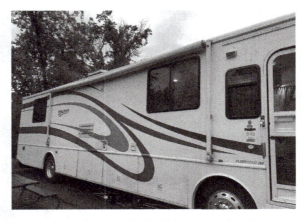

The broken awning back in its place, looking as if it was never broken in the first place, thanks to Theo.

willingness to try solutions that might seem unconventional. If we did it my way, we would have thrown away the entire awning set, and we would probably have struggled a lot more in taking it apart as well.

I went back inside, and we finished up our dinner, cleaned up the place, and settled in for a movie night. We kept a library of DVD movies for when Wi-Fi wasn't available, and I didn't want to use up my T-Mobile's

The awning gave me a new kind of headache, and I wasn't thrilled.

generous 50 GB data allocation. Sure, they call it unlimited but they severely throttle your Internet after 50 GB is used up. This affects my ability to make video relay calls for emergencies, such as calling 911. Hearing folks don't have to worry about the data caps for emergencies because voice calls will still go through if there is coverage. Voice calls are useless to us.

("Hearing folks"? If you're not Deaf, you might be wrestling with that strange new phrase, and trust me, I know how you feel. DeafBlind folks call us Deaf folks sighted, and they have a sign for it as well. It took me some time to process calling myself a Deaf, sighted person.)

My head throbbed and I had to put an ice pack on it while we watched the movie. We wanted s'mores, even though the campfire had died thanks to the heavy rain. We fired up the gas stove and toasted marshmallows over the small fire. Improvisation at its finest.

Stefania making s'mores using the LP stove.

The next day, we went back to Western Branch Diesel, and they replaced the leaky lower coolant hose, which took them a good part of the day to get done. Dan Greer surprised us by going over to the sawed-off striker bolt and somehow wrestling it off at no charge to us. We were so relieved that infernal thing was finally out so we could install a new striker bolt when we got back home.

The final bill for the coolant hose replacement was $628.93.

Chapter 12
ROCKETING TOWARDS
$10,000

MAY 23, 2018

- Mileage: **112,669**
- Previous total: **$8,426.74**
- D2 Governor and Spring Brake chamber: **$522.29**
- Tube assembly lower radiator and parts: **$628.93**
- Current total: **$9,577.96**
- Credit score: **700**

We thanked Dan Greer for making sure we were all safe and good to go, and we drove the RV back home safely. The trip went without a hitch, and we were buoyed by Dan's opinion that our engine still had a good life ahead. I was determined to replace at least some of the gaskets that had the worst oil leaks in them. Our next stop would be East Coast Repair in the small town of Union Bridge, Maryland. But I had to take care of several things first.

Theo quickly got to work on replacing the striker bolt and also tried to replace the door handle with a new kit from Fleetwood REV Group, but it didn't have the long lock bar we needed. We were not sure if REV Group sent us the wrong part or ours was a specially modified one. Eventually, REV Group refunded the cost, and we still have the useless part with us—it wasn't until two years later that I finally gave it back to the REV

Group. Theo managed to bend certain parts of the door that kept locking us out, and whatever he did worked great, so we kept the original latch.

Being a full-time graduate student along with being a single father to four kids in an eight-hundred-square-foot apartment on campus was challenging. I adored my apartment, which

The old door latch system had a welded-on extension that the new one didn't.

was just right for my family, providing that they stayed in their dorms and visited me once in a while. Unfortunately, Theo had to take a medical leave of absence that semester because of a condition that was affecting his eyesight, an experience especially harrowing for a Deaf person who relied fully on his vision. It took weeks and multiple doctor appointments with different eye specialists who all proclaimed his eyes in excellent health, but he was seeing spots and grid lines at times, and he was sensitive to light. He often wore sunglasses, even indoors. He couldn't continue taking classes while struggling to read and focus on watching teachers sign for hours.

I was really concerned. Finally, Theo saw a neurologist who quickly diagnosed his condition as a rare form of migraine without the headaches, which was probably due to a double concussion during his senior year at Indiana School for the Deaf. With the right medication, Theo began to recover rapidly much to all of our relief. I was grateful to have him home with

Warrick, Alec, and me, because he was such a huge help with our first RV purchase and repairs.

Theo's presence made my apartment fuller than usual, which I didn't mind. Stefania came by to visit and stay more often as the semester progressed. By the end of the semester, she realized she wanted to go to a different college so she could work in the space industry, perhaps with NASA or her first choice, Space X. What can I say? Elon Musk is cool. Our family watched the livestream of several Falcon 9 launches, and we all got together to watch the first ever Falcon Heavy launch, marveling when the video feed showed Starman in his red Roadster over Earth. An amazing sight.

With a full apartment, I struggled with finding me time, especially as an introvert. Many in the Deaf community who have taken classes and workshops with me will find that puzzling because I appear to thrive on socializing with others. I give out all my energy during my presentations, but I also need time to recover. Coming home to four kids with my battery depleted has often been a challenge for me. When you throw graduate school into the mix, it all added up to something that was simply too much for me.

The visual carbon monoxide and smoke alarm detector shows a high number.

One morning, I woke up to my apartment's kitchen in disarray. Plates and cups piled up in the sink, the countertops dirty and the floor unswept. I simply had enough. I took pictures of the offending mess and texted them to my kids, informing them I was taking my

Discovery out for the weekend—alone. I went to overnight at a parking lot next to Whole Foods Market in Fairfax, Virginia.

The next morning, I encountered a problem. I had a visual carbon monoxide and smoke alarm detector—actually, it did not really qualify as visual because it lacked strobe lights, and my only other option was to pay for a hardwired installation, an easy $400. I had ordered this one from Amazon, hoping for the best.

That morning, it was flashing a red circle saying there were 356 parts per million of carbon monoxide in my bedroom. I traced the source, and found it was coming from the drawers in the rear that I used to store my clothes. I remembered finding old work gloves stuffed into the floor opening under the drawers on the bottom. I had moved the gloves around, but apparently, I didn't stuff it in properly. The ten-gallon hot water tank was sitting right below this spot, and clearly the propane burner was giving off fumes that came inside. I wondered what I could do to stop this for good. I had an idea: duct tape to the rescue. I taped over the opening and threw away the old work gloves. The seal has held ever since then.

I also wondered if it was normal for the hot water heater to emit carbon monoxide fumes. The heater worked great, but the control board seemed warped, maybe a sign of an electrical short or improper heating melting the plastic molds. I would ask around before I did anything.

The next night, I joined Harvest Hosts for an annual fee of forty-five dollars. With that membership, I could ask to park overnight at participating wineries, breweries, and farms. I found a nearby brewery/winery, Quattro Goomba's, and I invited my friends to meet me there later that evening. When I arrived, I was dismayed by how incredibly full the parking lot was. I had forgotten it was Memorial Day weekend, and I tried to maneuver around the packed parking lot. With an employee's help, I eventually found a spot on the grass although I was a bit leery of the soft ground. It turned out great, and later that evening, when everyone left, I moved to a solid gravel area for the night. I enjoyed sampling their delicious beers with my friends and chatting up a storm. I relaxed, knowing that I wouldn't have to drive that night. My friends, who worked as certified Deaf interpreters, had to leave early for an emergency assignment. Feeling buzzed and aglow, I walked the few steps to my home and safely tucked myself in.

In the morning, I headed to Charlestown, West Virginia to overnight at Hard Rock Casino and Hotel. I am not much of a gambler and I don't usually go into casinos. I did that night, though, and I ate in one of their sports bars and played a few games of slots without luck. I was happy to go back to my comfortable retreat for the evening. I did my homework while on this trip, using Wi-Fi spots at Panera Bread and Starbucks to create videos for assignments.

At Gallaudet University, many assignments are submitted as videos instead of written papers. This is because ASL is a language distinct from English, although people didn't always believe this. Until the 1960s, most people were incorrectly taught that ASL was "broken English" or a shortened version of English. Thanks to the hard work of William C. Stokoe and his two Deaf assistants, Dorothy Sueoka Casterline and Carl Cronenberg, it was proven that ASL was a stand-alone language with its own grammatical properties and vocabulary.

In 1965, the researchers published *A Dictionary of American Sign Language and Linguistic Principles*, which shook the community. It took our community a long time, for many reasons, to come to terms with the fact that ASL is a full-fledged language with its own words, grammatical structures, and other properties, along with many other signed languages in the world—distinct from spoken languages. In fact, Gallaudet University only began to formally recognize ASL in its mission in 2007, after input from an accreditation entity.

Many Deaf people are bilingual or multilingual, like me; I am comfortable with both ASL and English, although ASL is my first language and the one I feel most capable in. I finished my assignments and then headed to Frederick to get our black tank (for waste solids) and gray tank (for bath and kitchen water) professionally cleaned. It took them about an hour and cost me $250. They gave me tips, including installing 360 siphon vents on top and using Angel Soft toilet paper given its easier dissolution in the holding tank. (By the way, there are YouTube videos comparing how different toilet papers break down.)

I then went up to the Catoctin Mountains just past Thurmont, Maryland. I know, I know… the mountains are more like hills to Westerners, but they're called mountains in Maryland. I loved every minute of driving through really narrow, yet beautiful, twisty wooded hills. After that, I settled in for the night at a Walmart north of Fredrick.

At this point, I felt it was time to head back home. I did get my alone time over the weekend although not so much relaxing. The refrigerator wasn't working, either so I had to use my cooler and eat out almost all the time. It wasn't perfect, but it was still great.

Chapter 13
FINE-TUNING AND DROP-OFF

JUNE 2018

- Mileage: **113,302**
- Previous total: **$9,577.96**
- Professional tank cleaning: **$250.00**
- Two 360 Siphon vents: **$23.00**
- NAPA chassis battery replacement: **$282.18**
- Current total: **$10,156.14**
- Credit score: **695**

Theo got to work installing the 360 siphon vents that I ordered from Amazon. There were a few things going on in our lives such as my youngest son Warrick's eighth-grade promotion ceremony at Kendall Demonstration Elementary School, located on the Gallaudet campus. He had plans to attend Model Secondary School for the Deaf for his high school, my alma mater. My other son, Alec, decided to return to Indiana to

Theo works on installing the vents.

stay with his mother. In the meantime, we began preparations to empty out our apartment by selling all our furniture, television, and anything we knew would not fit in the RV.

With that done, I looked for another excuse to take the Discovery for a short trip. I thought we could go to Kings Dominion and sleep overnight at a nearby Cracker Barrel.

Theo and his date Brianna joined me to head down to Virginia. We had a nice time, but the weather didn't cooperate. The new ride, Twisted Timbers, was having maintenance issues so it was out of commission. We got in a few rides then as the rains came, we headed out to a local pizzeria and taproom, Tap900, in Ashland. They had decent pizzas and a good selection of drinks.

The next morning, the Discovery wouldn't start. The chassis batteries had died. I sighed as we started the engine by switching to house batteries. We headed to NAPA and asked them to test the batteries, but we were told we had to remove the batteries ourselves. Theo, as usual, got right to it. He took pictures of the old ones and the wiring to make sure we put it back correctly.

The battery indeed tested bad, and after looking up the serial number, they said it was four years old. Apparently, batteries typically last three years. Hmm, okay, so time for new batteries. The total bill was $282.18. Moving on.

The next day, we went RV-browsing at Commonwealth RV Sales, just to see if we could find an RV with a better floor plan than ours. The lot had a huge selection of used Class A

Theo driving the Discovery in Washington, DC.

motorhomes, so it was easy to hop on and off each one, seeing a wide range of brands, quality, and, ahem, smells. They had Tiffin Phaeton, Newmar DutchStar, Fleetwood American Eagle, Fleetwood Excursion, Winnebago Journey, Monaco Diplomat and more. We visited nearly all of them despite the light rain.

At East Coast Repair, we saw a newer model of the Discovery and pulled in next to her.

After all that browsing, Brianna looked at me and said, "I don't know about you, but I love yours the best. I wasn't impressed with any others, even the more expensive ones."

Theo agreed, and I beamed as I replied, "I've been on over fifty Class A diesel pushers, and this one was the nicest of them all—the clean smell, the good-looking, sturdy floor and the floor plan as well as good decor."

We got back home, and I ordered a replacement solenoid for the PowerGear hydraulic leveling jacks. When we got the solenoid, Theo spent a good three hours struggling to get it off and back on, but it was a mess. The jacks refused to work. Dejected, Theo and I asked East Coast Repair to look at it along with replacing the engine oil cooling housing gasket and checking the belts and pulleys. I was already dreading what I knew would be an over-$1,000 bill even if they had lower labor rates and a small-town "can do!" mentality.

On June 13, the kids headed to Indianapolis and we timed our departure together so Theo could drop me off in Frederick, Maryland after leaving the Discovery at East Coast Repair. East Coast Repair, in nearby Union Bridge, was in the middle of nowhere, and was a beautiful, hilly drive. At one point, we all experienced a brief weightless pop while driving over a hill, which we absolutely loved.

Upon arrival, I talked with Bill, one of the two mechanics, via paper and pen asking for an estimate before they went ahead with the repairs. I also asked him if he could check our refrigerator. He agreed, although he couldn't promise when; he said it could be two weeks before they could work on her. I looked around, and lo and behold, there was another Discovery on the lot along with a few other RVs. We parked ours next to her; the other Discovery was a better and newer looking one.

Theo then dropped me off in Frederick, where I had a nice lunch downtown at Summitra Thai, enjoying my moment of solitude that I so desperately needed. I took a Lyft ride to the Rockville Shady Grove Metro Station to travel back to Gallaudet. I nervously wondered what the mechanics would uncover on the Discovery.

In the meantime, I waited. And waited.

I called Bill once each week, and each time, he would say they hadn't taken a look yet and that it would probably be another two weeks. I was becoming even more nervous. We needed the Discovery back in our hands by July 13, especially given that we were to move out of the apartment on July 16.

As I waited, I went through everything and tried to sell items as quickly as I could. Many items did get sold: bunk beds, a 65" television, furniture, my beloved 27" Apple Thunderbolt Cinema Display, and more. All the while, I began face-to-face classes, which was an all-day, five-day marathon that was both exhilarating and exhausting.

My professors were amazing and engaged, and it was clear they were committed to us. I had Ben Jarashow for both Deaf Studies and ASL Literature, and he brought a depth of knowledge and research to the class. I also had MJ Bienvenu, a legend in the field of linguistics and bilingualism. Being a Deaf

The combined 2017 and 2018 cohorts of Gallaudet University's Masters in Sign Language Education (MASLED) program.

lesbian from a Deaf family in Baton Rouge, Louisiana helped her pave the way in the fight against ignorance and inequality. She taught Critical Pedagogy and we pored over the works of Paulo Freire, bell hooks, Peter McLaren, and others, accompanied by mind-blowing classroom discussions that only began to scratch the surface of our internalized oppression, our privileges, and our assumptions about the world.

The last four weeks leading up to my last day on July 13 were intense and gratifying at the same time. Fast approaching the final aspect of my program, I desperately needed East Coast Repair to start working on my Discovery. I made it clear to them that we needed the RV back by July 14 so we could start loading our stuff and head to Indianapolis and Roscommon, Michigan, to see my father Mike and stepmother Sonja.

It was now the very last week of my program, and I was frustrated. I called Bill but couldn't reach him, so I spoke to Lonnie, his partner, and much to my relief, they had been working on my Discovery. He went ahead and replaced the engine cooling gasket and began the process of taking apart the hydraulic leveling jacks. He said the jacks were in bad shape—the shaft and core inside were stuck but they needed a part or two to get it running and unstuck.

We all were so relieved to be done with our graduate studies.

I was elated at first. Wait a minute... "I told you to give me an estimate first before going to work on it?" Lonnie wasn't aware, even if Bill knew. Later I found out that Maryland state law requires that shops provide an estimate before proceeding to work on the unit.

I was upset. But time was working against us. I told Lonnie to go ahead, and I was hoping for the best with the hydraulic jacks because a new one would set me back another $2,000. I reminded them to be sure to check the belts and hoses and the refrigerator. Lonnie told me point-blank that it was working "okay" enough at forty degrees—and if I wanted them to repair it, that would involve replacing the cooling unit at another $2,000 minimum.

Yeah, forget it. I asked them whether they thought the Discovery would be ready by July 14. "No, that's impossible. We are still waiting on the parts," Lonnie said.

"Monday then?"

"I doubt it. More likely Tuesday or Wednesday the seventeenth."

I sighed. I was worried about the cost, but we did need the Discovery in better shape.

Warrick chats with his mentor and former teacher Darlene Ewan during the MASLED closing ceremony. Theo is in the background at right.

The final day of college came, and my classmates and I hugged, celebrated, and let out a huge sigh of relief. We were now holders of newly minted master's degrees. We all were so relieved to be done with our studies.

For me, this represented a culmination of a long twenty-four-year creative detour that took me through the founding of three newspapers for Deaf people: *The Deaf Michigander*, *DeafNation*, and *SIGNews*. I had worked for Communication Services for the Deaf, in Sioux Falls, South Dakota, where I embarked on the unique journey of trying to build the world's first ASL-centric town in Laurent, South Dakota in honor of Deaf French pioneer and multilingual educator Laurent Clerc. I also had spent the past eight years as a Deafhood instructor developing two twenty-hour courses available nationwide… all of this while raising four beautiful Deaf kids who continued to make me proud every day.

Monday came, and the Discovery wasn't ready. I let the friendly folks at Gallaudet's Residence Life office know and they graciously allowed us to stay in our apartment.

Tuesday afternoon, on June 18, the call finally came. Our Discovery was ready. They had replaced all the belts and a pulley that was rusted stuck, causing greater friction, and the leveling jacks were now fully functional. They also replaced the wiring to the jacks and replaced the engine oil cooling housing gasket.

The final bill?

$4,492.64.

Chapter 14
WORSE THAN
A BODY-SLAM

JULY 17, 2018

- Mileage: **113,829**
- Previous total: **$10,156.14**
- Belts, leveling jack overhaul, engine cooling housing gasket, and more (labor alone was $3,307.50 for 36.75 hours): **$4,492.64**
- Hollywood four-bike hitch: **$564.60**
- Current total: **$15,213.38**
- Credit score: **680**

I felt like I had been body-slammed onto a hard concrete floor.

"What? Four thousand and..." I signed to the Convo Relay video interpreter, who was voicing for me to Lonnie.

Lonnie replied, "Yes, we spent a lot of time on everything."

"But you guys never gave me an estimate. I was expecting this to cost only $1,500 to $2,000."

Lonnie replied that they were working against my deadline, and they had to do what they could to get it done and ready for us. I sat there, stunned. We had to pay and get her back. We were pressed for time.

They did fix a lot of things, I rationalized. Not the refrigerator, though. I told Theo, "Man, the hits keep on coming. I don't know if I can do this much longer."

I remembered the conversation I had with him at the Cedar Point RV Park. We were outside grilling our dinner. He turned to me, and said, "Dad, maybe you need to seriously consider selling this RV and getting a smaller one?"

I just couldn't do it—at least, not yet, since the engine oil leaks were bad enough and would have hurt the asking price—and because I needed this, traveling and seeing the country and Canada and Mexico. I had been a single dad for a long time and even simple things like having my beloved kids with you could wear me down. I recall the example of someone asking you to hold a glass full of water with your arm extended, which is at first a piece of cake, right? But if you were to hold that glass for an hour? Two hours? A few days? It'd be brutal, and probably impossible, not to mention painful.

I needed this. I needed my Discovery. I wasn't ready to part with her. But I couldn't justify the climbing costs either.

The next morning, we headed up to Union Bridge. It was so good to have the Discovery back. Lonnie showed us the rusted parts and bad wiring, and they looked horrendous. He showed us the stuck pulley bearing, meaning the belts were running over it at high friction. It was a good thing they caught this before we put more miles on her.

We expected the oil leak to reduce since the engine oil cooling housing was one that Dan Greer pointed out as terrible: "but not puking oil, though but it's leaking bad." Theo and I took turns driving her back to DC, traveling on the pothole-filled George Washington Parkway then onto the eternal traffic jam of I-395 crossing into DC, passing through the tunnel under the U.S. Capitol onto New York Avenue. We took a right turn onto Florida Avenue, the Gallaudet University Tower Clock rising into our sight, and after the familiar bump on the front entrance, we were back home on campus.

With prior permission from the head of the facilities department and chief of public safety, we brought the Discovery up on the upper parking garage level of Kendall Apartments. Our Discovery's maximum weight was around 26,000 pounds and the parking garage could support up to fifteen tons. This made it easier for us to load our stuff out of our apartment.

The drive tired us, but we had to go straight to loading as soon as we could. Before we could even load our Discovery, the rain flooded the parking level. The drain had been problematic for a long time, and I always wondered why it was never fixed. I must admit that I didn't report this problem to the facilities department, either. Even so, it often would flood two to three inches all over. My friend John Skjeveland came over to check out our Discovery. He worked for Clerc Center as an accountant and had a passion for making sure the campus grounds were well-maintained.

The multi-talented John Skjeveland took only a few minutes to resolve the oft-repeated flooding problem.

Warrick, Theo, and Stefania help pack our apartment after my graduation.

He quickly noticed the flood. He walked through the water, fortunately wearing flip-flops on his day off, and found the clogged drain. He removed the cover and dumped out leaves and mud. The flood disappeared within ten minutes. If he hadn't come by then, we would have waited a better part of the day for the water to subside or would have had to move our Discovery to a different location on the ramp, taking us further away from the main door entrance.

Packing up for the move, we had to stuff everything into our Discovery. Even with John's ingenuity, the move took longer than we expected. We continued into the evening, and nearly all the next day. I was screaming at my kids, who wanted more breaks than I thought they needed, and one or two kept disappearing into thin air visiting a friend or two for the last time. This frustrated me to no end.

Theo oversaw loading the Discovery, trying to balance her out weight-wise. All of this was guesswork on our part. I still don't understand why the RV manufacturers couldn't build a weight scale into the chassis. I knew we would need to head to the nearest truck inspection stop to be weighed; there was one past Frederick, which was on our way.

We were already a few days late, and we needed to get going. At the last minute, I even sold one of three Sondors electric bikes to one of my neighbors. This also negated the need for four hitches, so we went with two, leaving the other two empty and in position so we could unload this portion when we got to my dad's home. His home had a nice side driveway with a 30-amp wall outlet ready for our Discovery. We planned to dry-dock her for a couple of weeks and install upgrades such as a dining table fashioned from my beloved office desk.

We also planned to unload a good number of things into my dad's basement. He and Sonja had a spacious basement that was an ideal location for my stuff.

The Discovery was loaded up to its gills. We worried that we had overloaded her, so we offloaded a few things into my 2007 Honda Odyssey that would remain at Gallaudet for Theo to use. "We need to monitor the radiator and engine cooling," I said to Theo. She would climb the "mountains" throughout Western Maryland and southwestern Pennsylvania before going through Wheeling, West Virginia onto more level roads.

My dream realized. This photo was actually taken later on October 19, 2018 while camped at Pea Patch RV Park in Branson, Missouri.

"I agree—and I think she should be okay this time, but definitely keep an eye on the engine temperature indicator while we are driving through these hills," Theo replied.

We finally pulled out of the campus late that Wednesday afternoon, July 17, headed for the beginning of a new life. We would go our separate ways of sorts by the end of August. Theo and Warrick would head back to DC to attend Gallaudet and MSSD. Stefania would drive our 1997 Honda Civic to Austin, Texas and stay with family friends Sami Jo Oates, Deb Kuglitsch, and Jodi Oates. Stefania planned to find a job, attend Austin Community College tuition-free—Texas is the only state we know of that waives the tuition for Deaf and hard of hearing residents—and work her way back into a university with a technical focus. Alec was to stay in Southport, Indiana with my mother and complete his high school education before attending Gallaudet University.

I planned to travel across the country teaching Deafhood classes and workshops while writing in the comfort of my

Discovery. I was eager to begin my journey westward, finding good spots to boondock off-grid for up to fourteen days each on Bureau of Land Management (BLM) and other federal properties. The resources for identifying areas where big rigs can be driven onto federal lands are sparse. I had an app on my iPhone that identified boondocking sites, but it didn't really show as many spots as I had hoped for; many locations required four-by-four vehicles.

For a while, before purchasing this Discovery, I had considered a Mercedes Sprinter van chassis such as the Winnebago View 24J. It got 16-20 mpg, had lower maintenance costs, but still cost higher than its gas-guzzling Ford F-350 and F-450 counterparts. If I were smarter, I would gain a greater ease of camping nearly anywhere, including stealth camping on city streets. The Class B Mercedes RVs are even better suited to stealth camping because they blend in easily on the streets, passing for regular vans.

My honking big thirty-eight-foot Discovery couldn't do this anywhere, unless it had a cloaking device, cleverly disguising the space occupied as cordoned-off road repair. Wishful thinking aside, I was also learning about how many sites in national and state parks would service big rigs of my size. I found out that my Discovery could fit into only 60 percent of the sites nationwide, according to a CamperReport.com article. This revelation came to me after I bought her. Despite my best efforts, I had overlooked this point. I really didn't want to full-time in a small RV like the Winnebago View 24J—the shower is tiny, the bathroom is cramped, and even the queen bed has a curved corner, losing some surface area. I would be stuck with a dinette booth providing subpar support for my back while writing. I love my Haworth office chair, worth around $700 new, which I picked up at a factory store in Holland, Michigan for only seventy-five dollars. The chair is so comfortable and supportive, I can last all day on one.

Granted, I needed to get out more often, and I wanted to hike on trails, go biking, and even climb mountains. I thought of even trying my hand at white water rafting, but I think I would probably enjoy kayaking. I wanted to get into shape.

With the extensive limitations of national and state parks, I would have to plan many months in advance to grab coveted sites at premium parks such as Yellowstone, Yosemite, and so forth. Planning that far ahead isn't my forte, and at this point of my life, I did not want to be stuck without an exit plan.

And this Discovery seemed hellbent on painting me into a corner with skyrocketing costs.

Chapter 15
DRIVING
OUR DISCOVERY

Theo and I loved driving our Discovery. Riding high above the road, floating over the roads (when they were good) and looking out through the expansive windshield as the vast landscape whizzed by... the experience is indescribable.

"She definitely has a pep to her ride," Theo said as we drove on State Highway 40 through Uniontown, Pennsylvania.

"I agree. I definitely agree," I said. "She has plenty of power to spare, even when climbing up steep hills and she just simply feels great."

"And the temps are holding below the halfway mark throughout these steep hills. She's in a good shape, radiator-wise," he responded. I nodded in relief.

We had been a bit worried about the hills. We had received tips from the Discovery Owners group suggesting manually downshifting to lower gears so the fan would run at a higher rpm, considerably cooling both the charged air cooler and the radiator. We didn't have to use that method at all, though—yet.

"I do wonder how she will take the Rocky Mountain roads in the west, though," I added. Just then, I recalled a friend, Jessica Kinney, saying, "Don't borrow worry. The future will take care of itself. You will only wear yourself down." Indeed.

We weighed her at CAT Scales in Hagerstown, Maryland and she was seven hundred pounds overweight on the rear axle, but overall she was two hundred pounds under the maximum weight limit. We tried to move heavy things to the front, but that

Theo driving the Discovery on State Highway 40 in Pennsylvania. Driving behind, I learned the brake lights would come on if the engine brake was engaged, even if my foot wasn't on the brake pedal. Cool.

only shifted about one hundred and fifty pounds. Theo pointed out, "Dad, we have four brand-new tires in the rear that are near maximum pressure so they should be okay for this trip."

Good point.

Yet the feeling of worry and being painted into a corner kept creeping up on me. It broadsided me several times in the middle of night, with me waking up in a cold sweat and chills, and I wasn't sure what I should have done differently up to this point.

I had planned to take three years off so I could remain on Social Security disability income (SSDI) benefits and request a total and permanent disability student loan waiver, available to those on SSDI with a seven-year medical review, which would wipe out over $53,000 in student loans for myself. The catch was I would be allowed to only earn up to $16,000 each year during the three-year monitoring period. I wanted to take a year off, being in solitude and with nature as I toured the country. I was considering Lamar University's doctoral program in Deaf Studies and Deaf Education; I could begin in the summer of 2019 with a seven-week program, and then transition to an online approach, meeting my cohort in person one weekend each semester. This would allow me the flexibility of traveling the country while doing my studies. The coursework would take up the last two years of the three-year monitoring period. By the end, I would become eligible to apply for a pre-tenure track faculty position at Gallaudet University and then work on my dissertation while teaching classes. The only issue I had was having to live within the poverty level for three years just to prove that I was still as Deaf as I had been since birth.

With the mounting costs of the RV, all on my personal credit cards, and my credit score dropping precipitously, would I be forced to cut my dream short and apply for a position that would take someone who only had a master's degree? That would mean a lower starting salary in addition to sacrificing the student loan waiver, easily adding back a $500-monthly payment for thirty years. If I were to accept a position with a $65,000 annual salary, the student loan payments would rapidly cut it down to $55,000 before taxes. With Gallaudet being in an ultra-expensive and hyper-gentrified neighborhood, I would be forced to live out in the suburbs and commute long hours daily.

There was a study by New Urbanists, a group of professionals trying to bring back traditional, compact and highly walkable and bikeable towns and neighborhoods. The study showed that for every five-minute increase in your daily commute, your happiness level markedly decreases.[3] So what would a one-hour commute do for my happiness? I had numerous friends who taught at Gallaudet but lived in Frederick, Maryland. They took the train to work, which easily required two hours a day for them. Ugh, no way.

That certainly wasn't something I wanted for my life. I have studied traditional neighborhood design and I can't imagine going back to the suburbs ever again. I want to have only one car

[3] http://www.thriveglobal.com/stories/is-your-commute-making-you-miserable

for the whole family. I want a large set of bikes. I want to walk to nearby amenities. And places like that cost a huge premium in the United States, unlike other places, particularly in Europe where vibrant, well-aged downtowns are highly walkable and the government subsidizes living downtown, making it so much more affordable.

And don't even get me started on universal health care. International Retired Living indexes affordable countries to live on one or two thousand dollars a month, with excellent health care, Internet services and a great expat community; these countries include Panama, Costa Rica, Belize, and Ecuador. In reading the magazine, I have often been tempted to do just that. I even considered driving down to Central America in my Discovery when I am just a bit more skilled at RV living. However, the drawbacks to these other countries are the severe gaps in accessibility for Deaf people. I would lose access to video relay services and many other top-notch accessible offerings here in the United States.

Challenges aside, the idea is that it is possible to live affordably in certain Central America countries, and I will find out one day whether this is feasible for Deaf people or not. I must also point out that these countries were colonized by Spanish, Portugal, and others, their cultures and languages banned, tampered with, and damaged in many ways—and the United States has been bad about this as well. So being a white Deaf United States citizen taking advantage of a cheaper lifestyle in other countries for personal gain while many remain in poverty does not sit well with me. I am sure they are welcoming of U.S. citizens and appreciate the dollars spent in their local economies. Yet I believe we must remain mindful of the larger picture and ponder what we should do about that.

Back to my current status: I was feeling powerless, painted into the corner financially. Not a good feeling at all.

I had already filed for bankruptcy in December 2011, doing the paperwork myself without an attorney. I was proud of myself for the few days it took to pull together all the paperwork. My family had been left deeply in debt as a result of losing health insurance and the failure of building the world's first sign language-centric town in Laurent, South Dakota. After many months of collection letters and judgments against me, I decided enough was enough. So I went through the process, paid the fees, and appeared before a judge who was a wheelchair user. The process went without a hitch.

But if my income was limited to $14,640 a year along with my disability income for the next three years and an ever-increasing credit card balance, would I face another bankruptcy? I couldn't even fathom the possibility. Besides, I couldn't file again until the required ten-year waiting period, which would end in December 2021. I told myself this was premature. "Borrowing worry," as my friend Jessica, would say.

I came up with a plan: I would take advantage of zero-interest balance transfer offers and consolidate my debts, buying another year of interest-free balances, and decide what to do then. I also would keep an eye on the market, expecting another serious crash that would affect everything, including RV sale prices—which would seriously limit my ability to sell the Discovery. Plus, we were already traveling to Indianapolis and Michigan so we couldn't even consider a sale at this point.

It was at that moment I noticed an oil leak again.

Damn.

Chapter 16
DRY-DOCKING
AND BIGFOOT

With the engine oil still leaking, we made our mandatory stop at Kings Island near Cincinnati. We needed our Diamondback fix as well as Mystic Timbers, The Beast, Banshee, The Bat, and Delirium. We left the generator running with the air conditioning to make sure our cat, Nauvoo, was comfortable as we excitedly sped around the park.

A glimpse of Gary Coleman in front of Theo and Alec. Gary, by now, had ridden Diamondback 15,500 times.

After Kings Island, we arrived at my mother's apartment in Indianapolis for a couple of days. Since there was no parking space for our Discovery, we parked next door at Meijer, but the manager frowned, shaking his head as he reluctantly allowed us to stay one night. So, we shortened our stay. Alec chose to stay behind with my mother, setting himself up with his PC so he could play Fortnite. His role model was Ninja, a young man making hundreds of thousands of dollars playing Fortnite on Twitch. It was around this time that another Deaf teenager Soleil Wheeler, aka "EwokTTV," became the first Deaf person to achieve high ranking in the world of Fortnite and streaming, amassing a huge following. Alec was cheering them on.

Alec could play that game very well, because he relied on the visual accessibility mode in the game, which turns off the sounds and replaces them with visual indicators showing where the bullets or footsteps are coming from. I told him I hoped he would make it big and play in large prize tournaments one day.

We said our goodbyes and started off for my father's home. We were ready to dry-dock her, and I was eager to work on a long list of to-do items on our Discovery as well as unload her. I had visions of a completed dining table, new vent fan in the kitchen, a Wi-Fi base station and antenna, and get this... (cue drum roll) a bidet!

Yes, a bidet.

You can't live without them after you've used one, seriously. Think about this... if you got crap smeared on your arm, would you be okay with wiping it off with toilet paper and nothing else? Eww, no. The bidet also does wonders for you if you struggle with hemorrhoids or irritation down there.

Why on earth would I take picture of our toilet? Because of the awesome bidet add-on that Theo installed, of course.

I had a Brondell Swish bidet ($250) with a warm water heater at my apartment, but unfortunately for our RV, we had to go with a simpler cold water Brondell model for about forty bucks. I loved it. I knew the bidet probably would pose a little bit of a challenge while boondocking, especially when trying to stretch water usage over longer stays. But I also knew we'd find a way through trial and error.

Nauvoo makes herself at home. Dealing with litter in a small space isn't pleasant, though.

As we drove up to Roscommon, Michigan, my dad texted us to meet at a diner across Higgins Lake from his home. We hugged as soon as we arrived, caught up, and enjoyed a nice dinner. I offered my dad a chance to drive my Discovery, and he jumped at the chance.

"It's definitely different than my Fleetwood Flair gas RV, especially those brake and gas pedals. It feels more stable, less rocking sideways," he signed as he expertly backed up the Discovery into the side driveway. We quickly found an old plywood board and shoved it under the engine area to catch dripping oil. We tried to level her but struggled a bit because the tires kept coming clear off the concrete. Dad got several old two-by-eight boards and we drove over these boards on one side. That solved it; she was perfectly level after the jacks went down a little bit.

Easy peasy. I said, "I want these boards." He looked at me for a minute before shrugging and saying, "Sure, why not?" Good. I didn't have to buy expensive leveling blocks; these boards would do just fine.

Nauvoo stayed inside the RV, the air conditioner running.

We were home, of sorts. None of my childhood homes has remained within my family, who has moved multiple times. My mother moved the most times, from Flint to Kalamazoo, Michigan then to Wentzville, Missouri for her final years until she retired and moved to Indianapolis. My father and Sonja moved from Swartz Creek to Clio then to Oscoda, and were finally now in Roscommon, a stone's throw away from the crystal-clear Higgins Lake. They had been at this location for seven years, and we always made it a point to come and visit every Christmas for a week or so. Every time we came, the lake was always frozen solid.

This had actually been only the second time we came in the summer. We all looked at each other and asked each other, "Why did we wait so long before we came in the summer? The lake is gorgeous!"

We took my dad's electric golf cart and drove half a mile down to the boat loading ramp at Higgins Lake. There, we drank in the breathtaking beauty of the lake against the backdrop of a setting sun. Why did we wait, indeed? Most of the summers we were pretty busy with travel and summer commitments including my teaching across the country. Besides, honestly, we weren't the outdoor type. We didn't really think about going out for long hikes, climbing hills or mountains or going canoeing. The reason was simple: bugs. As mentioned, my kids and I are serious mosquito magnets.

Another reason was simply the stress of organizing and taking care of logistics—tents, food, equipment, and herding the kids into van and then finally making the trip. But occasionally, when we did go camping, we always enjoyed the experience. Just not the stress leading up to it.

When the kids were younger, my ex-wife Jen and I were living in South Dakota. We joined a Deaf family-oriented, invitation-only camping group called Bigfoot. This was the brainchild of Russ and Melody Stein; Russ grew up in a Deaf

The laughter and family spirit we had at Bigfoot was unforgettable. Deb Kuglitsch with her late dog Gem and me, by the campfire.

family that had a similar group in New York, and they had some wild times. Russ and Melody wanted a family-oriented group, especially since there was a large group of Deaf families with children in Sioux Falls between 1995 and 2005, thanks to the largest Deaf-run non-profit agency, Communication Service of the Deaf. We took turns hosting the gathering, including selecting the campground, cooking for everyone on one night and organizing activities for children and teens as well as adults. Our family was initially invited as a guest then voted in as a full member. Each family received a nickname after a while. Know what our family was called?

The Survivors.

I chuckle at this now because it was so fitting. We barely made it through the camping weekend. Some of our equipment failed, and we forgot to bring certain foods or drinks. We had to borrow some of the equipment from others or share with others. Everyone felt bad for us. We just didn't have the skills. And we didn't go often enough in order to build up the necessary experience and skills, either. My father and Sonja went camping often, and I would go with them from time to time, alternating between loving it and being miserable from the mosquitoes or the crowds.

I recall one time when we decided to bite the bullet and buy a huge tent to fit all of six of us, and we went with Bigfoot to the Lake Thompson state park in South Dakota. The lake was huge; it had the feel of a Great Lake and you could barely see the shore on other side. The place was beautiful.

But oh, man... it was windy. We all settled in for the night after late hours of socializing where we sat in chairs all around the campfire as we chatted. The campfire was big enough for us to see each other, as visually oriented people, and was always a source of happiness for us.

It is always funny to walk around any campground seeing everyone else happy in the dark, talking and whispering around their fires. This isn't very convenient for Deaf folks. I get that for most of you, the dimness is a great ambience, especially when we want to be quiet and just observe the fire. But for conversations, nope—max out the lights for us.

The winds were picking up rapidly that night and we retired into our brand-new tent. We slept like babies, not privy to the noises out in the wild.

In the middle of the night, I woke up to something hanging two inches off my nose. The tent main support frame was broken, bent alarmingly towards my face. I leaped and ran outside, thinking I missed a hook-up. Nope. The tent support simply broke in half.

We had to scramble and reinforce the frame as much as we could, and then go back to sleep. It rained. By the end of the weekend, a huge thunderstorm came rolling in. We gave up on our tent long before that and had already packed up everything. But the other families waited, hoping to ride out the storm.

They had taken a bad bet. The storm was fierce. Everyone panicked and packed up as best they could but got soaked in the process. Some RV equipment was damaged as well. We met up at a nearby pizza place to dry ourselves and eat hot food. Soon enough, we were all laughing about it, trading stories of frantic departures.

The situation in Sioux Falls changed drastically for the Deaf community in the mid-2000s, when Communication Services for the Deaf began to lay off many of us, and also sold off a growing division to a new company in Clearwater, Florida. Many of us had to leave town, and this greatly affected the Deaf community in Sioux Falls.

By the time it was our turn to host, most of the families were already spread out across the country from California to Maryland, Indiana, and Minnesota. The logistics and timing made it more difficult for all of us, so we just let this group go quietly into that good night. I was disappointed that Bigfoot went away on our watch. But again, it was probably fitting; if it was going to happen, it would happen to us.

Back to today. I was determined to get back into the camping scene, but in style this time with my beautiful Fleetwood Discovery. My kids and I discussed the possibility of camping at the nearby South Higgins Lake State Park once we were done with the renovations. The campground stubbornly remained full, and the renovations... well, they took much longer than we expected.

And the engine situation wasn't remedied by a long shot.

Chapter 17
RENOVATIONS

JULY 18, 2018

- Mileage: **114,989**
- Previous total: **$15,213.38**
- MX57.com awning repair kit: **$414.94**
- Devaise slim file cabinet drawer: **$125.99**
- Wi-Fi CampPro 2: **$149.99**
- MaxxAir 7500 and three-year warranty: **$320.40**
- Miscellaneous items for repair or improvement (J-hook adapter for windshield wipers, digital cameras for side and undercarriage, marker lights, etc.): **$450.00**
- Current total: **$16,674.70**
- Credit score: **665**

We settled in and unloaded our things into my dad and Sonja's basement. We breathed a sigh of relief, knowing that our Discovery was now considerably lighter—well under the weight limitations for both axles. Drivers are encouraged to do a four-corner weigh-in with their motorhomes, rather than the typical front and rear weighs at CAT Scales. Unfortunately, that kind of weigh-in is difficult to find; usually the company that does four corner weigh-ins would come to rallies or RV events. We had no plans to go to these, for now.

We began our work on the RV, replacing the lightweight dining table installed by the previous owners. I was glad that the booth was removed because I wanted to work from my own office chair, and I already had a really nice and heavy wooden desk that would be custom fitted to our office/dining area. Theo and my dad went to work and made curved corners that exposed the particleboard. Theo sealed it with polyurethane and sanded it lightly. It ended up looking pretty good.

My dad sanding the edge of my favorite wooden desk as Theo looks on.

The support rack for the desk was kind of loose on the wall so my dad secured it with additional screws and moved it up to make the desk more level. With that reinforced, we then tackled the washer/dryer electrical lines. My mom and I tried to figure this out by working under the machine and identifying the wiring. We identified it but couldn't figure out where it went. It turned out that there was a central 120-volt fuse box under the refrigerator, with a clear label for one of the fuses: "Refrigerator 20-amp."

Geez.

My dad and I looked at this box, and it occurred to me that this box was an Intellitec model 900 load management system that automatically turned off specific appliances when at risk of being overloaded. When you have both rooftop air conditioning units running along with the refrigerator, you potentially run into a power overload situation and this management unit handles that for you by "shedding" or turning off the appliances in the order you set it up.

We found that the washer and dryer line was connected to the circuit board, and the relay was dead. We took that off and wired it up direct to the fuse. That fixed the washer and dryer!

I realized that the Intellitec system had never displayed how many amps were in use in the first place. This unit was broken before I bought her. I had wondered about the weird digits flickering at the front of the coach. Working properly, it would have lit up when I was on generator, or 30- or 50-amp shore power. It never did. I wasn't happy to find that something else was broken. The fuses were usable and in place so that was okay—but the ability to automatically shed power was gone until I had the circuit board replaced at a price of about $350.

M&M RV Electronics in Ohio City, Ohio does this kind of work, and they provide email technical support for Intellitec units. I did try to get my RV into their shop, but they were booked out for months and I was heading out west. I figured I'd live without the power management system.

I tried several approaches to fix the power management unit over the few days with no luck, so I just left the washer and dryer bypassing the circuit board. It worked just fine.

My dad and I drove to Camping World in Houghton Lake, Michigan and bought the MaxxAir vent. I got the store to match the greatly discounted price on their online store, saving $168. After reading some reviews on how faulty MaxxAir vents can be in the first year, I decided to spend extra on a three-year warranty.

Faulty devices are sadly commonplace in RVs, especially since RVs are literally rolling homes, vibrations shaking the parts loose. There is a major quality control issue on newly constructed RVs throughout the industry today, and there is no oversight agency such as JD Power to measure the initial and long-term reliability of RVs. I have read in multiple places it's better to

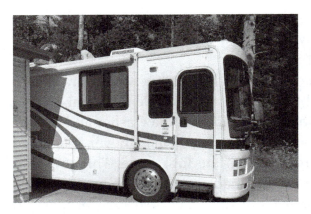

Theo and Stefania (on top) work together to remove the old vent fan for replacement by the MaxxAir Deluxe.

purchase an at least two-year-old RV because the initial buyers are the ones who must deal with the headaches of warranty repairs for everything done incorrectly in the factory. With a slightly older RV, it usually is in much better shape than one was right out of the factory. But like in my situation, *caveat emptor*. Buyers must do their homework and be sure the extended warranty package is worth its weight in dollars. The wait times for warranty repairs are seriously ridiculous so buyers shouldn't assume they are easily protected.

Speaking of coverage, I needed to fix our awning. I ordered an awning repair kit that would come with a section of awning roll. This repair was made possible by Theo's courage and foresight in saving the awning, and I was grateful for that. As the kit was being shipped, we went to work on the vents, replacing the marker lights, fixing a couple of broken electrical outlets, and trying to replace the rollers on my bedroom closet sliding doors. We replaced them all right, but by October, they were worn out again. The replacements along with their originals were cheap plastic rollers, designed for screen doors instead of the heavy mirror doors I had.

Days flew by while we worked on our Discovery, and I was eager to go out on the road to begin this new chapter of my life—full-timing in my Discovery with lots of solitude, reflection, and hopefully healing from a stress-filled, single dad life. But with the engine oil leaking, we had to do something. I called around and took her to Fick & Sons, a diesel repair shop in Grayling, Michigan. We had to bring Nauvoo inside my dad and Sonja's house and try to restrict her in the kitchen area. My dad is allergic to cats. Nauvoo didn't quite cooperate, so she ended up in the kids' bedroom upstairs at nighttime. For a sixteen-year-old cat that limped, she sure could jump up over the tall wooden board that was supposed to block her from doing just that.

At Fick & Sons, I told the workers my sob story of the inspection phase not catching so many issues. I told them I had spent way too much on this and I needed the cheapest, most cost-effective way to stop the oil from leaking any further. The manager, Garrett Joles, said he would have his team look at her and text me.

A day later, I got Garrett's text:

From what we can see sir I would honestly return this if you just purchased it. Believe the quote you already received will multiply greater once repairs started. We believe from damage that already occurred you will be replacing the motor in a short time to come.

I sat there in my father's living room, frozen in place. I looked at my dad and Theo in stunned silence before I went back to my iPhone. I could feel the color drain from my face. Again. I texted back, "What would it cost to replace the motor with you? I've seen a 3216b motor core for $7,500."

He replied, "Pending on mileage. $7,500 be a lil higher mileage motor. Be pretty extensive amount of labor because of position. The frame is scary to say the least."

Damn it. First the engine and now the frame? I asked, "I bought this from a private seller in April so there's no returning it. And the inspection gave it passing marks. Frame? As in chassis?"

Garrett clarified that he was referring to the house frame, not the chassis. "You could easily put twenty grand into this."

Great. I had already gone too deep at this point. I was pissed and tired of being punched in the gut and body-slammed several times. I just wanted the hits to stop coming.

I wearily replied, "So you don't recommend doing further repairs on it until we bite the bullet on engine replacement... I assume twenty grand on top of the eleven grand I already put in it."

"Yes, I think patching it will only buy you a short amount of time and waste your money and I would not want to do that to you."

"I truly appreciate your honesty. Any other ideas or advice?"

"Pending what your investment is in it. I would sell it as is," he concluded.

I had bought it for $34,000 with a NADA value of $31,650. Add the $11,000 I had already put in it… It wasn't looking good.

He added, "Won't get much for it. But if you have a lot into it, you might want to complete some repairs."

A moment later, responding to what I bought the RV for and what I put in so far, he texted, "Oh, wow. I am very sorry."

I wasn't ready to give up, though. "What would be the minimum work that can be done, given the amount I put in? So I can resell?"

> Really, I think you get into it, it will spiral into more and more issues. I could easily put ten into it and not be confident if would last days if not weeks without breaking down. We are more than happy to do the work, just don't feel right charging that kind of money and not knowing if it will not break down again that day. I couldn't have any kind of warranty on it from the moment it left unless it was fixed correctly. We take a lot of pride in our workmanship and want to do the best for you.

"Appreciate this. We will pick it up this Friday morning. Let me know what I owe you for looking at it."

"Owe us nothing, believe you occurred enough expense. If we can help more let me know," he graciously responded.

After a flurry of back-and-forth with Theo, I asked Garrett,

Would you be willing to point out frame concerns to us when we come by? We are aware of one that's rusted through the next to front left wheel and was told that was redundant frame. We had planned to weld a new one. But again the motor is a major concern. Used motors go for $2,500-5,000 on the Internet. But the labor to install will be costly.

He replied, "Correct, if you want a motor we can do it. We go through vendors that have limited warranty on their motors. More than happy to do repairs. Like I said, just don't want you think we would take advantage of you."

I asked one last question: "Curious. Engine vibration—normal or abnormal? It did feel particularly strong. But riding in the back of MCI buses, I did feel the same."

"Not really because of the multitude of issues."

Desperate, I needed something out of this nightmare. I asked, "I just contacted a law firm (800-Call-Sam) to see if we can pursue a case against our RV inspection company—I wonder if you could write up a mechanic's report so I could share with them? Again, thank you for being so honest. This isn't a good feeling at all. But it helps."

"We understand, and our hearts are with you. I assure you this isn't right." With that, Garrett signed off.

I sat there, stewing. I was in a foul mood for the next couple of days. I wanted to walk away from this damn RV, even if it meant I would be tens of thousands of dollars in the hole with credit card debt and nothing to show for it. No RV. No cross-country tour. No solitude and self-care time. No communing with nature.

To add insult to injury, the law firm wouldn't take my case. Since it wasn't a personal injury case, they recommended finding a firm with civil litigation expertise. Ugh.

Later that day, Theo looked at me determinedly. "Dad, I honestly disagree with what they had to say. The engine runs great—sure, it vibrates strongly but I think she would last a long time. I think the house frame issues can be fixed with some welding, grinding and paint job. I agree with them that our Discovery isn't in good shape at all, but she works." He reminded me that the Discovery had carried us across the Appalachians round-trip twice without complaining.

I said, "Well, except for that $1,200 and two nights in Ohio for the air brake system work…"

"I know. Still. Remember, Dan Greer thought the engine was in pretty good shape. Maybe ask him for his opinion again and share what Garrett had to say," Theo suggested.

A day later, I texted Garrett.

Hi. Our plans changed. We'd like to come and pick up my RV within the next hour. Could you point things out to us on concerns with frame and so forth? See you then? We are on the way now. And another thing we are unsure of is the fact that engine powered through east coast mountains two round trips in the past two months and the most recent trip was fully loaded, only 240 pounds short of its max load with our stuff. Engine didn't hesitate or struggle at all. We had to clean the radiator through three cycles of simple green and after that it didn't overheat. So… because we are 'screwed' by the inspection, I'm trying to make best possible decision here. The gasket around the hydraulically actuated electronic unit injection (HEUI) housing is definitely a concern because it allows mixture of unfiltered and filtered oil. If we leave that unfixed, it'll definitely shorten the engine life. As for frame, there are no weak spots in the RV floor anywhere. It's rock solid. We are trying to get a friend of ours who is a commercial welder to take a look at housing frame and give us his opinion.

Once we got there, Garrett showed us the areas of concern, and we thanked him for his time. Theo noted that our Discovery hadn't been moved from its spot when we dropped her off, so it was clear they didn't bring her in the bay and take a closer look at her. Maybe that was an issue. But I figured they knew what they were doing. If they could see issues on the surface, they must know there were a lot more to be found everywhere else.

I texted Dan Greer:

Hi Dan! Hope you are doing well. We made it to Roscommon, Michigan where my dad lives. We dry-docked the RV there so we could do additional work. The oil cooling housing gasket kit was installed by a two-guy shop who also worked on our broken hydraulic leveling system and replaced old belts along with broken pulley (it was sticking badly) and charged us $4,500 without an estimate. Needless to say. I was pissed but had to pay because we needed the RV back so we could move out of our apartment and into it. Anyway. Apparently, the new gasket made leaks worse in other place—most likely the HEUI and air compressor housing. We took her in at Fick & Sons in Grayling who took a look at the whole thing and told us basically to walk away from the RV. Devastating. They feel that if we continue to put in more repairs, it'll just spiral into more and more issues. They were also concerned about the house frame (lots of rust). They wouldn't even charge me for looking at it. I'm basically in a hard situation here. I can't sell her without losing money because I would have to honestly disclose that she's a "mechanic's special." Yet her floor feels absolutely solid everywhere. And she made two full round trips through east coast mountains without complaining. No hesitation or struggling. I'm trying to think through my options. Reman engine is $7,500 plus labor = $20k easy? Used engine maybe $3k but labor is what will be so costly. Any thoughts? Advice? Truly grateful for your help.

He replied quickly to my lengthy message:

I would charge $5,000 in labor for the engine. And I don't recall that unit being in that bad of shape. I guess I would want to look it all over and see but I can't see that being in that rough of shape to get rid of it. I would take a good look over it if you could stop by sometime. The leaks made worse might not be something that was there in the first place and might not be horrible to fix. Is the engine running good?

A brief flicker of hope passed through me as Theo nodded knowingly. "I told you so, Dad. We have people with different opinions, and I think we are okay."

"I want to say it's running well. But I'm not a mechanic," I texted to Dan. "Hmm. $5,000 labor even for a confined space in the RV? It's a bitch to work with, you know?"

He replied, "Oh, yeah, we have done them before, and they are not fun. They have to be dropped from under."

I asked, "Yeah. And what would you charge to replace the HEUI and air compressor housing gaskets? I think once I know the approximate cost of doing HEUI and air compressor gasket then I can weigh that with the cost of replacing the motor. God. I love that RV. It's really nice inside. Sigh."

He ended with, "Okay, I'll look it up and see. It did seem like a nice one."

Clearly, we couldn't drive her back to Dan's shop, so we needed an alternative plan. Our experience with Alban CAT Power hadn't been entirely positive, but I was reading a set of emails from Bruce Plumb, a Discovery Owners group member who happened to be traveling through Michigan. He had to make a repair stop at Michigan CAT in Kalkaska, about an hour's drive away. Bruce detailed his issues with HEUI, a certain oil pump bound to fail due to the lack of filtering. He praised Michigan CAT head mechanic Alan Spence for doing such good work on his engine, despite the $6,000 repair price tag.

If Alan was as good as Bruce claimed, then it was probably worth a try. Yet, I was dreading the $115 hourly labor cost, and there are no free estimates in the world of diesel mechanics. I called Jim Schultz at Michigan CAT before my dad, Theo and I went up there together to drop our Discovery off.

Chapter 18
MICHIGAN CAT

On August 7, with my father following in his Silverado truck, we arrived at Michigan CAT in Kalkaska without any issues. I backed the Discovery into the first open bay. Jim Schultz, whom I spoke with on the phone, wasn't there that day so it was Alan Spence who met with me. He said it would take a few hours to look through our Discovery's CAT 330 hp 3126b engine.

"I really need to find out what is the minimum I can do to stop the leaks and from further problems developing down the road," I typed to Alan on his PC, which was atop a mechanical tool drawer set. "Bottom line, we were told that she has weeks to live, if not days. And I need to know for sure whether it is worth doing more work on her or just replace the motor."

Alan nodded and went to work. We went for lunch at the nearby Trout Town Cafe, hidden a few blocks away from the main road. As I sat down with Dad and Theo, I said, "I just remembered what Jim Schultz said on the phone last week. After I explained everything, and I asked him the engine may have to be swapped out. Know what he said?" They shook their head in curiosity.

"He said he would be surprised that we would need to replace the engine if she still runs strong, managed to get through the Appalachians twice. So, he thinks the engine may still be in good shape but needs all the gaskets replaced," I said with a hopeful look.

Making funny faces to ward off high repair estimates at Michigan CAT in Kalkaska. The bedroom slide is pulled out to allow full access to the engine.

Yes, the RV's house frame was badly rusted in places, especially on the driver's side—there were some frames that were fully rusted through. But we could work with that, I felt. It wouldn't be easy, but with grinding, welding, and so forth, it could be done.

Theo said, "Basically, like I told you before, I think she has got at least 100,000 more miles in her. I think she's good to go after a few more repairs."

I wanted to believe him. I really did.

We finished our lunch and came back to Michigan CAT, lounging in the waiting room as Alan finished up. After an hour or so, Alan called us over to his computer in the bay right behind our Discovery, typing the verdict: "Good news. This engine model doesn't have the faulty HEUI issue. You are in the clear. The engine is running pretty well. I think she would have another 300,000 miles in her at least."

Theo triumphantly looked at me, "See, Dad? I was right!"

I smiled as I let out a breath of relief.

Alan continued, "We do need to replace as many gaskets as possible. We also will need to replace the air compressor unit—it's in pretty bad shape. We got a new one with a three-year warranty for about $700. I will put together an estimate for you if you can give me a few minutes."

Awesome. I swiveled to see Theo and Dad, who was sitting in his truck, and signed, "But I am afraid to see what the estimate will be... I think it will be in the $7,000-9,000, or maybe even $10,000, range."

Theo shook his head. "No, I think it will be $3,500."

Ever the optimist. I turned to Dad, and he sarcastically said, "One dollar."

"Oh, playing the *Price is Right* game, eh?" I said.

He nodded, grinning.

It took about another hour before the estimate came. And it was "only" $3,184.88. With a new air compressor. I was so relieved. My dad had won the guessing game with his one-dollar prediction. Theo had his "I told you so" look on, and I wanted to hug him. The world of diesel pusher repairs had really distorted my view of what was a "reasonable" cost. I was so used to the fact the repairs on our cars and vans rarely broke the $1,000 mark.

It was enough to make my head spin.

I told Alan to go ahead. We shook hands as I thanked him profusely. We left the RV there for at least a week and drove back home. In the meantime, we worked on the closet sliding doors. We weren't successful in finding factory replacements for the closet plastic wheels, but Theo came up with a homemade solution of using plastic wheels. Unfortunately, this solution didn't even last a couple of months. We should have bought steel ball bearing rollers.

My friend Ric came up from Grand Rapids for a visit that week. We went to Higgins Lake each night, chatting under the clear skies as we looked out at the clear water. Theo found a used vintage Jeep for sale down the road for the asking price of $4,500. Ric and I went with him to give it a look over and take it out for a test drive.

"I love the clean look of the instrument display and the simplicity of everything, including under the hood," Theo said in excitement.

Unfortunately, the rust on the frame and chassis looked scary enough. After a few days of thinking on it, Theo decided to walk away. If this Jeep was restored, the value could have climbed up anywhere from $8,000 to $18,000 depending on the level of restoration. But we didn't have time or place to really restore the Jeep, and Theo was heading back to DC in just a few weeks.

Ric, who works on his own cars and is a pretty capable mechanic, gave Theo some advice. Ric said at one point about his cars, "I am often confident in thinking I could do this and once I get into it, I sometimes find myself out of my depth… but I just keep at it until I get it fixed."

Confidence. Or overconfidence. Faking it until you make it. Was that something I could apply to the repairs?

Ric cautioned, "Although with diesel engines of that size, you often will need tools that we just don't have. And a lot of time, a lot of trial and error." True.

We did things around the house, including raking and cleaning up a lot of wood and leaves in the backyard, and repairing other stuff while waiting for our Discovery. I anxiously checked in with Alan via text message asking for updates. It did take a few days before an open bay was available and she was finally ready to be looked at.

I texted Alan on August 10 asking if he could do a tune-up since the engine was running with pretty strong vibrations— almost as if there was a mount loose.

"Yes, I am in right now and yes, we will adjust the valves." A short bit later, he sent two pictures and said, "I did get it all apart a little harder than I expected. I must replace the bolts. The heads are rusted but the biggest concern is the way the front cover is eroded at the air compressor mounting and at the speed timing holes. I can try to seal up with some sealer, but I don't know how long it will last. The front cover is pretty bad."

Sigh. I texted, "What would it cost to replace front cover? And that's the one that you didn't include in the quote, right?"

"You are correct. I was trying not to charge to do the labor of resealing. The radiator would have had to come out to do this. I will look up the part cost."

A moment later, he texted, "The housing is $909.55. I would have to order it in. The radiator would have to come out. You are talking about at least three days of labor, bolts and whatever else breaks coming apart. Basically time and materials."

Crap. I did some mental calculations and texted back, "Three days. Eight hours of labor each times $118 would be $2,800 labor plus whatever happens?"

"Yes."

Ouch. I had to think on this for a minute. I talked with my dad and Theo, and we went back and forth for a while. I figured it was probably best to leave the sleeping dog alone—if we were to open up her further, we would find more and more problems along with skyrocketing labor costs. The radiator was in bad shape but holding, and I figured we would want to buy some time before the radiator had to come out. That was when we could replace the front cover.

I texted back, "As opposed to using seals (RTV?) on the front cover, that would cost me nothing, but you are not sure how long it would last before the oil leaks again, right?"

I added, "By doing seals, you would be removing the front cover part the way—no need to take out radiator and seal up then back on the engine? For me, the question is also do you still think the engine would last another 300,000 miles after taking it apart so far?"

He didn't reply until the next day, clearly busy. "Basically, the repair going back together using a sealer will not cost you much more. Just the hardware that was rounded off due to corrosion. The leaks will definitely slow down and maybe even stop. But yes, I will use the gaskets, seals and an anaerobic sealer with it. You are correct that to change the pitted cover, the radiator would have to come out."

I pressed on, "You still think the engine will last another 300,000 miles?"

He said, "Looks clean. No sludge in the engine. I think there is a good possibility that the engine could outlast the coach due to couple of things. The engine is clean inside but the rust now... I have to put wrench on the bolts, and that part is hard to tell what you would be fighting with down the road."

So, okay... After another long night thinking on this, I decided to seal her up and leave things be for now, buy myself some time. Saturday morning, I texted Alan: "Good morning. I am leaning towards sealing the front cover. Will the new air compressor be secure? It is responsible for the air brake system and air bags, right?"

He replied, "Yes, the air compressor will be secure. The sealing surface is the only issue and the sealer should fill the void. And yes, the air compressor supplies air to the air system for everything that runs on air, suspension and brakes."

I told him to go ahead, and they said they would work on the Discovery on Monday. I had a sneaking feeling that they would exceed the estimate. Theo reminded me of a sign we saw at Fick & Sons stating that Michigan law required that we be informed of estimate changes any time the cost went over fifty dollars. I felt somewhat reassured.

I was so ready to take her on the road. Our stay at my father's had extended past three weeks and Theo and Warrick had to be in Indianapolis soon so they could drive back to DC with their mother. I became anxious. It was already Monday, August 14. Warrick needed to be at his new high school in four days, on Saturday the eighteenth.

Pressed for time, I worked on a back-up plan. The first thing on Monday morning, with some anticipation, I texted Alan, "Hi Alan. Hope your day is going well. Wanted to check in on my RV. How's it going?"

A quick reply: "It is going. I will let you know how far I get this afternoon."

Nothing came for the rest of the day, and I didn't want to bother Alan. I sat tight. Even my dad looked at me and said "Don't bother that guy, okay?"

The next morning, Alan texted, "I apologize for not getting back with you yesterday. I got the cam follower on HEUI pump, air compressor, power steering pump and ECM on. I still have to put in the push tubes, adjust the overhead, install the riser valve cover, fill with coolant, change the oil run, and check over."

I left him alone… for the time being.

A few hours later, I checked again. He was changing the oil and I asked if he thought our Discovery would be ready by the end of the day. He was cautiously optimistic.

A while later, he texted, "I do have it running. No leaks so far, but I do have the rough running that you were talking about. The #3 injector has current faults. I think it is the injector harness. I did order one for the morning."

Damn. Another day, more parts and labor. I asked him how much that would be. He held me off, saying, "Give me a few. Right now I am pulling the valve cover just to verify but that is my guess right now. I did order one in case."

A few minutes later, he texted, "It was just a wire end. I was able to repair it. You could plan on picking up in the morning. We still have to clean up."

Whew. Still, we had to wait until the next morning at 7:00 when they opened. By 6:00 a.m., I got a text from Alan: "I am just reading my email from last night and this is what I got: second shift steamed was running after and the miss came back. He removed the valve cover and rechecked the wiring after replacing the wire end and it was good, so Mike ordered an injector."

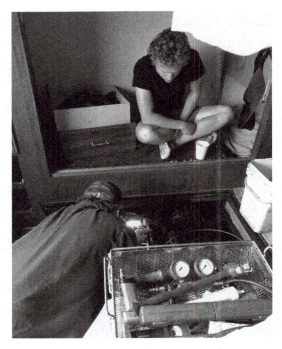

Alan Spence of Michigan CAT works on injector #3 as Theo looks on.

Okay. I was feeling the pressure and shared that with Alan, who said, "I am trying my best. I am still hoping for some time this morning to afternoon. You're welcome to come and watch and you can take it as soon as I get it cleared up. I think this is the intermittent rough running you were talking about. Now that I removed that riser to reseal it. Disturbing it made the miss show up more just every now and then."

I replied, "Okay. Glad you caught that and I'm not sure if it's related to what we were feeling—what we felt was pretty consistent rough vibration as if something was off balance while engine was idling. Deaf folks are more attuned to vibrations since we don't hear—but unfortunately, most of us aren't trained mechanics so we don't make those connections to the types of vibrations. But while engine is in motion, it's fairly smooth. We may come up and watch the work. My son Theo is curious. When do you expect the injector to arrive?"

"It is here."

Nothing more needed to be said. Theo and I hurriedly got ready and took my dad's truck. I texted Alan: "Don't wait for us. Go ahead and work on it. We'll come after we eat breakfast."

We arrived around ten and went inside the Discovery. The engine head case was open, exposing the wiring and injectors. We were fascinated by the innards—at least the upper portion—of the mighty (by my standards) CAT 330 hp engine.

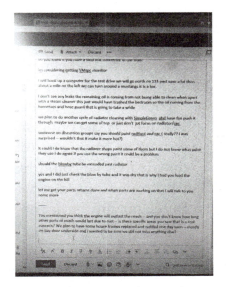

Alan and I communicate using his PC at the shop.

Alan came inside and greeted us. I was glad to see him. He motioned for Theo to sit nearby so he could observe Alan work on the injector. The remanufactured injector was massive. And heavy. I marveled at the thousands of different parts working together seamlessly to produce enough power to bring a thirteen-ton coach up and down the mountains.

After a while, Alan tested the injector and was satisfied. Alan typed on my iPhone, "Let us take her out for a drive. I will monitor all cylinders to see if they are running properly."

The engine compartment was closed up and floor covers back in place, the work area cleaned up. It took some time but eventually we were ready to head out.

I eased her out of their lot, onto the state highway and drove. Alan was in the passenger's seat along with his laptop and wire snaked to a port under the dashboard. Numbers were jumping around on the screen.

Alan gave us a thumbs up as he nodded at the screen. He told me to floor it while climbing up a hill, and I was happy to oblige. The RV responded happily as Theo said, "She feels great. Good power. Still peppy as ever."

Yup. We turned her around and came back. I backed her up into the same bay, stopping short before entering and parked her. It was time to see the total bill. I knew it would be a bit higher than $3,200 but it shouldn't have been more than $3,700 according to Michigan estimate law. Alan said it would be a while before he could bring us the invoice. He went inside, which I found out later was to talk with Jim Schultz, whom I had spoken with earlier on the phone.

While we waited, we cleaned the Discovery up a bit inside. I told Theo I was nervous about the final bill. Theo tried to reassure me, "Dad, nothing we can do at this point. Don't worry about it." After about half an hour of waiting, both Jim and Alan handed me a huge stack of sheets with the final invoice. I nervously swallowed as I thumbed to the bottom line.

$6,051.91.

Chapter 19
FLOORED, FOR THE UMPTEENTH TIME

AUGUST 15, 2018

- Mileage: **115,068**
- Previous total: **$16,674.70**
- Engine gaskets, front cover sealed with RTV, air compressor (without core charge refund), and over 37 hours of labor: **$6,051.91**
- Current total: **$22,725.61**
- Credit score: **645**

---

reeled at the total, and immediately became pissed off. Weren't they supposed to give me an estimate and get my express authorization before going ahead with the job?!

I really respected Alan, and I appreciated his willingness to communicate with me. He did his job well, but I just... $6,051.91?! What the hell was this?

Alan and Jim spoke to each other, and I was not sure what was going on at the moment. Alan typed on the computer, explaining that the air compressor was so badly rusted through that they couldn't even send the unit back in for a core charge refund of approximately $900. I lost $900 alone simply because the rust was too nasty.

I fought back. I typed angrily, saying they were supposed to, by law, give me an estimate and get my express authorization—which I never received.

Jim nodded, and typed back, "I know. We were supposed to do that. I am sorry. I already cut nearly $3,000 from the invoice by flat-rating the labor. The hours our mechanics put in her were too high, way over thirty-seven hours because of the rust. The bolts and nuts kept rounding off, forcing drastic measures."

I was dumbfounded. My invoice should have been over $9,000? Because of the stupid rust?

Jim continued, "But as for the air compressor, what we can do is to look around for a used one and send that in as a core charge. I am confident that we can find one for about $200, and you should get $700 back in a week or two."

That helped... a bit. I looked at Theo, who looked as shocked as I felt. He quickly reasoned, "You know what? The engine has stopped leaking oil. He did what he had to do. The rust is worse than what we thought. I honestly think it's a good thing they cut $3,000 off the invoice in the first place."

I stood there for a few minutes, seething. I had to stop myself for a moment. Alan probably did me a favor by trying to rush the work. They were willing to do the additional work of finding a used air compressor for us. That wasn't cheap for them, labor-wise.

I took a deep breath and relented. "Okay, I'll pay."

Jim nodded. Alan was talking to one of his co-workers and I became concerned that Alan would get in trouble for not providing the estimate for my approval. I typed to Jim, "On one condition."

Jim looked at me quizzically as I continued typing, "You don't dock his pay to help cover the amount you cut out of the invoice. He did a great job, and he was great about communicating with me as a Deaf person via texts. I felt I was on top of things while he worked on the engine."

Jim smiled, and he called Alan over, sharing what I had said. Alan laughed, and we shook hands. At that point, Jim had to go back to the office and finalize the invoice for us. I winced slightly as I handed him my credit card.

Alan motioned for Theo and me to follow him deep into back of their shop. The place was huge. They must have had over twenty-five bays for trucks and heavy equipment along with a large warehouse for parts. Alan walked to a brown box and showed what was inside.

There it was. Our air compressor, in all its glory.

The air compressor unit was so badly rusted that the unit couldn't be sent back for rebuild, sticking me with a core charge.

Holy mother of God. The unit was in such bad shape that it wasn't even funny. It was rusted out on the outside on many layers, and almost everything was flaking off. I immediately understood why they couldn't send it back in for a core charge.

Theo's eyes widened at the sight, and said, "If this is in such bad condition, what does it mean for the rest of the coach?" I grimaced; I didn't want to even think about it.

Alan then told us to follow him back to a semi-truck undergoing a major engine overhaul. We could see pistons— massive pistons nearly the size of bowling balls—on the worktable, and the chassis of the semi-truck look pretty weathered. There was rust in a lot of places.

I typed on my iPhone, using Cardzilla, a fantastic app developed by Tim Kettering, who is Deaf. "So… I see rust everywhere here, also."

Alan nodded and typed on my phone, "This truck has two million miles on it, and is undergoing an engine overhaul for the second time. She actually has less rust on her than your coach."

What?!

Sickened, I looked at the truck in disbelief. We wrapped things up, and Jim was kind enough to offer us two free baseball caps. Theo picked a white cap with the CAT logo emblazoned on it, and I picked a weathered CAT logo cap in dull gray that I planned to give to one of my other sons. We shook hands with Jim and Alan and thanked them.

I turned to Theo. Grinning, I cracked, "Well, we got ourselves $3,000 caps."

It was time for beer. Theo had just turned twenty-one a few weeks back, so he suggested that we stop by Paddle Hard Brewing Company in Grayling on his dime. I wasn't going to turn my son down. Theo and Warrick had school to go to, and I had my next chapter of my life to look forward to, right?

Chapter 20
SAYING GOODBYES AND HELLOS

Me, Warrick, Theo, Sonja, and Dad on the last morning of our stay.

We finished up the awning, which took a lot of hair-raising effort because the torsion rollers inside the awning roll on one side could come loose and spin out the wrench, potentially hurting or even killing someone. I actually yelled at Theo and my dad for taking the liberty of trying to spin it without a safety pin inserted.

"I don't want to lose one of you! I'm serious. This isn't worth making a mistake over." I glared at them as they shrugged my words off and continued working. It took us a few hours of trying to get it right, but we finally rolled the awning back in place only to find out that the locking pin was facing the wrong direction. Even though I was upset, Theo wanted to leave it as it was. I insisted on fixing it in the event I wanted to rent her out via RV rental websites one day to recoup some of the expenses.

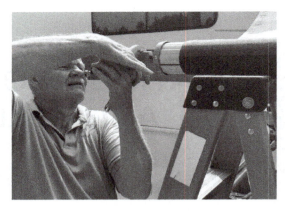

Dad carefully adjusts the torsion before we roll the awning back into place.

Dad went ahead and redid the whole thing: drilling out the newly riveted end cap, turning it around, and putting it back the next day. I worked frantically to tie up loose ends, like installing a gutter spout extender on both sides of the front end. I did the passenger side, and it went without a hitch. I had to the driver's side gutter next. I dragged a six-foot aluminum ladder my dad borrowed from his Deaf neighbor, Jerry, so we could have two ladders holding up the awning roll. I set that ladder up on a rather uneven surface, half on concrete and the other half on grass. I climbed up, mindful of the instability, and tried to reach the gutter spout near the roof line. I couldn't quite reach up there, so I had to go into the "no-step" zone—the top two rungs of ladder—and I was able to install the gutter extender and caulk it in place. I was all done just as Theo came around and asked if I was okay.

"Sure, I'm almost done."

Of course, as soon as he walked away, I lost my balance. I remember thinking, *Oh, shit!* as I fell nearly six feet, hitting the grass with my left leg slightly bent—fortunately, I hadn't hit the concrete part straight on. Even so, the impact was unbearable. My other leg swiped the ladder, and I was rolling on the ground, moaning loudly, cursing and holding my leg, rubbing the calf.

All of my worldly possessions in Dad's and Sonja's basement.

I couldn't get up. And I couldn't yell for my family members. They were blissfully working on other things and of course couldn't hear me.

I had to crawl across the driveway before they noticed me and ran over. I said, "I fell from top of the damn ladder as soon as Theo turned around and left." My dad looked at the ladder and saw that the bottom struts were all bent inwards. We would have to buy a new one for Jerry.

I was in such pain. Sonja came up and worriedly said, "I hope you didn't fracture anything."

Me, too. Dammit.

They helped me inside the house and got ice packs on my legs, loaded me up with ibuprofen and naproxen sodium, and I was miserable. We were supposed to leave that day for Indianapolis. Meanwhile, Theo took a power nap. My dad came around and talked with me for a while before he continued to load things up in my RV. After about an hour, I was feeling better. I could walk around.

I went downstairs and took a picture of our stuff. Clearly, I had a long way to go before I could rival India's independence movement leader Mohandas Gandhi in keeping things to a bare minimum.

We said our goodbyes. I wanted to stop at a gas station in downtown Houghton Lake because they had the cheapest diesel fuel in the state at only $2.89 per gallon. I filled her up, and then we headed south to Indianapolis. It was lunchtime, and I was in the mood for sushi. It had been weeks since we had good sushi.

We stopped in downtown Mount Pleasant at a sushi restaurant on Main Street. Unfortunately, even though Google Maps said they were open, they were closed until 5:00 p.m. We instead ate at a sandwich shop next door, and our sushi craving would continue until we pulled into Fishers, Indiana that evening for dinner at our favorite place, Wild Ginger on 116th Street. Their sushi rice is just right, the salmon buttery, and their Mistake Roll is a family favorite. We highly recommend this place, along with Sushi Masa on Phillips Street in downtown Sioux Falls, South Dakota where I first fell in love with sushi. But if you want to experience the best sushi in the country, go to Takashi in Salt Lake City. Heavenly.

Stuffed, we headed to my mother's apartment. We unloaded some things and then parked in Meijer's parking lot, and their customer service grumbled about it as usual, but I told them it would be only for a few days. I had every intention of heading out west as soon as I could.

Within a day, Theo, Warrick, my mom, and the children's mother Jen left for Washington, DC in a rental car. Unfortunately, they found the car in bad shape, brake-wise, and the tires were iffy. Instead

Let sleeping cats lie. Our Nauvoo.

of heading south after dropping off Warrick and Theo at MSSD and Gallaudet, they went straight back home. I was enjoying Mom's place, especially the quiet time with Alec. Nauvoo purred happily on my lap.

Upon their return, it was time for me to get ready for my new life and adventures. With a full apartment, I decided to hop over to Aunt Laura's place nearby. There, I had my own guest bedroom and access to an awesome soaking bathtub. I also could park my Discovery on their street, although not on level ground. Since the refrigerator wasn't working right anyway, it was turned off.

On Wednesday, August 22, I decided to do a dry run by camping at Monroe Lake State Park near Bloomington, Indiana for a week. I wanted to see if I had everything I needed, including riding my Sondors electric bikes into Bloomington to do some food shopping. I was concerned about the Sondors bike's limited range; they could be ridden for only a 15-18-mile range, and I couldn't use them if the battery went dead. They had no gears, either so it was very difficult, especially on the fat tire one, to bike anywhere. I needed to be sure it was feasible to park my Discovery and bike into town. I even installed collapsible metal wire frame baskets on the bikes to carry grocery bags.

It was now time to camp for real. I made the reservation and drove my RV to Fresh Thyme where I spent over $200 to stock my weakly running refrigerator. I then stopped at Camping World store to pick up a battery-powered refrigerator circulator fan to help further chill the fridge. With that done, I was ready.

I got onto I-65 and within minutes, the check engine light blinked on.

For the first time since I owned her, I felt an actual loss of power. The Discovery shuddered, struggled to pick up speed, and then outright slowed down. The check engine light was blinking. What the hell was going on?

With a loss of power for the first time, the Check Engine light came on several times.

I thought Alan Spence of Michigan CAT had blessed her roadworthy, so I quickly texted Alan as I pulled into a high school parking lot. I ran outside and looked underneath the Discovery. There were no leaks. No blow-out. Nothing. For a minute, I swore that the engine looked as if it had dropped a few inches. But that couldn't be. I must be imagining things.

Alan texted back, "Turn the engine off and cruise on hold the set resume switch and count how many times the engine light flashes. You should get a quick flash then a pause and more flashing. So, something like five flashes and pause then five flashes would mean a 55 code. It will give you this code three times before moving on to the next code."

He quickly added, "You might have to play with the cruise control buttons to get this to work."

I texted back, "I'll get that code." And boy, did I have to fumble around with the cruise control several times before it worked. After a few frustrating minutes, I texted back, "73." I continued, "Injector fault 3 and 4 based on that code. Is it safe to drive if it's acting normally again?"

"Yes," he responded.

Okay, great. I was going to the damn campground! I hadn't camped by myself at a real campground, and I wasn't going to let anything stop that. I drove her over a mile before the loss of power happened again.

"As if it's coughing. I am pulled over on the side of road right now," I texted.

A tow truck hauls the Discovery off to be looked at.

"I bet you will need the injector harness."

"Crap" was my texted reply. I tried for a few minutes more to get the error code, and it was the same 73 code. Dejected, I texted, "Should I bring it to the nearest CAT shop? MacAllister CAT, I believe."

"Yea, that would probably be the best. That is our sister company owned by the same guy. Let me know which branch you will be going to, and I could maybe call them."

"The engine light is on all the time now. I can definitely feel a loss of power. Can I limp along for twenty minutes to MacAllister CAT to drop it off?"

"I would if that is the only code and the coolant is up and oil pressure is good," Alan said.

After several tries in driving her, I gave up and I parked in a strip mall. It was time to make good use of Good Sam's Roadside assistance. I called them via Convo Relay on my iPhone; thankfully the signal was good. A tow truck would be deployed later at around nine that night. My mother came and picked me up, and I got things off the RV, including the $200 worth of food I had just bought.

I was pissed. The hits just kept on coming, and coming.

Later that evening, the tow truck company called me and said it was getting late. They suggested we tow her the first thing in morning. I had no idea why they couldn't make it that evening. I told them sure, no problem. I was already sleepy and I was glad I didn't have to go out that evening.

Immediately after that call, the Good Sam's Club Roadside Assistance automated system called asked me if my RV was towed yet. I responded in the negative, and it transferred me to an agent who then insisted that my tow be canceled and I request a new one in the morning. I didn't have any idea why aside from their saying that this was policy. This meant they would have to put me on a waiting list, so the tow could be much later than the agreed upon 9:00 a.m. time. No way.

I blew up. I told the agent that was not acceptable. The tow company and I had already agreed on a time for pick up, and there wasn't any need to go through this all over again. The agent was unmoved and insisted on canceling my tow. I signed furiously in ASL to the poor Convo interpreter, who flawlessly translated what I said to the agent. Apparently taken aback, the agent put me on hold and after a few minutes with their supervisor, they came back on and said, "My supervisor says I can keep the case open until tomorrow noon."

Thankfully, common sense had prevailed—for now.

In the morning, the tow truck came and handled my Discovery as if she was a feather. I was stunned, seeing how she was lifted up so easily. The driver took out my axle shaft and connected the brake air line to the air brake system, then latched the wireless brake/signal lights onto the back of the ladder. I thoroughly enjoyed the show, and it was an easy drive to the beautiful and massive complex that is MacAllister CAT. As I drove around the campus, I ogled the total number of service bays—fifty, and many of them cavernous. The tow truck seemed to know where he was going, driving straight to the very back of the campus, and parked the Discovery next to a couple of diesel pusher RV and semi-trucks.

I went inside and spoke with Richard Crowe, the service manager, who said they would look at her in a few days. I groaned, even though I knew nearly nothing was ever available immediately in

A powerful painting by Nancy Rourke in 2014 showing the infamous Alexander Graham Bell in a county jail for murdering ASL on Eyeth.

the world of diesel maintenance. I thanked him and returned to Aunt Laura's home using her roommate's car. I got myself settled, even bringing over my beloved Haworth office chair and some other stuff so I could begin writing this book.

I had always wanted to write a book. I wrote many short stories and even tried to write a novel during my young middle school years and teenage years; I still have these faded, dot-matrix printed pages. Naturally, I cringe at what I wrote back then, but the point is I had written page after page. I wanted to do that again.

While in graduate school, I made a half-hearted attempt during NaNoWriMo—the National Novel Writing Month in November—to write fan fiction about Doctor Who visiting the legendary Planet Eyeth, a world full of Deaf people running their lives successfully.

Eyeth is a version of a story that has been passed on for decades within our Deaf community, a Martha's Vineyard kind of tale, but taking it to the maximum where Deaf people are the vast majority and hearing people are marginalized. According to Paddy Ladd, Ph.D., he writes in his book *Understanding Deaf Culture: In Search of Deafhood* that history shows that the Deaf community mingled with hearing leaders in Paris during the 1800s and there were discussions on the idea of requiring all people in Paris to learn sign language. On Martha's Vineyard in Massachusetts, everyone knew sign language well enough to the point that Deaf people out-earned their hearing peers, were relied upon for legal and writing expertise due to their formal education at American School for the Deaf in Hartford, Connecticut, and were active in local politics and church. Deaf and hearing people intermingled easily, and everyone signed.

The inclusion experienced by Deaf Vineyarders lasted for over three hundred years, despite Deaf people being only three percent of the island population. Even though the last hereditary Deaf person on the island died in 1952, Martha's Vineyard continues to serve as a real-life example of real and meaningful integration and inclusion. I believe we can accomplish something even better.

I wanted to elevate the *Eyeth* story to a new level to explore what a world populated by Deaf people would be like; what would be the differences? Writing that while in graduate school was not too bright of an idea, though. I faltered after a few thousand words. I did not have a consistent writing regimen in place and developing this new habit during times of stress wasn't ideal.

However, since getting the RV, I had been writing at least a thousand words daily for at least thirty minutes, no ifs, ands, or buts. The only exception was when I taught my all-day Deafhood classes. As for NaNoWriMo, I'll try again soon. It will be a real challenge. World building requires ideas, research and taking inspiration from other well-conceived stories by Deaf people, such as *Bleeva* by Benjamin Bahan, a Gallaudet ASL and Deaf Studies professor. *Bleeva* is a unique one-man show that combines a new genre of lecture, performance, and storytelling. In this show, Ben presents intriguing ideas and concepts based on real-life history. I was blown away by his work, and he's been working on publishing it.

Stories like those not only explore the "what ifs," but also aid us in our Deafhood journey, exploring what it means to be Deaf in a world that is hell-bent on wiping out our people, our signed languages, our cultures, and our unique identities. What would it be like if the world accepted us? What if everyone learned American Sign Language in the United States along with Black ASL, Mexican Sign Language, Plains Indian Sign Language and others? What if our society was multilingual, like Finland and Sweden? Plenty of research clearly shows that if a person grows up knowing more than one language, that person has significant cognitive and reasoning advantages over monolingual folks.

With that in mind, I was determined to build a daily writing habit. I had my trusty office chair. I had a desk space in my guest bedroom. I figured I might as well get started while in a holding pattern over Indianapolis. Throughout all this time, I wasn't in great shape, emotionally or spiritually, what with all the constant setbacks and delays. I desperately craved my alone time, being "out there" in nature and going hiking, climbing, kayaking and more. I felt somewhat trapped in a such loving and comfortable home. Aunt Laura and her roommate Dari both gave me plenty of space and never pestered me or continued to talk to me when I wanted quiet. It was fantastic. Yet I was dejected. I felt bad because clearly, I wasn't appreciating what I had now—a beautiful home with comfort and amenities—albeit with one horror story.

Aunt Laura had bought her new home that previous May, and so it had taken a few months of settling in. In my guest bedroom, when I went to bed, I'd turn off the lights and look up while I drifted off to sleep. One night, I noticed glow-in-the-dark scrawling on the ceiling. My overactive imagination jumped right in. *Is that a Satanic pentagram I see?* I nervously peered at the ceiling as the scrawls came into clearer view. The message was handwritten, something obviously created by a bored teenager. I don't quite recall what it said, but the fact that it was scrawled in big letters was a bit creepy. From that night on, I didn't leave the light on for too long to ensure the words wouldn't glow. My aunt eventually painted the ceiling, so all was good the next time I stayed there.

The weekend morphed into a Monday, and it was time for MacAllister CAT to look at the Discovery. I had to wait until Tuesday before the estimate came, though. After they looked at the engine, it was determined that I needed a new injector wiring harness. Michigan CAT would pay for the part. But I still had to pay for labor and other parts. The estimated total?

$2,200.

Chapter 21
BREAKING FREE FROM
THE HOLDING PATTERN

AUGUST 31, 2018

- Mileage: **115,572**
- Previous total: **$22,725.61**
- Injector wiring harness: **$2,200.26**
- Porch light with motion sensor: **$50.00**
- Dashcam: **$35.00**
- Brake system check and lube and fuel/ water separator at Speedco: **$76.07**
- Four 6V sealed AGM Duracell batteries for house battery bank: **$762.06**
- Current total: **$25,849**
- Credit score: **640**

With my Discovery being worked on, I unloaded two Sondors electric bikes into my aunt's garage, and I decided it was time for me to bite the bullet and buy the FLX electric bike I had my eyes on for some time. Their Trail version touring edition was what I wanted, but it was sold out online. I contacted them about the remaining white bike, but it wasn't what I wanted so I asked if they could give me a discount for taking the bike off their inventory. They turned me down, and instead offered me an open box item: a black Trail touring bike with a larger 17Ah battery for two hundred dollars off.

I replied, "Has this bike been examined and cleaned by your team to make sure everything is in it?" I didn't exactly have a good experience with a used purchase, after all.

The reply was affirmative. I ordered that bike. I planned to sell both Sondors bikes to help offset some of the cost of the new bike. I knew I would need something that had much longer range, in the thirty to ninety-mile range, depending on the power level I used.

I waited for my Discovery's injector harness to be replaced, which took about a week. I was hoping to take her up to my father's home so we could get the house batteries replaced with four 100-amp hour AGM sealed batteries—no more filling the batteries with distilled water and cleaning off the corrosion—because I love maintenance-free stuff. Sam's Club in Traverse City had the batteries in stock (unlike in Indianapolis), and this would give me a chance to travel to the Upper Peninsula and cross the Mackinac Bridge before driving around Lake Michigan to Wisconsin for my next Deafhood 101 class at Water Tower View, a Deaf senior citizen apartment complex, in the Milwaukee area.

The day finally came, and the Discovery was ready. Dari and I drove over to MacAllister CAT, and I paid the $2,200.26 invoice. Before I could take the RV out of the cavernous bay she was in, the mechanic had to jump-start the battery. Apparently, there was some kind of parasitic draw somewhere, despite shutting off her master system for days. With her charged up, they pulled her out of Bay 44 and I hopped on quickly. As soon as I pulled alongside Aunt Laura's home, parking halfway on the grass to give more room to passing cars, the brakes kicked in. The "Low Air" light went on.

What the...?

She lost all her air pressure. I couldn't move her any further. My plan to leave for my father's on that day was totally shot. I quickly emailed and called Richard Crowe asking what was happening. Given that it was already late in the day, they promised to send a mechanic the next morning. The next morning, the mechanic climbed underneath the RV, squeezing in like a pro. After a few minutes, he emerged, having identified the culprit: a worn-out air brake hose.

No wonder. Alan Spence did point this out to Theo while we were at Michigan CAT. The mechanic went back to his shop and picked up a brand-new air

The air brake hose was bad.

hose. Within half an hour, the mechanic wiped his hands, done with the replacement. He then made me very happy when he said the service was at no charge. I breathed a deep sigh of relief and thanked him. He said, "Bless you on your journey. God has taken a liking to you, my son." He also asked me to thank his supervisors, Wade and Richard, for waiving the service call. I promised him I would, and I did.

While at Aunt Laura's home, I noticed that the chassis batteries were being drained quickly. I mentioned this to Mom, and she said there probably was probably a short somewhere in the house. We tried to track this down, and it was next to impossible.

We looked under the dashboard, at the relay switches, and at the fuses. Aunt Laura and I struggled to get the dash cover off, and after a few tries—thanks to the Discovery Owners group again—we found a couple of screws hidden inside the carpeted wall. We got that off and looked around. No luck. We decided to look elsewhere for the problem.

The porch light was flickering a bit so my mom climbed up and looked at it. Sure enough, it was burnt. A short. She out the wires and wrapped them. I decided to go to Camping World and pick up a motion-detecting porch light

Mom uses a stepladder to repair the porch light as Aunt Laura looks on with a screwdriver.

on sale—but it wasn't an amber light so it would attract bugs. I made a mental note to find an amber light cover and bulb soon.

All of this was done while we waited for the mechanic to come and look at the brake situation. Unfortunately, somehow, I broke our slide-outs during this process. They wouldn't come out or operate at all.

With nonfunctional slides and the refrigerator on its last legs, I scheduled a cooling unit replacement at National RV Refrigeration in Shipshewana, Indiana for right after my trip to Michigan and Milwaukee. I had to come back to Indiana to pick up my new electric bike, anyway.

This appointment was my second try. I had originally scheduled the cooling unit replacement made by the Amish people on that coming Friday, but I was sidelined by the broken air line. I would have to make do with a barely functioning fridge by putting things in the freezer, if need be, and keeping some food "chilled" at forty-five to fifty-five degrees, way above the thirty-two to forty degrees normal operating range. I used my cooler as well, but I decided I would just eat out rather than taking risks with potentially spoiled food.

For weeks, I struggled to decide whether to replace this refrigerator with a residential refrigerator, a move popular among Discovery owners. However, residential refrigerators run only on electricity—no propane—which meant I would have to invest a lot of money in an upgraded battery bank. I did not have the space for the bank, either. On top of that, I would need to invest $1,000 to $2,000 for 400 to 800-watt solar power, and because I was stuck with an underpowered Tripp-Lite Work Truck utility 1250-watt inverter, I would either need to get a separate inverter just for the refrigerator or replace this inverter with something I had been drooling over, a Magnum Hybrid 3000W inverter. This would have set me back another $1,900 plus installation and rewiring for it to power everything in the Discovery. More importantly, this new inverter was a pure sine wave inverter as opposed to cheaper units like the one in my Discovery that ran on modified sine waves. The latter was known to play havoc with sensitive electronics such as laptops, phones, tablets, and even refrigerators.

I asked for advice on the refrigerator via the Discovery Owners group, and Bruce Plumb graciously gathered information on potential residential refrigerator replacements. He also made a key recommendation for Duracell 6-volt AGM sealed batteries available at Sam's Club in Traverse City, Michigan—the reason I was headed to my dad's.

Most people sang praises about their residential refrigerator installation, which would create additional installation headaches for me. A window would have to be removed to allow the new refrigerator, typically on the driver's side. My dad and I would have needed additional muscle to help us to do that. I worried about that for a while.

Group member Bob Horvat posted this piece of wisdom:

One more thing: The refrigerator choice is "to each his own." I believe Bruce has done extensive, real-life testing and is giving you good, reliable, numbers to go by. For some, if not most, a residential fridge is the way to go. But for the rest of us, who boondock as much as possible, absorption fridge is the only way to go. I don't want, nor have, 600 to 800 watts to put into just running a fridge. Maybe someday, not today. Yes, there have been fires caused by the absorption fridges in the past but it is also a true statement that the industry would still be using them if not for their bottom line. The manufacturers are switching to residential to put more money in their pockets, plain and simple. A $1,000 versus $4,800 fridge the new buyer never thinks about—until he dry camps for the first time! Only then does he realize his "go everywhere, see the country do everything we've ever wanted to do" brand new unit, has to be plugged in or listen to a generator two to four hours a day. We are all friends, and both have pluses and minuses. I choose to boondock as much as possible. Parks are OK but I feel cramped in them. I spent thirty-eight years in the rat race and I love the peace and quiet that boondocking gives me and the missus. Got nothing to do with money either—visit Quartzsite this winter. Brand-new 400k motorhomes with solar panels on the roof! Just enjoy the trip! Oh, and get some panels up there!!

That did it for me. I found the Amish made cooling unit replacements that ran better than the original manufacturer's equipment and came with a standard three-year warranty. I contacted Pines Refrigeration and was referred to Leon Hershberger at National RV Refrigeration. He quoted me a total of $1,500 installation and disposal price.

Sold!

That was scheduled and rescheduled for the trip after Michigan and Milwaukee. I was happy to head up to my father's, and everything was working well. I stopped at Speedco, known for its reasonable cost on diesel motor oil changes. I asked if they could do a transmission drain and fill but they wouldn't for automatics. I asked them to check my air brake system and lube as well as replace the diesel fuel/water separator. The bill? Only $76.07! This was my first under-$1,000 maintenance charge for the Discovery.

I stopped for a quick dinner in north Lansing, and as I came out of the restaurant, the clouds were impressively menacing. It

A rapidly approaching storm in Lansing, Michigan.

was beautiful. I knew there were more sights to see as I traveled through the country, and I appreciated the beauty of Mother Nature, however bad the storm was. I continued north until I arrived at a rest area just south of Alma, Michigan and set up for the night there. I slept like a baby that night despite the heavy rains and semi-trucks moving in and out of the area.

The next morning, I stopped at Tim Horton's for breakfast, and after a frustrating night with my wipers and rain, it was time to dump my Rain-X blades for the highly regarded Bosch Icon blade. I went into a nearby auto parts store and picked some up. It took me a couple of tries before I realized I had the wrong blade part number. Earlier in the summer, my dad had helped install a J-hook adapter that made it possible to use auto wipers rather than the special ones for semi-trucks. With the right blade, it went in its place easily.

Wow, what a difference! I was happy with the new blade on the driver's side. I left the Rain-X on the passenger side for now. Within a couple of hours, I stopped again for a fill-up because it was the cheapest by far in Houghton Lake, Michigan. I then continued to my dad's home.

Sonja told me that Dad had been restless, waiting for me to arrive back home, and that warmed my heart. I told him he missed me and my to-do list. He smirked at me, and we went to work. We took apart the four house batteries that were flooded with lead acid, and the corrosion was everywhere in the battery compartment. We cleaned that out as much as we could, and of course, we took a picture of the battery cables before we took it apart so we would know how to put it back together. At this point, I was glad we were going to pick up the new sealed AGM batteries.

Cables were carefully removed and laid out on the cement floor to ensure proper re-installation.

Dad works on the new batteries.

With the wiring out and the compartment relatively cleaner than it was before, we headed to Traverse City, stopping at the Trout Town Cafe in Kalkaska, Michigan for lunch. I have always thought Traverse City is blessed with some of the nicest views around, including the bay leading to Lake Michigan and the hills and forests. There are a good number of wineries in the area, and many places sell cherries, a leading crop in that area.

We then went to Sam's Club and picked up the four batteries. We went around the back and unloaded the old, ratty-looking cell batteries in the recycling center. Both new and old batteries were heavy as hell at over sixty pounds each, and it took some effort to lug them over. While carrying them, I was so tempted to splurge for Lithium Iron Phosphate (LiFePo4) batteries, but at $900 each, I would be happy with my sealed, maintenance-free batteries. It was getting late in the day, and the rain came along so we called it a day.

The next morning, Dad went to work after I loaded the batteries—did I mention how fricking heavy they were?!—into the clean compartment. I loaded them one by one, and then we secured them.

It was at this point that I finally found that 300-amp fuse. The fuse had been sitting right in front of us in plain sight all this time. I immediately texted Theo a photograph. He was astounded that it had been right under our noses.

The "mythical" 300-amp fuse discovered!

We finished up the batteries, and we connected everything back on the inside. And… nothing worked. My heart dropped.

I went inside to start the engine up, and nothing came on. I went back outside, "Dad! Nothing is working!"

He grimaced, and looked at the wiring and batteries, tugging at them. He turned back to me. "Everything is wired up right. It can't be?"

I panicked a bit. Earlier, we did try to find the source—a broken fuse or something—that was preventing the slide-outs from working. Did we break another fuse somewhere? I checked the 300-amp fuse and it was intact.

It suddenly occurred to me: I had forgotten to switch back the main and auxiliary switch located right above the driver's dashboard. *D'oh!*

In front of the Mackinac Bridge on a beautiful day.

I turned both on, and everything lit up. Everything was good, except for the non-operational slides. I told dad, "Forget the slides. We tried." I said I would try again later in Milwaukee when I had free time.

With the new batteries in place and running well, I was ready to head up north and see the Mackinac Bridge. I had flirted briefly with the idea of taking the Ludington ferry across Lake Michigan, but the cost and the desire to see Upper Peninsula overrode that.

We said our goodbyes and hugged, and I was on the open road once again, even if I wasn't quite free from my commitments to return to Indiana—I had to replace the cooling unit in the refrigerator and pick up my new electric bike.

Upon arrival in Mackinaw City, I made a brief stop at Fort Michilimackinac. I biked around the town, taking in the sights. I was tempted to get on the ferry to Mackinac Island and eat at a sushi restaurant there. But with the ferry cost, the extra charge for bringing my own bike and the dinner cost—common sense prevailed. Instead, I dined at a Mexican restaurant in St. Ignace.

The day was getting darker, and the time came to find a place for the night. I could stay at a rest area right off U.S. 2, but I had found a U.S. Forest Service campground in a wooded area on a beach along Lake Michigan. With my lifetime federal parks Golden Access pass, I qualify for half-off campground rates. I pulled in and noticed a huge swarm of mosquitoes.

Did I mention yet how I hate mosquitoes?

I drove through the park and found the site, a fairly level one, and I realized most of the sites were hidden away from the beach and the tree cover was so intense that I couldn't see the beach. I had to circle back to the entrance, but the skies were buzzing with mosquitoes. I ran outside trying to avoid that swarm so I could take the payment envelope and run right back inside. I drove to the site and backed her in, and groaned. The air was thick with mosquitoes everywhere. I had to fill out the form and go outside to stick it to a post. *Damn it.*

After that, I discovered there already was a swarm inside the RV. I would be miserable all night. I leveled the RV with ease, grateful that Theo installed an extra camera underneath so I could stay inside and observe the jacks being lowered down. Next, I set things up inside, foregoing bringing her slides out. *But still these forsaken mosquitoes inside,* I muttered to myself. (Yes, you can mutter in sign language.) I swatted at them and decided to use the vacuum cleaner to suck them off the ceilings. I vacuumed like mad until I was satisfied I had caught every single one. I went to bed after I turned on the blue light fan unit to draw any bugs that then got sucked inside and air-dried themselves to death. Not the quickest way to go, I guess, but... after being bitten a thousand times in my life, I had little sympathy for them.

I woke up in the middle of night, and there were more mosquitoes. Aggravated, I had the vacuum out again, sucking in those critters as much as possible. As I crawled back into bed, I realized I hadn't been bitten at all. I looked closer and the mosquitoes were smaller than your average mosquito. They looked similar but were not quite the same. Later when I was eating at Bayside View Café, I Googled it and learned they were harmless midge flies. The Upper Peninsula typically has huge swarms of them during September.

Oh. Even so, they continued to get inside the Discovery. I wasn't sure how they were getting in, maybe the windows or slide-outs. I vacuumed after them for more than four days; it wasn't until I was in Milwaukee that they finally dissipated. Sheesh. I swore that the next time I saw a huge swarm of anything, I would continue driving until I found another place.

I drove westward on U.S. 2, taking in the beautiful scenery. I also stopped at Manistique to look at the lighthouse way out there on the lake. The waves splashed on the long concrete pier upon huge rocks, and I was thrilled by the fresh windy air, water spritzing all over me. The water seemed to draw out the stress and pressure from my body. I walked around the lighthouse and felt refreshed.

This was the life I wanted—a taste of things to come, I hoped. With my mood lifted, I headed westward towards Green Bay, Wisconsin. The roads were gorgeous with lakeside views until I hit a highway deep inland, and things got boring rather quickly.

I spent the night with electric hookups at Oneida Casino for fifteen dollars a night. I had to sign up for their players club in order to camp for the night, and I had to hand over my driver license. Okay, whatever. With that done, I set up for the night and I was comfortable, aside from still furiously vacuuming the errant midge flies. They were *everywhere*.

When I woke up, I pulled up the jacks and headed for a brewery in Appleton, Wisconsin to eat an Impossible Burger. I then went straight to the Milwaukee State Fairgrounds to check in for the next five nights. The site was basically a parking lot with full hook-ups. I asked the clerk to give me as level of a site as possible, and she smiled, handing me a check-in sheet with the site number already listed. I did get a fairly level site, so I was happy. I leveled the RV easily, but I again couldn't get the slide-outs to operate so I made do with a cozier environment. I was comfortably writing, editing, and revising my presentation. I took my Sondors thin bike and rode all the way to downtown Milwaukee via a bike and running trail, and the views and winding trail were wonderful. I have always appreciated the good urban bones and continued development of mixed-use living in downtown Milwaukee. I even biked to a sushi restaurant right on the riverfront.

I had to keep an eye on my bike's range, though, especially since there were no gears. I was definitely ready for my new FLX bike, which promised a 60-90-mile range with power assist. After lunch, I biked about six miles back to the state fairgrounds and settled in. I was starting to feel at home no matter where I was, but not quite. I still couldn't stock up on food or cook yet.

The next day, I rented a car to get around. It was about five miles each way for the Deafhood 101 class, and I wanted to do some shopping as well. I could have biked, but I wanted the flexibility of having a car handy. I called Enterprise to schedule a pick-up time. They told me that my confirmed rental wasn't available, nor did they have other cars.

"What? I have a confirmation number here."

"I know, I am so sorry, but we don't have any cars on our lot. The national reservations made that confirmation while not having an up-to-the-minute report of car availability here locally." The representative then transferred me to the national reservations line, and the new representative apologized to me again and booked me a car at a different local Enterprise. I then called this new location.

Same thing: no cars available. I was flabbergasted. I told them the national reservations line assured me that there was a car available. Same explanation: the system wasn't in sync.

I called the national line again and after bouncing around within their system, they finally said they were out of cars in the area. I had to go to the Milwaukee airport, a good hour and half away on the city bus. I went with Lyft, which cost me about twenty-five dollars one way but took only twenty-five minutes. I got ready and thumbed through my credit cards one by one, and slowly realized I didn't have my driver license.

Crap.

I frantically searched around to no avail, and suddenly realized where it was: Oneida Casino in Green Bay. I had handed over my license to the clerk, and he never gave it back to me. I had to walk to Lyft and let the driver know I was canceling the drive; that cost me a five-dollar cancellation fee.

I called Oneida Casino and confirmed my license was there. I asked them to hurry and mail it to me at the state fairgrounds, figuring it would take two days. Nope. It didn't arrive until Tuesday next week, after I was already long gone. Luckily, Indiana BMV is one of the fastest services among many DMVs in the nation—it's easy to get in and out within twenty minutes.

With the rental out of the picture, I had to use the fat-tire bike to class, and I had to be sure it was fully charged up for the next day. It was easy to bike to the class and back, even at nighttime. The city streets were well-lit. The class went well, and because I've been teaching Deafhood since January 2011, I sometimes forget how powerful Paddy Ladd's work is and the impact it has on people. They often are blown away, seeing our Deaf communities and our peoples in a new light through a different set of metaphors. I was feeling pretty good by the time Sunday rolled around, but at the same time, I was also running on fumes. I give my all when I teach these classes so I was grateful for the home I could come back to in my RV—the familiar, the comfort and the quiet.

Monday came around, and my license still hadn't arrived. I went through the process of pulling up the jacks, cleaning out the gray and black water tanks and filling up the freshwater tank. Within an hour, I was ready to head back to Indiana. I wanted to drive through Chicago on Lake Shore Drive. I love taking in the city sights, the beach, the urbanity—and I knew I wouldn't have a problem driving through Chicago.

Sure enough, I loved every minute of it. But, man, as I get older, there are some days I gotta pee—often. I was in the middle of a traffic jam on Lake Shore Drive and I was sorely tempted to park her in the middle of the road—the cars weren't moving for a good minute—so I could use the toilet. But no, the timing didn't work out. I had to wait patiently, and it was turning slightly painful to hold it in. The traffic jam eased finally past the Navy Pier area. I pulled over on the shoulder just past the Millennium Park and quickly took care of my business.

I continued onto the Dan Ryan Expressway, which turned into the Chicago Skyway tollway to Indiana, again taking in the sights while I drove. The huge windshield made all the difference. If roads were in bad shape, the ride could feel rough despite the airbags. The Discovery would rock back and forth a bit too much for my taste. I kept wondering if I should replace the front shocks. They were five-year-old Bilsteins. Was it time?

One day, maybe.

Chapter 22
IN AMISH COUNTRY

SEPTEMBER 15, 2018

- Mileage: **115,572**
- Previous total: **$25,849**
- New Amish-made cooling unit installed: **$1,565.81**
- Current total: **$27,414.81**
- Credit score: **640**

After the sights of Chicago, things settled down into the typical Midwest scenery as I made my way into northern Indiana, stopping at a turnpike service plaza about thirty-five minutes away from the exit into Shipshewana, Indiana. I was happy to settle in for the night between semi-trucks, and after watching *Gold Rush* on my iPhone, I dozed off. The next morning, I went into the service plaza and picked up breakfast before getting on my way.

I passed the National RV Museum in Elkhart, and I told myself I would go there one day. I pulled off at a beautiful country farmhouse. There was a huge metal pole barn with a sign that said National RV Refrigeration, which served as their shop. I backed up right next to their open bay, and I met with Leon Hersberger, an Amish man who was polite and helpful. We got down to business right away.

Leon pointed out that he needed the slide-out to work. I explained that I couldn't find the short in the system. He

The National RV Refrigeration building is located amidst Amish farmland.

responded that they couldn't do the work, even when I offered to remove my desk and chairs from the area.

Oh, heck, no. We were doing this today. I remembered that Mel Kimbrell, a member of the Discovery Owners group who contacted me offline to help, told me the slide-out could be jumped with a cable to another 12-volt source. I took out the key plate for the front slide-out, and I showed it to Leon even though I had no idea how to jump it.

He nodded, and he went inside and got a piece of long wire and then crawled under my dash to insert the wire into a bracket with a live 12-volt current. Next, he connected the wire to the amenphole and touched one side of it.

Boom. The slide-out pulled out nicely. I let out a huge breath of relief. I was floored, again, by how much space we gained with the slide-out.

An Amish teenager, probably fifteen or sixteen years old, came in and swiftly began the work of disassembling the front cover and frames. Within the hour, the refrigerator was out and laid down on the blanket protecting floor of my Discovery. Their speed and efficiency impressed me, and I went inside their office, sat in their comfortable recliner chair for a short bit. I then took my bike out so I could go out for lunch at a nearby Mexican restaurant. By 2:30 p.m., everything was back in its place.

Leon tested the refrigerator by letting it run for a while then he came inside to check the temperature inside. I approached him, asking him if he could fix the interior lamp that wouldn't come on when the door was open. He fixed that, and I asked if he had spare plastic shelves for my refrigerator. He only had one, and that went in as well. I paid a little extra for these parts, of course.

At that point, Leon furrowed his brows while checking the temperature and went inside the freezer unit, took out the cover plates, and bent the metal piping to level it properly. An hour later, he told me all was good, and I was free to leave. He also gave me the 12-volt jumper cable and showed me exactly where under the dash to insert the wire.

I asked him to show me the level tolerance range for the Discovery when the refrigerator was in operation, and he did.

A teenage worker took out this refrigerator with such speed and efficiency. The old cooling unit had already been removed.

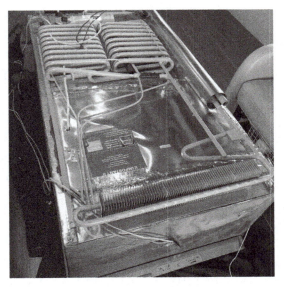

A brand-new, superior Amish-made cooling unit waiting to be installed in the RV.

The refrigerator ran on both LP and electricity, and because of that, the cooling chemicals inside were sensitive to non-level operations—if you park the RV on unlevel terrain for more than three hours, the refrigerator potentially could "freeze up" and lose its cooling capability. If this happens, one of the fixes is to take out the refrigerator and turn it upside down for a week to let the chemicals move to where they need to be. So, no, thanks. With Leon's help I knew what to do now, much to my relief.

I went in and paid the bill of $1,565.81, which was well worth the cost. They were professional, efficient, and communicated well with me.

I headed to Bontrager's RV Surplus in White Pigeon, Michigan to see what they had to offer. I was blown away by what they had in stock, although they didn't have everything and sometimes their inventory could be a haphazard mix of things. I walked through the aisles, and I was this close to buying a ladder for the back of the RV at only forty-five dollars, but there wasn't one that would fit. I decided not to continue the search for the ladder, a decision I regret to this day. Later, I went to Colaw RV Salvage, and they wanted $110 for a used ladder. Nope. I also saw that they had a triangular skylight roof cover for only twenty dollars, but I didn't have the measurements and it was getting late in the day. I let the exhaustion get to me, and I again regret this decision.

I drove south on State Road 13, and it was dinnertime so I was thinking about where to eat. My refrigerator was working like a charm, bringing down the temperatures quickly, but I wasn't in the mood to go food shopping. I decided to eat in Goshen. I made my way on Route 4, which had a lot of construction and detours, taking me away from Goshen a bit and onto incredibly narrow country roads. Driving on them gave me a huge thrill, yet I had to be cautious. As I turned on Monroe Road headed towards Goshen, I noticed the Elkhart 4-H County Fairground on my left side. As I admired the huge space they had, I noticed that there were several RVs parked. I suddenly spied a Discovery—cool!

A beautiful sunset peeking through the passenger side window against the backdrop of the Indiana countryside.

And there was another one right next to it…and another one! What a coincidence. Then another one, and…

Wait a minute. I realized they were mostly Fleetwood Discoveries of varying model years and conditions, although there was a lone GMC motorhome sitting in a corner among the sea of Discoverys.

It hit me.

This was where the Discovery Owners Association was holding its annual rally, right here in Goshen! I had seen their flyers and announcements, but I had thought it was in Elkhart, Indiana. My heart skipped a beat. *Should I turn around and go in? Maybe I will bump into some people I have met through the email list…*

But then doubts crept in. This was a big rally and the admission fee was hefty especially for a short visit. My worries chattered in my head. I knew there probably weren't very many—if any at all—who would know ASL, making communication a bit more difficult. Plus I was still in maximum introvert mode, wanting to be alone and simply chill. In the end, I chickened out. I kept on driving towards downtown Goshen, still elated that I had passed among my Discovery brothers and sisters. I ate at a delicious Indian restaurant before heading south via Route 13, taking me through the countryside with the sun setting to my right.

This was the life I wanted. The views. The quiet. The purr of the powerful Caterpillar engines pushing my Discovery forward as sure as anything. For once, I felt as if everything had finally begun to work right, and the pieces were falling into place. Even if nothing on the Discovery was brand-new, the engine had been repaired, hoses and belts replaced, I had a new air compressor, a new injector and a new wiring harness along with new tires and front brakes. But there were still a lot of other things that could, ahem, not go quite right.

I thought of a quote by Daily Zen (@dailyzen): "Self-care isn't about trying to heal yourself or fix your problems. You must have time to simply be. It's as necessary as food or water."

Yep. Just to be surrounded by the beauty of nature. I was ready to begin my journey westward.

Chapter 23
A FINAL
HOLDING PATTERN

Our Discovery at Aunt Laura and Dari's home.

I pulled in at Aunt Laura's home, and she wanted me to park in her sloped driveway instead of on the shoulder of the street. I made it work—turning into the driveway was tricky, and tree branches scratched my Discovery as I steered her into her final parked position, up close to the garage doors.

The driveway was slanted upwards like crazy, and it was a good thing that I hadn't yet used my refrigerator; so, it remained off. We ran a long extension cord from the garage to my Discovery so I could keep her charged and prevent the batteries from draining. I also ran the dehumidifier for several hours each day to make sure she remained dry inside.

I unloaded my things and, naturally, my office chair into her guest bedroom for the next week. I turned to Alec, who was staying with my mother, and asked, "Wanna go to Cedar Point for two days? Check out their Halloween Haunts while we're at it?" Alec smiled, so off we went. I borrowed my mother's car and we drove for four and half hours.

We got in Friday night, and naturally, we made a beeline for GateKeeper before going to Millennium Force and Steel Vengeance. The wait for Steel Vengeance was over an hour, but oh, man, the ride was wild and absolutely worth the wait! Everything else had minimal wait times. Coming out from Steel Vengeance, Alec and I were absolutely gobsmacked, laughing and discussing the ins and outs of the ride that wouldn't let up until the very end—with only a brief breather during its mid-course braking run.

Alec, Amanda, Jake, Haylie and I wait in line for the Halloween Haunt ride at Cedar Point.

We were walking towards Skyhawk when someone grabbed me from behind, hugging me hard. *What? Who the heck…?!*

I turned around and it was my cousin Jake Ward, Aunt Laura's son who identifies as a hearing Child of Deaf Adult (CODA). It was wonderful seeing him, his wife Amanda and their oldest daughter, Haylie, along with their friends. After we caught up a bit, we parted ways, yet we continued to run into each other over the evening, so we took a picture together while waiting in line.

We stayed until nearly midnight, and we were tired, so we called it a night and headed for a motel. I did calculate whether we should have taken the Discovery for this trip, but the cost of diesel fuel for the round trip was much higher than using a car and staying at a motel. And the stress of driving her for more than four hours in the same day would have tired me out by the time we got to Cedar Point. Alec didn't have his driver's license, just a learner's permit, so he wasn't comfortable driving a big rig yet (and I certainly wasn't going to hand him the keys, either).

We stayed until the next afternoon when we were ready to go home. My next trip would be out of the country, so I needed to get ready for that. I was due to travel to Rio de Janeiro, Brazil to present at their national Deaf education conference. I had been working with the Brazilian Deaf conference planners, and they asked for my passport information to process my visa. I had never traveled to a country that required an entry visa so this was completely new for me. I would leave my Discovery at my aunt's for the week while I flew to Brazil. My FLX bike was due to arrive right after my return from Brazil, and with the bike in hitch, I would then begin my trip westward.

The day came for me to fly to Rio, and I realized suddenly that I didn't have a visa. I had contacted the planners the previous weekend, but I received no response. A low-grade panic started to spread through me. They paid for my United Airlines flight, so I had a flight ticket, but no visa. I asked my friend, Ella Mae Lentz—world-famous ASL poet, co-author of the widely-used *Signing Naturally* curriculum, and visionary founder of the Deafhood Foundation—along with her wife, Judy Gough, who had contacts in Brazil and knew the conference organizers, particularly Ana Regina Campello, Ph.D. Ella quickly contacted her through another friend, and Ana responded just a few hours shy of my departure. She said I should have received a visa long before, but someone must have dropped the ball.

I went to the airport, talked with the United ticket agent and for an hour tried to secure a visa, including applying online, all to no avail. At that point, the trip had to be canceled. I was disappointed, yet I also had some concerns about traveling overseas while feeling vulnerable, lacking self-care lately. This meant I could do some self-care. The conference organizers asked me to create a five-minute video message instead, and I was happy to oblige. With the video sent, I could then relax.

Campello texted saying the video and especially the message I had was well-received. She then texted something that was inspiring to me (keeping mind that English is her third language): "They warned me that you are beautiful!" I was so warmed by that. I still hope to fly to Brazil one day and bring the message of consciousness raising and healing.

I had another issue to deal with back home as well. While Alec and I were at Cedar Point, the bike I ordered arrived. I had asked my mother and Jen to open the package so they could charge the battery for me. They texted me pictures of a damaged bike. My heart sank.

"This bike is not new, for sure. Did you order a used one? It looks damaged," Jen texted.

We got home and I took a good look at the bike. Sure enough, it was damaged goods—with a broken, non-functioning brake light and a scratched, bent battery case.

I was livid. I sent off a disappointed email to FLX support, which began a long two-week affair, emailing back and forth daily before we came to an agreement: they would send a brand-new battery, a new brake light, black paint to cover the chips, and a few other things. They also paid for my bike to be tuned up by a bike shop. I was still unsure if I should return the bike, but they didn't have any

The "Bent-Case Bike."

in stock. Instead, I had to hammer the battery casing frame back into shape. Even today, it's still slightly bent. I guess I could call her "The Bent-Case Bike," a nod to a certain television show on Netflix. All of this for $300 off the list price. *Hmm.*

I did wonder why I got a damaged Discovery with so many issues, yet the

Rainbows emerge over a replica of the Eiffel Tower at Kings Island in Mason, Ohio.

inspector caught absolutely none of them, and now an open box electric bicycle despite prior assurances that the company had cleaned and inspected it before shipping to me. Why was I attracting broken things? I clearly needed to address a part of myself in a healing way.

With the Brazil trip canceled and the FLX bike situation up in the air, I asked Alec if he wanted to go to Kings Island. He broke into a wide smile and invited his childhood friend, Courtney Skjeveland (whose dad rescued our Discovery from that parking lot flood last July). Courtney had never ridden in our RV so she was thrilled.

Off we went. As always, we loved driving and riding our Discovery—the feeling of gliding over the open roads, taking in the sights, and appreciating the freedom. We got to Kings Island on Friday night, and it was raining lightly. We knew the rain would let up, so naturally we made a beeline for Diamondback, the best coaster in the park. There was a double rainbow, which inspired us.

We didn't want to wait any longer and ran to the ride entrance where the line was short. A perfect evening for us all. We took rides on the wonderful Mystic Timbers, the classic Beast—a spectacular nighttime ride—and made our way to the other end of the park where we rode on Delirium, Banshee, The Bat and Drop Tower. We went in a few of the Haunts as well.

We stayed until almost one in the morning, and we were worn out. Feet aching, we made our way to the Discovery. The slide-outs weren't working, still, but we made do with the cozy space inside. We all were comfortable when we drifted off to sleep in the Walmart parking lot.

We slept in and got off to a late start then we drove back home during a beautiful sunset the next day.

It was getting late in September 2018, and I hadn't even started full time living in my RV. I flew to Rochester to give a keynote and Deafhood training to St. Mary's School for the Deaf

students during their first-ever leadership retreat at a beautiful campground just south of Rochester.

While there, I got together with Ritchie Bryant, who was then teaching at National Technical Institute of the Deaf. We went to a vegan

Ritchie Bryant and me at a vegan restaurant in downtown Rochester.

restaurant in downtown Rochester and caught up on our work and travels. Ritchie is a renowned trainer and presenter on interpreting, and at the time was part of the Registry of Interpreters of the Deaf (RID). In 2021, he became RID president, the first Black Deaf man to lead RID, the nation's main certifying body for sign language interpreters.

As we chatted, Ritchie shared his work on creating a visual gestural communication curriculum. He was the first Black Deaf person to publish a sign language curriculum along with the late Nathie Marbury, a Black Deaf female leader. With that trip a success, I still wanted to maintain a low profile; I was still feeling introvertish. There were more friends in Rochester area who I would have liked to see, but I needed to pace myself.

Once back in Indianapolis, I turned my attention back to test-riding the damaged bike and finding a welder to address the severely rusted-through front-end house frame supports on the

The house frames are badly rusted through.

The horribly potholed dirt driveway at EDCO Welding caused my RV to lurch, damaging all of my dishes.

Discovery. And there was the bent battery shelf, which Discovery Owners group member Doug Poad pointed out could become a fire hazard if the top shelf dropped down and came into contact, causing an electrical arc.

A few weeks into owning the Discovery, I had asked Steve, who sold my RV to me, about the rusted-through frame. Steve told me that it was a redundant support frame, and he thought it would require about $250 by a mobile welder.

Sheesh.

After a few unsuccessful leads, I found EDCO Welding and Truck Repair in Indianapolis, and I was told to come in that afternoon. I had my mother follow me as I drove the Discovery there. They were deep in an industrial area and their long gravel driveway was so pockmarked with potholes that my Discovery shook back and forth to the point where my kitchen cupboard spilled out and broke everything.

My favorite tea mugs, my favorite Kings Island shot glasses, and plates and bowls—all gone. My mother swept these up while I ran inside and spoke with their front desk person, Christine. It turned out she knew ASL, so she and I communicated easily. She got one of their guys to come out and look at the rusted frame and the bent-shelf battery case.

Bryan estimated the welding work would cost me about $500. That was less than the $800 quoted to me at another place that was booked until much later. I was happy to tell Bryan to go ahead and do it. I brought the Discovery into one of their bays, and their gravel pavement was so muddy that it took some doing, but she was backed into the bay neatly.

We went home, and Christine called me after a couple of hours. They were already done.

What? Wow. Since they were about to close, I said we would come by tomorrow and pick her up. The next morning, we did just that. I was so ready to bring her home. I walked in, and I told my mother to go ahead and leave.

Christine came up to me and said, "They are trying to put her batteries back together, but they haven't been able to start her up."

Oh, no. They had to take out the batteries to weld the bent-shelf case. Apparently, they didn't connect everything back together properly. I showed them a picture of the wiring that I took earlier, and they compared everything to it— and they did it right. Still, she wouldn't start.

The brand-new frames, all secure and solid.

Damn. Bryan kept at it, searching for broken fuses *somewhere.* It took him a couple more hours of trying. I was FaceTiming Theo to update him that they were able to force-start her engine from the rear, but the Allison Transmission shifter was still off. No light came on. Theo waved at me frantically while I was looking at something else, "Dad! There's a fuse on other side of the Discovery, next to the PowerGear leveling jacks. The wiring for Allison unit is in the bay."

How the hell did my son know that?! I went to Bryan and got him over to the wiring bunch in the rear right bay door. He looked at it, and he smiled at me, nodding, "Yup!" The fuse had broken. In his process of searching for broken fuses, he found a total of four broken fuses, and he replaced them all.

As soon as I sat down on my driver's seat, I quickly noticed that the radio was now functional. The thought struck me… if the radio is now working, then…

"The slide-outs!"

I ran back to my bedroom and tried the slide-out switch. *Boom!* The slide-out moved. *Oh, thank you, sweet heavens!* The culprit had been the broken fuse all along, despite my efforts to fix and replace relay switches and other things along with Mel Kimbrell's help.

I ran up to Bryan and said, "Man, I owe you a case of beer!" He grinned, and he showed me where the fuse was replaced under the dash. The handiwork was good—the front frames were secure, and the battery case shelf consisted of simply adding another metal plate and welding it on top of the bent-shelf case. That worked.

It was time to pull my baby out of the bay onto the muddy pavement. I said a brief silent prayer that she wouldn't get stuck in the mud. Nah, she powered through with ease. The total bill? $490.78. A deal!

(As I write this, I realize I still need to send Bryan a case of beer.)

Chapter 24
NORTH-WESTWARD HO!

OCTOBER 1, 2018

- Mileage: **115,572**
- Previous total: **$27,414.81**
- Welding for front frame and battery shelf, and bonus slide-out repair: **$490.78**
- Current total: **$27,905.59**
- Credit score: **633**

With the welding on the Discovery done and my FLX bike in better shape but not quite perfect, the deadline was looming over me to be in Madison, Wisconsin by October 10 for a Deafhood in Allies workshop with interpreters and Deaf people. I also had to head to Oconomowoc for Deafhood 201. I said my goodbyes to Aunt Laura and Dari, their two cats May and June, and their lovable dog Karley. I also went over and said goodbyes to my mother, Alec, and Nauvoo.

As I was leaving, Alec cracked, "You'll be back early given that Discovery's recent track record."

I growled at him.

On October 6, 2018, everything was loaded, including my trusty writing chair. I stopped at a Kroger in Brownsburg, Indiana to shop for groceries. The refrigerator was humming along nicely, keeping food cold.

I drove westward on I-74, taking in the vast expanse of farmland as the sun set beautifully. After a fill-up, I eventually pulled off into a rest area in Illinois for the night, just past

Alec, holding Nauvoo, with my mother and me as I get ready to leave for Wisconsin.

Champaign-Urbana. Owning a diesel pusher really distorts any sense of normalcy in terms of spending and maintenance— even simple fill-ups require pumping twice, hitting the commonly-set $100 limit in order

My first breakfast as a full-timer! I cooked an omelet with mushrooms, spinach and onions.

to reach a full tank, usually anywhere from $150 to $180. My highest was $209 at one point. The days of forty-dollar fill-ups for my Honda Odyssey were fond memories at this point.

The next morning, I woke up from a peaceful sleep, other than slight annoying pinholes of light streaming through my dark blinds, right into my eyes. For Deaf people, any light or flickering during the night is probably the equivalent to annoying, constant noise for hearing folks. I added masking tape over the column of pinholes, and that solved the problem.

I cooked my first breakfast in our Discovery—this time, I had everything I needed to cook a meal. The food seemed to be extra delicious as I savored the quiet moment, sitting in my writing chair and taking in the view of Illinois farmland.

After that, I cleaned up and washed dishes, and put them away into cramped cupboards. I told myself I needed to figure out a better way to organize my food, dishes, and cups. For now, the set-up would do. I stepped outside to check the tires, jacks, and anything else underneath to make sure all was clear before I drive off. I made that a habit after nearly ripping out the electrical cord from a campground post after thinking I had stowed away everything. And that was my father's RV from last year. Whew.

I drove on back roads all day, making my way towards Madison, with a brief lunch stop in Gridley, Illinois. I drove through Dixon, Illinois where I stopped to watch the raging, swollen river. The sight was breathtaking. The lower sidewalks and ramps were flooded, and I took all of it in. I recalled a news clip showing several RVs being washed away in a flash flood somewhere out east, and I shuddered at the thought of being caught up in such a fierce current.

The scenic drive continued all the way to south Madison, where I parked at the Lake Farm campground in Dane County. The sites offered 50-amp hook-ups, but no water or sewer so I pulled into an empty

I quickly got used to this lifestyle.

site and paid for the next few nights by depositing the envelope in their mailbox. I filled her eighty-gallon freshwater tank from a pump nearby, and I was all set for the next few days. I would be comfortable with my water needs except being unable to wash clothes. A single load can easily consume 20 percent of the freshwater tank and fill the fifty-gallon gray water tank another 30 percent. I told myself I could wash my clothes on the last morning, and then go and dump the tanks and fill her up again.

I settled easily into my new life and the routine. I would wake up, cook my breakfast, and clean up. Then I would tackle my book writing, being committed to at least one thousand words each day—sometimes exceeding that by a large margin easily and struggling on other days. I find it easier if I get up early in the morning and get my writing done then, but occasionally, this isn't possible. So, I try to make it up on the other days.

I rented a car, and the rental agency was to come and pick me up. I would have the car for the whole weekend. There wasn't any campground near Oconomowoc, so I decided to keep my Discovery at Lake Farm and commute fifty minutes each way for the class over the weekend. I wanted an electrical connection so I could leave a 60-watt light bulb on in the water bay to prevent the water from freezing as well as keeping my heat on over the cold weekend.

I biked Madison's amazing bike pathways throughout the city connecting directly to Lake Farm, and it was truly a remarkable network of bike paths, unmatched by paths in other urban settings I have seen. I easily biked into downtown Madison and ate at Muramoto's, an excellent sushi restaurant with an exceptionally unique take on house's hot sake; theirs was infused with honey and ginger. I then biked back with a good buzz and warm feeling.

The next day, I walked around the campground and noticed a warm orange tabby lying down in someone else's motorhome, absorbing all the sun's rays. The warm fuzzies continued, knowing that I would see many more of these kind of sights as I made my way through the country and Canada and perhaps even Mexico, if I am brave—or stupid—enough. I knew I would be going to Mexico this winter to have my three cavities filled—hey, don't judge... I love sugar—and the cost would be around forty-five dollars per filling as opposed to nearly $700 "discounted" in Indianapolis. But I didn't think I would cross the border with my Discovery. I had to do some checking around first.

Both my Deafhood workshop and class went well over the weekend, and I made the fifty-minute commute fairly easily. I did have to adapt to the rainy weather by bringing inside my electric bike to make sure she stayed dry.

One evening, I had a craving for an Impossible Burger so I looked on the Internet, and the highly rated Salvatore's Tomato Pies came up. I was intrigued. They had Impossible Burger crumbled on their pizzas. I went there, and I wasn't disappointed. The beer was great, also.

The pizza was of a different style from my favorite pizzeria, Mozzeria in San Francisco, the only Deaf-owned and operated Neapolitan pizzeria with a custom-made Stefano Ferraro oven imported from Italy. Mozzeria was founded by Russ and Melody Stein, the same folks who founded Bigfoot Family Camping in South Dakota. Since then, Mozzeria has opened a second location through a partnership with a Deaf-run nonprofit, Communication Services for the Deaf, in Washington, DC. The San Francisco location has converted to a trolley (food truck) and is doing well.

Sadly, successful retail businesses owned by the Deaf people are few and far in between, largely due to the massive damage inflicted upon our peoples by oralism—a totalitarian ideology banning the use of sign languages and Deaf teachers that continues in full force today across large swaths of the country and worldwide. Oralism has long been led by hearing specialists such as audiologists, speech therapists, and special educators with the Alexander Graham Bell Association at the forefront. A huge majority of the Association's membership and leadership are made up of the same specialists, and the remaining are well-meaning hearing parents who have been led to believe they could deprive their Deaf children of what World Federation of the Deaf now recognizes as a natural birthright to their signed languages, their Deaf cultures and healthy identities. Whether it be Black ASL, Mexican Sign Language, Plains Indian Sign Language, or ASL in the United States. Sign language is not universal—most countries have their own sign languages—but what is universal is that Deaf babies have a birthright: their natural language of sign.

We are beginning to come out of the long shadow of a war lasting nearly two centuries, filled with hatred and revulsion of signed languages and Deaf cultures, and we are seeing more and more Deaf-owned businesses popping up across the country, including Crepe Crazy in Austin, Texas and its franchise in Baltimore, Maryland and Streetcar 82 Brewery in Hyattsville, Maryland.

With the class a great success, I pulled up my jacks and dumped my tanks and filled up with fresh water, then I hit the back roads south for Nauvoo, Illinois.

Chapter 25
NAUVOO AND SPIRITUAL EXPERIENCES

The Discovery in front of the Nauvoo Temple of the Church of Jesus Christ of Latter-day Saints in Illinois.

Nauvoo, Illinois holds a special place in my heart. The Church of Jesus Christ of the Latter-day Saints (LDS), commonly referred to as Mormons, settled in this town and built their second temple here. Situated on the western border of Illinois along the Mississippi River, the city flourished, and the new city was actually bigger than Chicago at one point. Due to intolerance and persecution from their neighbors, the Mormons were forced to migrate westward, eventually settling in the Great Salt Lake Valley.

My children's mother and I converted to the church around the time she was pregnant with our oldest, Theo. We had been active for a good number of years before deciding that as much as we loved the church and how it operated, there were a few things we could not support or abide by—their position against LGBTQIA+ communities and their opposition to marriage equality for all, for instance. I believe there will be a "Spencer W. Kimball" revelation moment for the church in the future regarding LGBTQIA+ members—similar to when Black people were finally allowed to hold priesthood in June 1978, despite historically having already given priesthood during LDS founder's Joseph Smith's time.

Many are familiar with the LDS church's former practice of polygamy, and the fact that they deny priesthood to women, which continues to be somewhat controversial within and outside of the church. Many people assume that women are oppressed within the church and that may be true in different ways, but many people also overlook the role of women leaders within the church as well.

For example, who was the first female state senator in the United States, and which states granted women the right to vote first? The answers may surprise you. The first two states to grant women full voting rights were Wyoming and Utah, two states with large LDS populations. Martha Hughes Cannon, a medical doctor and LDS member, became the first female state senator. She also was the fourth wife of Angus M. Cannon, a leader in the Latter-day Saint community. She even ran against her own husband in the election and won. Interestingly, she served on the board of Utah Schools for the Deaf and the Blind and passed legislation funding a health center for the school.

There are plenty of surprises about the LDS church, and plenty of head-scratching paradoxes, but it is what it is. I still have a warm place for the church in my heart, despite its cultural and doctrinal imperfections. I have always loved the idea that the church is led by revelation through prayer. Church leadership has three members: the bishop (senior leader of a large congregation) has first and second counselors, and they pray and make decisions together. I have had firsthand experience with this process, having had the privilege of serving as a second counselor in Grand Rapids, Michigan when Theo was a baby.

These experiences are considered by the church to be sacred and are not typically shared outside of the community, but I feel the experience is too important to not share. Leadership and positions within the church are determined by prayerful consideration and the person given the calling, and it is up to this person to accept the calling or not. Each person usually serves two to three years per calling before being released. No one ever "applies" for any position within the church. No one has an "ambition" for specific callings. Dropping hints of your interest in specific callings is not acceptable. The callings come to you, and it is up to you to accept them or not. That's it. The church is led by lay clergy; no one studies for any position. Every person often has a full-time job outside of the church.

The time came to release our branch's Relief Society president. The Relief Society is a woman-led organization and considered to be the largest women's organization in the world, with its own presidency and leadership structure. The Relief Society president is selected by the branch presidency (or bishops and their counselors for larger congregations called wards; branches are much smaller, typically between twenty-five and one hundred members).

For the first time in history of the Grand Rapids, Michigan branch we had an all-Deaf branch presidency. Patrick Phillips served as the first Deaf branch president, and Jerry Hunsburger served as the first counselor, and I was the second counselor. We got together and discussed prospective Deaf and hearing women members for the position of Relief Society president within the Grand River ASL branch. Then from that point, the new Relief Society president would call her own counselors and leadership.

We discussed candidates, and my wife at that time, Jen, came up. We all quickly agreed that we need to pass over her because she just had given birth to Theo, and it was an incredibly long and difficult birth. She had back labor, her tailbone broke while delivering Theo, and she was having a rough time recovering from this. We discussed others and their challenges as well.

We were vexed. We wondered who should be called for this position because each woman had her challenges or potential conflicts of interest, such as being the wife of the branch president and so forth. There were approximately nine women in the branch, so we decided to submit their names to a prayer circle, each taking turns being the prayer signer. After mentioning a name, the signer would pause and we all would bow our heads, close our eyes, and meditate quietly, being open to any feelings and thoughts that came to us. Then after a moment, the signer would resume and close the prayer.

Several names were submitted through collective prayers, and nothing happened. It was Branch President Phillips' turn to sign the prayer and he submitted my wife's name, and paused for all of us to close our eyes and…

I was on fire.

I remember goosebumps all over me, powerfully washing over me in waves. I panicked and quietly thought, *My wife? Are you serious?!*

The answer came peacefully yet with such power, "Yes."

No way. This has to be coming from my pride and my ego.

"Okay, then. You have two other grown men to agree with you."

Oh, right. Good point. Relieved, I opened my eyes, and I looked up to Jerry Hunsburger, who so often provided comic relief with his facial and body expressions at times, and he

Beautiful views by the Mississippi River in western Illinois.

grimaced at me—half apologetically—"Ooh! Your wife!" He then shrugged with a half-smile.

I was agog, and quickly turned to Branch President Phillips, who was visibly shaken. "Y-y-yes," he signed. "Your wife... will be the next Relief Society President."

As taken aback I was then, I am still filled with warm fuzzies from that moment, and I have always admired how the process removes raw ambition and replaces that with humility and willingness to serve.

I do wonder if the Deaf communities could take a page or two from the church's leadership style, with our own culturally appropriate modifications. I truly believe that everyone could access the divine source—whether it be our Heavenly Father and Mother, our universe, our Great Spirit, or our collective consciousness, or any other deity. If we engage with this greater power in a humble way, I think the potential for transformation and healing is huge.

With that in mind, I wanted to figure out a way forward with the healing for my Deaf and signing community, starting with myself. Unfortunately, my plan to stay in Nauvoo for a night or two had to be scratched. The state park campground was virtually deserted, and it was a tight space as well as having no cell signal at all. Frustrated, I continued my trip south towards

Quincy, Illinois, passing many beautiful roadside areas by the Mississippi River—but the signage clearly said no overnight camping anywhere along this route. An unfortunate waste, especially off-season.

I settled in for a night at Walmart in Quincy and cooked myself a meal. I shopped for a couple of things from the store. I really wish they would pay their workers a much better wage, stop gaming the system, and depriving the workers of much needed benefits. I sometimes joke and call Walmarts Evil-Marts because of the poor working conditions and pay while the owners reap huge profit margins. Yet, as an RVer, I am grateful that they welcome RVers to stay overnight in their parking lots, so I do occasionally shop there. Life is full of complicated trade-offs, and I wish I could live a life in a completely principled way. Maybe one day.

There are alternatives to parking at Walmarts: Cracker Barrel restaurants, some highway rest areas (though not all states allow overnight parking), and some scenic turn outs. I also am a member of Harvest Hosts where I can stay a night at a local winery or brewery or even a farm, but thus far my location has never lined up with an available Harvest Host—maybe I should help them out and sign up more breweries and wineries while traveling.

I ended up at a Cracker Barrel in Columbia, Missouri because the local Walmart didn't have a level parking lot.

Chapter 26
GETTING ON RIDES IN SILVER DOLLAR CITY

I was in Branson, Missouri simply because of the Silver Dollar City amusement park. I wanted to ride their promising new wooden roller coaster, the Outlaw Run, that actually turns you upside down and takes you on corkscrews. I certainly wasn't interested in their music offerings, or the garish tourist traps everywhere. Passport America, a national membership program that gives you half off on your RV stays at participating campgrounds and RV parks, had several locations in the Branson area.

Looking up at one of several Branson's neon-lit water towers from the Pea Patch RV park.

I headed for a campground on top of the hill ridge, but it was fully booked. I then called around and discovered most campgrounds were also booked. A small RV park, Pea Patch, right in the heart of a suburban strip off the Branson near the Titanic and Ripley's Believe It or Not museums, had one site left, so I grabbed that one. No discount, though. Their Passport America special rate didn't kick in until

Wildfire, a Bolliger & Mabillard floorless roller coaster in Silver Dollar City, Missouri.

after November. The owner offered me a weekly rate and I took the deal.

The place was on a steep hill. The sites were leveled out in a staircase fashion. The owner gracefully helped me pull in and set up, and he even fixed my leaky water filter by removing the small hose that came with the filter and replacing it with the new water pressure regulator I picked up in Illinois. A good thing because the park was right under a huge water tower, and clearly the pressure was intense.

I went to the Silver Dollar City amusement park first, and I discovered that if I went to the guest relations office, I could get free admission because I was Deaf. I agree with this approach because many of the amenities in the park are offered only in spoken English and not accessible in ASL. Until amusement parks commit to becoming fully accessible twenty-four hours a day, we shouldn't be paying full price at all.

I got in a few rides on the Outlaw Run, and I was blown away. I loved the ride—the intensity, the smoothness, notwithstanding the slightly vertigo-inducing ending. I wanted to come back another day since the newest ride, Time Traveler, was down for the day. I went to set up at Pea Patch.

The next couple of days brought rain, so I worked on replacing my leaky kitchen faucet. I had bought a new Moen faucet for $150 at Menards, a Midwestern hardware store, in Madison, Wisconsin and I didn't get around to installing it until

Branson. The rainy day provided a perfect opportunity for me to stay inside and do some home improvement projects.

The incorrect measurements using Apple's Measure app were exasperating.

The old faucet was removed, and the area around the mounting was cleaned thoroughly. The installation of the new faucet went so easily and smoothly that even though I didn't have the right tools to tighten one pipe, it never leaked (but I did tighten it a few days later). The new Moen faucet worked far better than the old one, creating less splash and it moved around with such ease. It was easily worth the premium price.

The next project was to replace the washer and dryer shelf with a new customized oak shelf to hold my beloved Big Berkey water filter system. By this time, Apple had released its new iOS 12 update, which included a brand-new Measure app using augmented reality. I thought it was such a nifty feature that I used it to measure the shelf length and depth, and I went into Menards and confidently picked up an oak board. It turned out the measurements were not correct, and I had to return this board for the correct size. Good thing I checked before I left the parking lot.

While the rain continued, I went ahead and removed the old shelf. The removal took some effort; it required repeated chiseling to remove the wooden splinters that had been glued onto the frame. As soon as the weather cleared up, I went outside and cut the shelf to the correct size, and I realized I needed to round off the shelf so it wouldn't stick into my ribs as I entered

The final result. I added foam to the bottom to reduce the vibration that could untwist the filters. I added duct tape to hold the fluoride filters in place. The foam is a bit unsightly, but that's a project for another time.

the bathroom. Although I didn't have a jigsaw, I had a handsaw, and it went much easier than I expected.

The corner then was well-sanded to round off the sharp corners on top and bottom. A clear coat of spray paint went on the shelf, which took all day with repeated coatings, two hours between each. With adhesive caulking and two screws, the shelf went in easily and within the weekend, the entire shelf and water filter was secured in place.

I felt a certain pride for completing these handyman projects—I was not particularly handy, but I was compelled to do as much as I could to save money.

Saturday came fast. I was scheduled to give a two-hour presentation on Deafhood via video conferencing to the Deaf community in Anchorage. I had to find a place with excellent Wi-Fi; online reviews pointed to Starbucks having the best Wi-Fi speeds since they partnered with Google. Second best? McDonald's. I'll go with Starbucks any day. To do this, I had to bike with my laptop in my backpack clear across town to the old downtown Branson's Starbucks location. Luckily their Wi-

Alaskan Deaf community members watch my Deafhood presentation.

Fi checked out fine. I ran over next door to a sushi place and ate there for dinner before the presentation.

A Deaf technician, Aaron Stribling, met me online an hour prior and we worked out the logistics of giving the presentation with slides minimized at times to maximize my signing for the audience, and switching back again so the audience could read the slides as well. This required a dance between each mode, and Aaron pulled it off without a hitch.

I had never done a live video conference using Keynote, and it went well. The videos I used on my slides did skip and stutter at times, but the viewers understood the gist of everything that was shown. Relieved, I celebrated with a nice beer back at the RV after biking across the suburban wasteland during the chilly night.

I went back to Silver Dollar City the next day by biking over steep hills from Pea Patch to the amusement park, and my FLX bike handled it with aplomb. Pleasantly surprised, I felt a good amount of relief after spending so much time trying to make the bike "right." The only drawback was that the park didn't have a proper bike rack. The park was in a place that was readily accessible by car but not for pedestrians, so they probably didn't consider cyclists, either. I had to chain my bike to a wooden fence post behind a small staff entrance.

I got in way more rides that day, including on Time Traveler, which proved to be such an enjoyable surprise. The ride initially appeared to be the type that induced vertigo by spinning riders willy-nilly throughout the track, but no, the spins were perfectly timed to make it even more interesting and less vertigo-inducing.

Of course, I got in seven rides on the Outlaw Run—my favorite in the park, except for the dizzying ending. I felt satisfied that day, and the bike ride back home was as easy as the initial trip.

Though I had two more nights paid for with the weekly rate, it was time to pull up the leveling jacks and head out. I wanted to make my way westward towards Salt Lake City by October 30 in time for my friend's favorite haunted house, Nightmare on 13th Street.

Chapter 27
COLAW SALVAGE AND ROUTE 66

OCTOBER 27, 2018

- Mileage: **118,202**
- Previous total: **$27,905.59**
- Freightlighter cover and air cleaner (Tip: Check salvage yards for used items to save money): **$206.81**
- Harbor Freight tools: **$24.83**
- Intellitec Model 900 salvage unit and gas props for cargo bay doors: **$225.93**
- Current total: **$28,363.16**
- Credit score: **628**

Heading towards a Freightliner shop in Springfield, Missouri, I spotted Lambert's Cafe, known for their "throwed rolls." I knew I had to make a pit stop there, despite not being a fan of country cooking because of the heavy meat content. I had to see the famed flying dinner rolls for myself, and I wasn't disappointed. The rolls were so buttery and heavenly. I crafted a meal out of the vegetable sides, and it was halfway decent, though not something I would crave. But man, the rolls…

I lost my rear tire cover somewhere on the road before Quincy, Illinois and a local Freightliner shop helped me find a shop with the cover in stock. It was in Springfield, two hours east on I-72. I made my way there and picked up the new cover and air brake dryer cartridge that I intended to install myself.

My new Freightliner wheel cover.

The tools required to tighten the wheel cover weren't in my tool set, so a stop at Harbor Freight was next. With the right tool, the wheel cover was completely secure and in place. So shiny.

After stopping at HyVee, a grocery store, to stock up my refrigerator and taking a power nap in the parking lot, I continued to a rest area just before Colaw RV Salvage where I spent the night in peace and quiet.

The next morning was a short drive to the salvage yard to see a huge array of parts. Some of the things were way overpriced, in my opinion, such as factory Xantrex Freedom 458 inverter/charger units that retailed for $999 new; Colaw listed salvaged ones at $750. They also only offered a ninety-day warranty on anything they sold, so no thanks. But they did have several Intellitec Model 900 electrical boxes in stock with the necessary circuit boards for power management and shedding. The Discovery's box was broken before I bought it.

I was told by Intellitec that certain circuit boards would go for $350 new. Colaw listed them for $150 so it was an easy decision right there. I would have to take out the fuse box and replace the entire box... *wait a minute... why don't I just pop out the circuit board and replace that? Keep the fuse box as it was?*

That could work! I spent some time replacing the gas props, asking the store clerk to help me size them correctly. It took some trial and error before I replaced all the weak ones. I also wanted to replace a missing windowpane that fell out of my bedroom window the night before. Aunt Laura and my son Warrick had glued that pane in earlier in the year, but it wasn't strong enough. I really hope it didn't cause any harm or damage when it fell out on the road.

The missing glass pane staring at me, annoying the heck out of me.

Josh Phillips, a Colaw Salvage employee, confirmed he had a replacement window, but I would have to replace the entire thing for $225 plus labor. They were willing to remove my window, but I would have to go to another RV shop across the highway for the installation. I thought I would rather find another solution, knowing that most RV shops have a long backlog for service, and I didn't want to wait.

I asked Josh if he had cargo bay door tabs that would hold the bay doors in place and prevent them from shifting. We went out to my Discovery, and I demonstrated the problem. Apparently, the demonstration went too far. The bay door shifted so far to the right that it couldn't go back in position.

Panic set in; no amount of slamming the door moved it back into its original position. Josh looked under the door and pointed out a metal bar that was interfering.

Ugggggh. Further efforts still yielded nothing.

It was time for a lunch break. As I heated up leftovers for lunch, a million-dollar Prevost coach pulled up alongside and parked. I texted my family, "The universe is mocking me. I'm trying to get the cargo door back in place and a million-dollar Prevost RV pulls up next to me."

It was time for Dremel power.

I pushed the bay door too far, and the door wouldn't go back in its original place.

As I struggled with my cargo bay door gone wild, a million-dollar Prevost bus conversion RV pulled up. The owner was cool, and he said he absolutely loved his bus.

I cut off the offending metal plate and figured I could replace it later. The bay door slid back into place, and I let out a huge sigh of relief. I wrapped things up, and I decided to head for a local RV park right off Route 66: the Casa RV Park. With the Passport America discount, it was just twenty dollars for the night with full hook-ups.

The Intellitec circuit board needed to be replaced that night before I headed out to Denver to ensure everything worked right. If it did not, I still could easily return to Colaw—fifteen minutes away—and replace it under their ninety-day guarantee.

I arrived at the quaint and clean Casa RV Park and checked in with ease. The owner gave me the most level site they had, and I pulled her through and leveled her, got the slides out and hooked her up. The place was clean and comfortable, and the owner told me I could have firewood for free as well. They had a nice outdoor pool, but the weather wasn't good for it. I longed for a hot tub.

I went right to work in removing the metal cover on the fuse box and pulled the broken circuit board. I pulled the newer circuit board from the box I had just bought, and I was about to swap them, but...

The part didn't match. The four pins were different. My circuit board was made in 2000, and the replacement was made in 2006.

I cursed to myself.

Colaw was closing in less than hour. I quickly pulled in the slide-outs, pulled up the leveling jacks, disconnected her, and drove back to the salvage store. I brought the box to Josh and pointed out the difference in the circuit boards. He told me to go ahead and pick another unit off the shelf and he would open it to ensure I had a match. I grabbed two units and brought them back to the checkout desk. The first box he opened was empty. The second unit checked out with a 2002 model board with pins that matched up perfectly. Josh let me leave with this new one.

It was dinnertime so I stopped in town for a beer and pizza. The beer was good, the pizza, not so much. The crust seemed factory-made.

Back at the RV park and all settled in, I finally swapped the circuit boards. I plugged everything back in its rightful place including the washer and dryer, which had previously been running on bypass wiring due to the damaged board. I anxiously plugged in the 50-amp power. After a delay everything lit up—and everything worked!

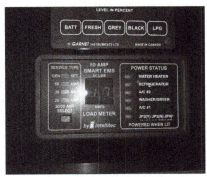

The display finally shows the correct amp load.

I switched over to 30 amps, and the unit actually counted the amps I was using. The same went for the generator. After a delay, the amp usage was shown and each unit for shedding—a process of turning off power to the refrigerator, hot water heater, and air conditioner based on available load—lit up in succession. The feeling of a hard-won victory washed over me. Finally, a working power management system, as opposed to a weird, glitchy light show that did absolutely nothing to manage power. It took us over six months to fix, but by waiting, we saved quite bit of money compared to buying a new circuit board.

The campfire for the night was canceled because of approaching rain, and I didn't want to have to clean up a soggy wet mess on my portable fire pit. I was happy to settle in for the night, reading a book and watching Netflix.

In the morning, after reading responses from the Discovery Owners group about the window replacement, I thought I probably should go back and look at the $225 window Josh offered. Maybe I would buy it and hold onto it until I could find a time and place to have it replaced, or possibly we could replace it ourselves. As I prepared to leave the Casa RV Park, I went through the steps: stow away the gear, get the slide-outs in, unhook the power cord and stow it, empty the gray and black tanks, fill up the freshwater tank, and finally, retract the leveling jacks. After running the engine at a slightly higher idle to fill up the air tanks, I pulled her off the pad.

She didn't want to move. She struggled, rumbling as she moved slowly. Something was wrong. I pulled onto the shoulder just few hundred feet from the pad, hopped out and looked around. The air bags hadn't inflated at all.

Oh, no. Theo and I had discussed this earlier and agreed that the airbags might need to be replaced within the next couple of years as they showed signs of cracking and slight dry rot. Maybe this time, they had broken down for good.

Ugh. Damn it!

I climbed back in, and I looked at my dashboard, desperately checking the air pressure. It was good, well over 120 psi in the front and rear, which meant there wasn't a leak in the air system.

I checked the leveling jacks control pad and the video monitor showing the underside—the best thing we ever added because it allows me to remotely monitor front and rear jacks.

Wait a minute. A thought came to me, and I shifted my gaze to other side of my steering column, and there it was. I had forgotten to turn the air suspension to auto in order to inflate the airbags, after releasing them last night. Duh.

The switch flipped, the Discovery began to rise gracefully, and I took a walk around outside to verify that everything was good and dandy.

I sent a message to my family letting them know that the safe operation of this huge and lovable beast required a checklist so we wouldn't miss any steps. I also made a mental note to create a label and put it right next to the leveling jack controls as a reminder to release/build air suspension. On the way back to Colaw, I noticed two used Discoverys in good-looking shape at the RV consignment dealership across the road. I wanted to stop and check these out, especially to compare the rust—or the lack of.

Back at Colaw, I rode with an employee in a golf cart—their salvage lot is huge, and it was a couple minutes' drive—so I could visually inspect the replacement window. It turned out they had a 2002 Discovery as

The cooling and engine area had melted down in this salvaged Discovery.

Both RVs had disastrous fires, one in the engine and one over the entire back end.

a salvage. She looked just as good as mine externally, except for the telltale salvage yard code spray painted on her body.

I wondered what was wrong with her, and so I decided to take a walk around her. Ah, there it was.

The cooling system had a meltdown—quite possibly the engine had blown out as well—and it wasn't pretty. Clearly, this Discovery was totaled after this happened. The RV next to the Discovery had it even worse—there was a huge fire in the back, taking out nearly half the coach.

Yikes.

Clearly, there are many good reasons to be vigilant in checking the safety systems on the Discovery to prevent this from happening, including buying a more expensive foam fire extinguisher as opposed to dry powder ones (onboard, we had the dry powder one).

I made another mental note to rectify that sooner rather than later. It also reminded me of another safety system that needed to be addressed: the smoke and carbon monoxide alarms. Being Deaf, I need alarms with strobe lights, but they are expensive and require extensive hard wiring to work on a 120-volt system. There are wireless systems, but they give off false alarms from other types of sounds.

This is a source of frustration for the Deaf RV community. The engineering required to add LED strobe lights on battery power is relatively simple, but this still hasn't been done by any of the major alarm system makers. Clearly, we need to contact our legislators and see if we can't pass a bill requiring this on all battery-powered systems. This would make these alarms even more accessible for all of us at a much lower cost.

The employee climbed inside the salvaged Discovery, and I followed his lead. I had to step over debris all over the floor to reach the bedroom and look at the window. The smell inside was atrocious.

The window had improved handles that would extend and retract the windowpanes, but the seals were all damaged and screens were torn in many places. This window didn't look good, and I asked the employee if Colaw would repair the seal and screens before handing it over to me, and the answer was no, it was sold as is.

Dejectedly, I told him, "No, thanks." We tried to find another window of similar size in their yard without any luck. But I did see there were plenty of Freightliner rear wheel covers—dang. I could have picked these up and polished them up for much cheaper than I paid at Freightliner. Lesson learned.

With that done and over with, I wanted to go across the highway to the consignment RV sales and check out the two used Discovery units on their lot. Would they have same amount of rust as our Discovery? If so, what would the visible differences be?

Chapter 28
THE INTERIOR OF
THE DISCOVERY

A cross from Colaw, I toured a 2006 Discovery. It had a nicer interior, better kitchen layout, and double wide slide-outs that made the interior space larger. This model also offered another five inches in ceiling height, which made the space even more comfortable. I also especially appreciated the much-improved bedroom closet mirrored sliding doors— clearly with steel ball bearings and better locking mechanism than our 2001.5 model. Though the original carpeting was still in place, it looked somewhat decent. All in all, this Discovery looked, smelled, and felt pretty great.

There was no question that we loved the Discovery's interior look and feel. The only thing I would change about this space is to replace the driver's side jackknife sofa with a newer expandable L-shaped sofa so we could easily watch TV. Unfortunately, even used, these sofas sell for over $2,000. I saw one on eBay for $375 but the L-shaped

A 2006 Discovery 39J interior with a dinette booth, a feature we did not want, and original carpeting.

Our 2001.5 Discovery with hardwood flooring; despite only having one main slide-out, the space feels roomy and clean.

expandable section was on the wrong side. I learned later that these sofas aren't quite comfortable, so I have given up on this idea. I also would love to have the extendable kitchen counter/drawers like the 2006 model.

Another thing on my wish list? A tub. I even measured the bathroom area, and it seemed possible to install a freestanding bathtub—this one from Menards for $719 fits the bill nicely at sixty inches by thirty-two inches.

The total length of bathroom area is approximately sixty-four inches. To fit a tub, we would have to remove the shower stall, the bathroom cabinet and sink and replace it with a narrow, "floating" sink above the tub, and tile the walls. This would be a weird compromise, but I would be able to take baths whenever at full hook-up campgrounds.

But this also means I would have to replace the current ten-gallon hot water tank that runs on both gas and electricity to a tankless hot water heater. The plumbing work would have to be creative to make the sink fit right above the tub.

Our 2001.5 Discovery, looking toward the front end with a HDTV.

I'm still tempted. Especially after seeing photos of the Foretravel Luxury Villa Spa model for a mere $800,000-plus price tag. One day, perhaps, I will be stupid enough to try this stunt.

Unfortunately, there are other upgrades I need to make to this Discovery if I continue full-timing with her. These upgrades—or my wish list—include some key safety features we need or increases our capacity to boondock:

- Solar panels (roof): $1,000 (400w) to $2,000 (800w) plus installation cost
- Inverter: Replace puny 1200-watt inverter with Magnum Hybrid 3000-watt pure sine wave inverter for $1,800, or back to Xantrex 458, the factory default for $1,000
- Rewiring: Rewire so all outlets operate with a new inverter, rather than just select GFCI outlets for an unknown cost
- Tire monitoring: Six tire pressure monitoring system for $450
- Stabilizer: SteerSafe or Safe-T-Plus for $500 installed, which will help with driving fatigue and provide stability in the event of a tire blowout

- Electric heat: CheapHeat 30/50 amp heating add-on to furnace heat for $400, saving money on LP heat while at campgrounds or with hook-ups.
- VMSPC: Computerized monitoring of engine and transmission functions for $450, including Windows tablet
- Drawers: Replace all drawers with slow-close drawer bars, for $50-$75
- Water pump: The Shurflo pump has struggled at times, so about $100-$150
- Welding: Additional house frame welding and grinding to remove excess rust and strengthen frames for $1,000
- Radiator & CAC: We will eventually need new ones at $4,000
- Shocks & air bags: Replacement within two to three years for $1,500

All of this is on top of regular maintenance, such as oil changes ($300), transmission fluid ($300), air cleaner ($75), lube and brake checkups, and other expenses.

Diesel pushers are magnificent beasts, and they require serious upkeep—although I could have done with a lot less "upkeep" in the past eight months. But would I have learned lessons in patience, letting go, celebrating with my children, coping and so forth along the way if I had a different, lower-maintenance Discovery?

Chapter 29
TIME TO HEAD WEST

My stay in Missouri had come to an end, and with it, the power management system fixed, gas props were now holding up the bay doors, and the rear wheel cover was in place, though I had yet to find a solution for the missing windowpane. The time had come to head west to Provo, Utah to meet up with friends for a trip to a renowned haunted house on October 30.

I drove through the changing landscapes of Kansas and made a stop in Czech-populated Wilson, Kansas, home of the world's largest

In front of the world's largest painted egg in the small town of Wilson, Kansas.

painted egg that measured twenty feet high and fifteen feet wide. After a power nap and a tour of the egg, I made a stop in Hays, Kansas at a university-operated Starbucks for the best possible Internet connection. I was giving another video presentation to the Alaska Deaf community, educators, and policymakers. Unfortunately, this event had to be rescheduled so more people

Two Discoverys sitting next to each other. The one on the left is a 1999 model.

Brown duct tape on the edges of the main slide-out floor. It looks nice, if I may say so myself.

could attend the workshop. With that, I was done for the night, and I pulled onto the Walmart parking lot in Hays. I noticed that I was pulling up next to another Discovery. This one was an older, but clean, model.

Their curtains were drawn, and I was tired also, so I closed up everything and retired to my comfortable bed for the evening. I didn't bother with putting out the slides. I wanted to take off the first thing the next morning.

After a good breakfast and a good writing session, I started the process of going through my departure checklist—making sure the leveling jacks were retracted, the air bags inflated, and doing a walk-around. Before I did that, I finally got around to duct taping the edges of the slide-out floor. There was a wooden trim on it before, but I didn't like how high the bump was. I wanted a smooth transition from the slide-out floor to the main floor.

Me, Claudia Booth, and Dick Booth in front of their 1999 Discovery 36T. Mine is on the right.

The brown-colored duct tape worked well. I would have liked to use real copper tape, but most of what I found online was too thin and I was afraid it would break up easily.

As soon as I stepped outside, I saw my neighbor watching his slide-out retracting. I went up to him and introduced myself—typing on the Cardzilla app—"Hi! Nice Discovery! My name is Marvin Miller, what's yours?"

He typed on my phone, "Dick Booth." His wife, Claudia, came around and talked with him, indicating that they had something to tell me. Dick typed, "As you pulled in last night, we heard a clanking noise."

Uh-oh. "Really?" I looked underneath, and I saw that the makeshift sheet metal Theo installed on the underside of the front radiator fan had fallen apart. I removed that. Dick and Claudia weren't sure if that was the issue, though. I mentioned to Dick I had been having issues with the leveling jacks' light remaining on despite the jacks being fully retracted. I wondered if this was the noise they heard.

Nope. But, referring to the light problem, Dick said, "That's an easy fix." He went inside his Discovery and pulled out hydraulic fluid and tools, and he showed me where to unscrew the fluid cap and add more. We had to add quite a bit. And the blinking jack light problem was solved.

I was so grateful. While Dick was looking for his tools I gave Claudia a tour of my Discovery, telling her what a headache it had been for us. Claudia loved *Chicago*'s interior, and we chatted for a little bit. They were headed to see friends in Colorado then to California and the southwest.

They wanted to be sure the noise problem was eliminated so I started *Chicago* up and moved her forward and back, and they reported that everything was good.

It turned out they were also members of the Discovery Owners group. We took a picture together, wished each other good luck, and said our goodbyes. Dick had been a great help. He even left me the remaining hydraulic fluid. I only hope I can pay the kindness forward to other Discovery owners I come across during my travels.

Leaving Hays, Kansas with a warm, fuzzy feeling, I headed for Denver. After an hour, when I stopped at a nearby rest area for a quick lunch and a power nap, I realized I didn't tell Dick and Claudia about a good-sized engine oil leak underneath their Discovery while I was admiring their coach, comparing for rust—their coach was far in better shape than mine. So I emailed Claudia to let her know about that, just in case. I also shared a picture with her.

She replied later,

Thanks so much for the picture! You may have had issues with your Discovery, but I'd trade the inside of yours for ours any day! Beautiful!!! Yes, Dick is aware of the leak, but thanks for the reminder. We've found so many "angels" in our seven snowbird travels. People in motorhomes know what it's like to be in

Going up and up on the Interstate 70 west of Denver was a hair-raising experience, especially in monitoring the engine temperature.

difficult situations! We wish you well in your travels and happy writing!!! Until we meet again, keep on smilin'.

Oh, Claudia—she had no idea how much that meant to me, having gone through so much with the Discovery.

As I drove towards Denver, I considered my plans. I would only be in Denver for one day. I wanted to conserve my energy, and I still craved alone time. I reluctantly decided to forego contacting my friends, with one exception: Amy Novotny. She is the director at Rocky Mountain Deaf School (RMDS), one of the handful of Deaf-led charter schools in the nation serving Deaf children.

The last time I visited Denver, RMDS had completed its fourth, and possibly final, move into a brand new, state-of-the-art Deaf-space school building in Lakewood, just across from an elite private high school. Amy led the transition team, juggling many hats while managing the school as well as the huge building project with help from Derek Sevier, a Deaf man in the construction industry, and a few others. The transition went smoothly. I had the privilege of teaching my first Deafhood 201 twenty-hour class in the brand-new school building within a week of its opening in December 2014.

The elevation steadily increased as I continued westward and uphill, and I noticed that the engine temperature indicator was slowly creeping towards the halfway mark. I recalled the advice from members of Discovery Owners group to downshift and force the engine into a higher rpm, thereby turning the fan at higher speeds and cooling the radiator more. "Runaway" overheating usually happens when the indicator climbs past the halfway point. From there the engine can quickly jump past the three-quarter mark and much closer to the dreaded red overheat light coming on.

Time to downshift. The engine rpm climbed higher and kept the temperature indicator in check even past Limon. Limon was at a higher elevation than Denver.

So far, so good. The real worry would begin going through the Rockies just west of Denver the next day since the climb continued through the Eisenhower Tunnel at 11,158 feet, and Vail Pass at 10,622 feet.

I pulled into in Lakewood safely. Amy and I went out for dinner at a pizza place in Golden, and we caught up with each other. The next morning, I tried to see if I could wash the radiator once more before making my way through the Rockies. Unfortunately, the outside water was shut off for the winter at her house, so I decided to just go ahead with the drive and see what happened.

The black and gray water tanks were emptied at a campground in Golden to lighten the coach's overall weight by a few hundred pounds. Would that be enough?

With grocery shopping done and tanks emptied, everything was a go for the mountain climb. I eased our Discovery onto Interstate 70, climbing up the hill steadily and the temperature indicator pushed its way towards three-quarters mark fairly easily. I panicked a bit.

Taking a quick stop to enjoy the scenery just before Frisco, Colorado.

I pulled her off a ramp and waited a little bit to allow her cool down a bit before pressing forward. While I waited, I FaceTimed Theo and shared my progress.

"Dad, I think she will be okay since no red light has come on at any point. Just keep going forward slowly," he said.

"Yup, I plan to stick to thirty to thirty-five mph uphill and at lower gears," I agreed.

Pressing forward, the Discovery made it past Idaho Springs without any warning lights coming on. I turned on the engine brake (which downshifts to lower gears) for the downhill portions, and she handled these with ease.

I took advantage of a couple of beautiful scenic lookouts, pulling over and allowing her engines and radiator a break while I took a walk around and took a power nap.

The breathtaking scenery in Frisco, Colorado prompted another break. I stopped in town for a few things I needed, including finally replacing the broken reverse taillights. I wanted to get to the Iron Mountain Hot Springs resort in

The incredible hot springs at Iron Mountain.

Glenwood Springs for the night, so I drove into the sun. I wished I had an electronic sunshade since I had to pull over and manually adjust the visor flaps a couple of times. I wondered if there was a third-party add-on for electronically adjustable sun visors. I looked online, and sure enough, there were some units for sale around $150 to $200. *Hmm.* I would live with manual adjustments for now.

Iron Mountain Hot Springs was a blissful experience for me, soaking in amazing waters filled with the smell of sulfur at varying temperatures in different pools. The contrast between hot water and the cold air was refreshing! Since I had arrived late in the evening, a staff member gave me a free ticket, so I went back the next morning as well.

I was still in stealth mode, and I didn't contact any friends in the area. I just wanted this time to myself. After the first night at the hot springs, I headed back to a rest area I had passed, the No Name rest area, and parked there for the night. Leveling the Discovery took some doing because the road was sloped.

I woke up in the morning, cooked my breakfast and got in my daily writing as I enjoyed the view outside my RV. This is what I was aiming for—the views, the scenery, the ability to walk around or bike whenever the mood struck and having a beautiful and comfortable interior space.

Parking overnight at the No Name rest area just east of Grand Junction, Colorado, and enjoying the scenery.

It took many months of detours and false starts, but I was finally living the life I had wanted for a long time, after getting my first taste of solitary RV life with my father and Sonja's thirty-two-foot Forest River Class C motorhome more than a year and half earlier. I had to remind myself that the journey was the destination—not wherever or whenever I arrive. And I was so looking forward to more adventures like this.

With my writing done, I headed back to the hot springs for a good couple of hours followed by pizza and a beer. Heavenly.

It was time to get back on the road and head further west. I wanted to stop at a specific liquor store in Grand Junction because they carried Avery Brewing beers, and I didn't get a chance to stop at in Boulder this time around. I picked up a six-pack of Avery Lager and a six-pack of Avery Reverend beer. I liked the Reverend better than the lager, and I also picked up six bottles of Paulaner Octoberfest.

Parked at the No Name rest area, working on this book amidst beauty.

I stopped by the Bureau of Land Management office in Grand Junction, but arrived after the 4:30 closing time. I looked through their brochures and took a few. I noted that they had dispersed camping sites right off Exit 2—just two miles before the Utah state line. I thought, "Why not? Why not try boondocking on federal land for the first time for one night?"

By the time I got to Exit 2, everything was pitch black. A nervous lump developed in my throat. Did I dare and take the exit, and drive into pitch black and try to identify areas I could park just for the night? I hate to admit this, but I chickened out.

Instead, I pressed westward, looking towards a rest area after a long gap of no service for forty-two miles or so. I crossed into the state of Utah, the furthest west I had traveled with her. Did I want to push her forward to Pacific Ocean this season? Maybe. But serious wildfires and diesel fuel prices ranging from $4.50 to $6.00 a gallon gave me pause for now.

Chapter 30
UTAH!

As I drove closer to Provo, Utah, the scenery continued to be majestically breathtaking.

crossed into Utah in near-complete darkness, and I drove on for another forty-two miles or so before reaching the Utah Welcome rest area where I parked for the night.

The next morning, I had a scare. *Chicago* struggled to start up; I stomped on the gas pedal, and she coughed up a huge cloud of white smoke. It was as if she was asthmatic. I told Theo via FaceTime that I was concerned.

Theo replied, "Dad, it is normal for older diesel engines starting in really cold. You probably should have started up the generator and turned on the engine block heat for at least thirty minutes to avoid that issue."

How on earth did my twenty-one-year-old son know this off-hand? Had he secretly driven buses and semi-trucks while growing up?

Turns out he was right. Diesel engines hate starting up in the cold and heating the engine before starting helps considerably. Gotcha. Now I turn on the engine block heater religiously before I leave the campgrounds, taking advantage of electrical hookups to do that.

The drive through Utah was splendid: the open skies, the desert climate and the dry air, which meant way fewer bugs. Now, I felt guilty for contributing to climate change with a diesel-guzzling coach getting only seven miles per gallon. At the same time, I reminded myself that I was managing my resources far better than people in their average home: better batteries, turning on and off the water heater to use only when needed and carefully managing my water usage to stretch out my boondocking capability. Eventually I would even install solar panels. In a way, living the RV life has taught me how to be more resourceful, and I am grateful for that.

The road through Price, Utah took me through bluffs, canyons, and mountains, and closer to Provo where I would stay for the next few weeks before heading further south. The views were breathtaking. I daydreamed about if I were to settle in here and created a self-supporting ecovillage—something I have wanted to do for years, create a village where everyone spoke sign languages. But I considered how we would struggle to farm and raise crops in this arid climate with limited water.

Let's be honest—I would fall flat on my face. My Deaf grandpa, David K. Smith, was a gardener and farmer all his life while he worked full time as a roofer for Slatile Company in South Bend, commuting over an hour each way from his farm in Marcellus, Michigan. He grew amazingly tasty tomatoes, cucumbers to be pickled later, corn, green beans, and more. Sadly, I inherited none of his gardening skills.

The suburban sprawl along the Interstate 15 corridor in the metro Salt Lake City and Provo areas is depressing: consuming acres upon acres of land because everyone wants a fenced backyard with their own private play sets. We are content to get into two-ton gas guzzling machines and spew pollutants to drive a mile to an ice cream shop. Worse, this is what our daily lives look like when we go to work, shop, drink, eat and more. However, the suburban stores with their oversized parking lots made it easier to navigate my large Discovery. There are better ways to build our towns and cities, even if it meant more challenging driving for large RVs.

Even with all those thoughts on my mind, I was happy to see civilization as I neared Provo. My long drive across the country would take a brief hiatus here; Provo would be my home for the next few weeks while I flew out to Chicago on the first weekend of November for a Deafhood 201 class, then Atlanta the following weekend for another 201 class, and finally a 201 class in Salt Lake City after that. I had never given back-to-back Deafhood 201 classes three weekends in a row, and I knew this would be challenging energy-wise. I had to be sure I took care of myself during this intensive schedule.

This meant a lot of alone time back in my Discovery. While teaching classes, I would need to alert the participants that I would need some quiet time during the breaks and lunch. This flies against the norms of Deaf culture and community—socializing in person is highly valued—but being an introvert, I needed the time to recharge my batteries. And I later found that participants were very understanding.

I pulled up to my friends Ben and Kat Jarashow's home near the base of the mountain overlooking Provo, and the view was just exhilarating. Ben had graciously agreed to accept packages for me while I was traveling, so I picked up my new inflatable

The view from the Jarashow home near the top of Provo was gorgeous.

kayak from SeaEagle, and a few other items. I was looking forward to kayaking with my son, Alec, who was joining me in Las Vegas on November 25; I hoped the temperatures in the area would still be reasonably warm then.

Both Ben and Kat are Deaf. Ben is a nationally renowned ASL storyteller and comedian, and he has brought many an audience to laughing with tears. I know. I was one of them, literally drooling from my mouth, laughing so hard. He pokes fun at hearing people—in a good way, I assure you—and even at himself. At the time of my visit, he was teaching at Utah Valley University, although his family and he has relocated to Rochester, New York after a brief stint in Florida.

Kat is an artist and craftsperson, specializing in knitting. Kat grew up in the Deep South; in fact, only one member of her entire family was from the north—her grandmother. She waxes about Southern cooking and loves sweet tea, although she admits she now mixes it with unsweetened tea.

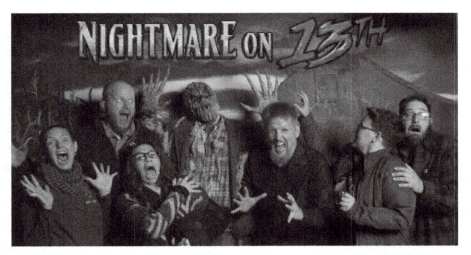

Raychelle Harris, David and Chrystee Davenport, me, and Kat and Ben Jarashow ham it up at a haunted house.

After a tour of their lovely home, I headed to Lakeside RV Campground, and settled in for a couple of days. It was a really nice place, with full hook-ups.

Ben and Kat graciously offered me a ride to the Nightmare on 13th Street haunted house. We met up with David and Chrystee Davenport and Raychelle Harris at the local bar Lucky 13, which offered excellent vegetarian options and great drinks. David taught ASL at Utah Valley University and served as an adjunct media professor at Gallaudet University's Master's in Sign Language Education (MASLED) program. David also taught me how to use cameras and other techniques to produce high-quality videos. Chrystee teaches at Jean Massieu School for the Deaf, which was originally a charter school but later merged with Utah Schools for the Deaf and the Blind.

Raychelle, who has a doctorate, founded and served as the director of the MASLED program at Gallaudet. She has published several academic videos—an innovative approach to academic publishing, rather than the typical dry and, ahem, oftentimes boring English-based papers. Her videos are highly watchable and digest complex ideas with such clarity. Best of all, these videos are presented in our natural language, ASL. I hope to see more academics producing such works. Raychelle is also one of the five authors of an ASL online curriculum called TRUE+WAY ASL (www.truewayasl.com).

After the bar, we headed to the haunted house. It turned out they were closing, but they were gracious enough to let us through. We loved the experience, especially with the upgrade we paid for. Totally worth it.

That evening made the long drive across the country worthwhile. The Jarashows dropped me off and I gave them a tour of our Discovery with the slide-outs open, revealing a spacious interior. They seemed impressed by the interior and said, "Whoa...you actually have a washer and dryer?!" The washer and dryer are one of my favorite surprises for guests.

The next morning, I had my own nightmare in broad daylight. There was a coolant leak in the back of the Discovery.

Chapter 31
SCRAMBLING

Well, crap. This didn't look good. It was Wednesday morning. I was flying to Chicago on Thursday, getting up at 3:00 in the morning to catch a 5:00 a.m. flight on Frontier to Denver, then O'Hare.

I knew the radiator was in rough shape—this was one of the few critical systems overlooked by the inspector when I bought her. Still, I was hoping for a few more years before the radiator needed to be replaced. But there it was… dripping orange fluid everywhere. The coolant fluid tank was low, so I added the last of the Shell Extended Life Coolant into the tank, bringing it above the minimum level.

My friends wanted to visit another haunted house that evening. I decided to go ahead with my plans for the day, including a massage appointment that afternoon. But first, I called around for a good local diesel repair shop; a few had completely full schedules, and some had sky high hourly labor rates. I settled on J R Diesel Repair,

Coolant leak dripping all over the back cover flaps of the RV.

which was highly rated on Google Maps. I spoke with the manager and owner José, who looked at my RV that evening before closing at 6:00.

After my much-needed massage appointment, I took another look at the coolant leak, and it had dried up. Weird. I brought the Discovery to José. He looked at the leak and the piping around the radiator. He came out, looking solemn and said, "Not looking good. You may need a new radiator."

I felt sick and pleaded, "Can't we pour in a stop leak of some sorts? Buy ourselves another one or two years?"

José replied, "You can buy six months at most. That's it."

Damn.

"Okay, why don't you keep her for the weekend and take a closer look at the coolant leak and check her engine oil leaks also?" I replied.

"Sure."

I asked José why the coolant had stopped leaking while I was driving her around, and he said it apparently leaked when it was cold. The only bright side about this whole thing was... free parking. I could park on the street across from their shop. I gave José an extra set of keys and explained that she had to be kept level for the refrigerator to keep food cold. I set the heat at fifty-five degrees to ensure the plumbing didn't freeze over the weekend. José agreed to make sure she stayed level.

Well, all good. All set.

Using the Discovery, I headed to Salt Lake City for a hike up Ensign's Peak before picking up friends and heading to another haunted house. The ride up there through beautiful (and expensive) homes just past the state capitol was quite steep and thrilling. The Discovery's Caterpillar engine powered her up the steep hills with such ease.

There wasn't any dedicated parking space at the Ensign's Peak trailhead park, so I parked her on the street right next to some fancy homes. The trail up to the peak was steep, scenic, and thoroughly enjoyable. LDS prophet Brigham Young reportedly hiked this trail after being sick for weeks, right after declaring "This is the place" for Mormon settlers to establish their city. The Mormons built an impressive community in the West with a strong dedication to their belief in building God's kingdom on Earth.

Unfortunately, this move meant wiping out many of the indigenous tribes and their settlements, another horrible legacy of white men's colonization and imperialism in taking lands as if they were ours to begin with, and never quite understanding that we all are stewards of our only home, Earth.

When Raychelle and her friend Rachelle Settambrano-Wallis, an ASL professor at University of Southern Florida, were ready to be picked up, I drove back down the steep hills, passing the beautiful Utah State Capitol. The scene was so beautiful that I pulled over and took a picture of the Discovery with the state capitol in the background. I decided I wasn't going to share my coolant leak issue with my friends that night. I just wanted to enjoy the evening together.

We went to get a bite to eat. The food was decent—not the best, but decent. The haunted house was a disappointment with substandard décor. The level we paid for included a lot of touching—but Deaf people are used to people in our community touching and hugging us, so for us, the novelty wasn't there. There was a lot of yelling and talking from the actors, as well as signs on the doors saying, "For Actors Only!" This broke up the illusion of being in a real haunted house. The actors did try their best to scare us, but… it wasn't enough.

Despite the haunted house being a dud, the fact we got together one more time and enjoyed each other's company was worth it. I dropped my friends off at their hotel and headed back to park across from J R Diesel Repair. By the time I packed my clothes, got ready for the trip and finally settled in to sleep, it was one in the morning. I had to wake up two hours later for my flight to Chicago.

The flight was no fun. Seriously. I have said this so many times, but I swore to myself that this would be the last time I took such an early flight—no matter how tempting the low fares were. I was so tired that I nodded off too many times to count, and the sudden movement of nodding off would jerk me awake, and then the cycle would begin again. After a long flight and layover, I was happy to be on the ground again, viewing the iconic Chicago skyline.

The warm and brilliant people in this group absolutely saved the weekend for me. The participants included Illinois Association of the Deaf president and 2Axend owner Corey Axelrod, and his wife Jennifer Buck Axelrod, a school psychologist working at a local mainstream program serving Deaf and hard of hearing children. Other participants included Harper College Director of Disability Services Jason Altmann, De'VIA (Deaf View Image Art) artist Rosemary Parker Edwards, Chicago Hearing Society counselor Michele Cunningham, Illinois Registry of Interpreters of Deaf President and an ASL professor at a local university Teri Hedding, and her husband Steve Trapp, a certified public accountant.

They were all Deaf and proud of it, and their work and struggle for equality and justice for all in Illinois continues to this day. Many of them grew up orally, meaning sign language was strictly forbidden—a practice that continues to this day in many places, depriving our Deaf and hard of hearing children of their natural signed languages, their cultures, and their ability to form healthy identities. All of the participants were well-aware of the real urgency and need to reframe so many things we had been struggling with for decades.

And it was their work to reframe an ongoing controversy of certain educators pushing cued speech at the expense of ASL at the Illinois School for the Deaf in Jacksonville.

Corey and Jason, on behalf of the Illinois Association of the Deaf, along with others wrote a groundbreaking letter to the school superintendent, who isn't Deaf herself, focusing on the grave concerns of audism and systematic oppression by the school against the students and Deaf staff.

The letter was unique that it didn't engage in the typical "ASL versus oral/cued speech debate" trying to figure out which approach is better. No. The idea of the whole thing being up for debate is ludicrous—ASL is our powerful and complex language, period. Any effort to minimize, marginalize, or to treat unequally our language, our Deaf cultures, and our healthy identity development must be treated for what it is: revulsion and even hatred. And this is not acceptable.

The Chicago group's approach—and the actual application of lessons from Deafhood 101—made this class stand out among others, and it was with 201 that we dove into issues even deeper. I found myself leaving the city with greater hope and a stirring belief that we can end the centuries-long war on signed languages, Deaf cultures, and our peoples.

That, and I had a great date the night before I flew back home with a smile, having no idea what I was heading back to.

Chapter 32
THE NOVEMBER SHOCK

NOVEMBER 10, 2018

- Mileage: **119,822**
- Previous total: **$28,363.16**
- Coolant hose clamps, valve cover gasket, rocker box gasket and pressure test system: **$621.27**
- Current total: **$28,984.43**
- Credit score: **640** (improved, thanks to the disability discharge of student loan, although I was still under a three-year monitoring period).

My Lyft ride from Salt Lake International Airport pulled up to my home on wheels.

"Home, sweet Discovery!" I thought to myself, feeling a mixture of pride, elation and relief. She was parked on the street across from J R Diesel Repair service, all leveled. The area was industrial, so it was quiet yet well-lit at one o'clock in the morning. I had talked with José Gutierrez and asked him to be sure to level her so her refrigerator would run properly. They had replaced the hose clamps to fix the leaky coolant system, replaced the valve cover gasket, and filled her up with additional oil and coolant, all for $621.27. I told José that I would get in late Monday night—actually, early Tuesday morning—

and I would sleep in my Discovery. I offered to pay the bill via phone with a credit card. He waved me off and told me to just come in the next morning. I had given him an extra set of keys to my Discovery.

I walked to the front door, and immediately noticed a red light blinking on my motion-detecting porch light which indicated that my chassis batteries were too low.

Crap.

Inside it was freezing. I had left the heat on at fifty degrees, yet it was much colder than that. Shaken, I tried to start the engine. No go. Generator. Silent. I checked voltage: nine volts, which meant the house batteries were almost completely drained. The general rule of thumb for deep cycle batteries— whether sealed or flooded—is to never go below 50 percent.

Even worse, the refrigerator was off. I ran and opened the door and sure enough, the stink of spoiled food quickly filled the air. I slammed the door shut, only opening it once again to take out water bottles, and the stink quickly filled the Discovery. The fans wouldn't turn on. The heat wouldn't even come on.

I had thought since the refrigerator and gas furnace ran on liquid propane, they would be fine, but clearly, they relied on at least some electricity to keep them running.

There was a switch that allowed me to start her engines with the backup—house batteries—in event of dead chassis batteries, but it didn't do me any good; both were completely drained. I had suspected there was a parasite drain on the chassis batteries somewhere in the system. There were several times when she couldn't be started after being parked and left alone for two or three days, but the backup switch always saved the day.

Not this time. Everything was dead.

What should I do? Could I even sleep in thirty-eight degrees? Going to the bathroom was literally a freezing experience. The water pump was off, so the water bottles from the refrigerator helped replenish and clean the toilet for the night.

Luckily, I had a thick down-type comforter on my bed. I was exhausted: my flight had been delayed twice. So, my pants came off, but my socks and shirt stayed on. I climbed inside and furiously rubbed my legs on the sheets to

I parked overnight on the street across from J R Diesel Repair.

warm up. To alleviate my thoughts and to stay warm, I focused on remembering a special moment from the night before. With time, sleep came.

The morning crept upon me, but the shop didn't open until 8:30 a.m. Around 7:00, my son Theo, checked on me via FaceTime and I shared everything that happened. I also relayed my surprise that the 400-amp house batteries drained almost completely over the three-day weekend. This meant I couldn't possibly just park her at the airport for my upcoming trip to Atlanta (a five-day trip) without switching off her master and auxiliary (house) battery switches, which would shut her down completely. This meant the refrigerator wouldn't run at all, forcing me to either use up the remaining food inside or find another way.

"If, as you told me before, there seems to be about a 45- to 60-watt draw on the house batteries when everything is turned off, it wouldn't last more than two full days according to my calculations," Theo said.

I snarled. "I thought the 400-amp hour Duracell 6-volt AGM deep cycle batteries were plenty. I turned off the hot water heater. Only the refrigerator was running, and it was on LP gas.

Along with the heat set to fifty degrees. That shouldn't have taken so much out of her batteries."

"I know, but the draw is enough to kill it dead, it seems," Theo said, apologetically.

Sighing, I asked, "Seriously, what's the solution to keeping food inside the refrigerator while I fly out of state for weekends at a time?"

Theo replied, "Solar panels, maybe."

"That's about an $1,000 investment for a 400-watt solar panel system, not including installation," I pointed out. "Even then, will 400-watt panels be enough to keep her topped up for days at a time?"

"You need a sophisticated battery monitoring system so you can measure the draw and try to identify parasite draws somewhere," suggested Theo.

Yeah. The chassis battery drain needed to be identified somehow, for sure—it shouldn't be losing so much in only couple of days; the batteries were only a few months old. What would be the best way to find and identify the drain somewhere in the system? I probably would have to take her into an RV repair shop somewhere.

I got up and went into the shop, where José was. Using Cardzilla, I told him that I needed a jump. I explained that everything was dead and told him about the spoiled food. That was completely on me, I told him. It had not occurred to me to ask José to keep an eye on battery levels and maybe run out an extension cord to her to keep her charged through the weekend.

He grimaced and apologized. I shrugged. A rookie mistake. I made a mental note to develop a placard with instructions for leveling and keeping her batteries charged for future mechanics. We settled the bill, and José charged her chassis batteries up.

We started her up, after waiting a bit for the diesel glow plugs to warm up, and she started without complaining much. Though a white cloud of smoke appeared, there was much less than the last time. José said the smoke was typical for high-mileage diesel engines in cold weather.

She was running, and her generator started without any hitch. Suddenly, everything started to work normally inside. The heat came back on. The refrigerator was running again. I took a deep breath with momentary relief. I cleaned the food out of the refrigerator, about $125 worth, that filled a trash bag. What a waste. That was the tuition cost for my learning experience, I guess.

A gentleman walked by and was curious, so I communicated using Cardzilla to tell him what was happening. He looked sympathetic and pointed to his 2005 Alfa diesel pusher that José was backing out of the shop. He introduced himself: Pat Brown. He had bought an RV last May. Pat told me not to be too worried about the house batteries because deep cycle batteries were designed to take that abuse, but not for long, though, and I felt a twinge of relief. We shook hands and wished each other good luck.

All seemed to be running well. I kept the generator running while the engine was turned off so José could check her oil levels, which were a bit higher than expected. I then remembered that my brakes made this funny clanking noise almost every time I had to brake harder than usual, or sometimes even under normal braking conditions. I wanted to know if I should be concerned.

José looked at the brake system and found that the right front brake was out of adjustment, and the rear ones were slightly out of adjustment as well. He adjusted them then and there, and I was grateful for the quick service. I told him I would pay for that service, and he told me, "No, it's on us. I feel bad that your food was spoiled. Thank you for coming to us for service."

With much gratitude, I was able to shower and clean up, and then sit down to do my daily writing. The generator continued to run, charging her batteries. I planned to head to Salt Lake Marina State Park for one night with full hook-ups so she could be charged properly before I left her in the airport parking lot for the weekend. I decided I would turn off her master and auxiliary switches and leave her off for the five-day weekend. If her chassis batteries died, I theoretically should have the house batteries in good shape for backup.

Would that be enough? I wondered. Should I also disconnect her batteries or unplug the inverter? Why couldn't I leave my refrigerator running without killing my house batteries? What was the amp draw there? Clearly, I didn't have the tools to tell me, except for the Intellitec power management system, which showed how many amps I was using while running off the generator. I was surprised that when I switched on the hot water heater, her amp usage increase by 11 amps. I had thought our hot water only ran on gas. (I learned later that the hot water tank had been replaced in August 2015 with a gas/electric unit. This was good news, saving some money on LP gas while hooked up at campgrounds.) After the water was heated, with the refrigerator on gas and the water pump on, her average amp usage would be pegged at two amps.

Would these two amps be enough to kill 400-amp hour batteries in three to five days? Clearly, I had more learning to do. After checking in with the Discovery Owners group—again, the absolute best twenty dollars I ever spent in my life—it turned out the problem was the blower on the gas furnaces that required electricity. Therefore, the batteries were drained in a hurry. *Sigh.* Group members said I probably could get away with running just the refrigerator for the week, but not with heat.

This meant I would need solar panels, an investment of one thousand dollars for 400-watt panels that could handle partial shade. These panels would keep the batteries charged, and hopefully keep up with the furnace blowers if I set the temperature low enough (but definitely above freezing).

Now that the Discovery was running normally, it was time to shop for food. I planned to head out to Great Salt Lake State

Park for the next few days to commune with nature. This was my third time at a state park campground with the Discovery, and this one was a real charm. A simple five-site RV park with 30/50-amp electrical and water hook-ups, and dump nearby. The views were expansive and breathtaking. And the sites had fire pits as well. Time for some serious campfire experience—sans s'mores. My dad bod didn't quite need that, methinks.

A nice toasty campfire with Antelope Island in the background.

I had gone food shopping, getting what I needed until I flew out to Atlanta. My plan was to park in the airport economy lot and shut the Discovery down completely, switching off the master and auxiliary switches, meaning the refrigerator would also be offline. Since it was already empty—well, mostly—due to that recent failure, I only bought what I would consume within the next two days.

I checked in, got her all set up, and took a walk to the Great Salt Lake shore. On the agenda for the evening was a real honest-to-goodness campfire with a breathtaking view of Great Salt Lake and Antelope Island. I built the fire following the Tim Ferris method: stacking the biggest logs on the bottom, medium logs in the middle, and smaller logs on the top along with kindling and a fire starter. This method usually takes care of the fire for the rest of the evening.

The grille prevented me from building a full stack, yet the fire was quite satisfying that evening. Accompanying my

A view of the Great Salt Lake State Park campground from the salty, sandy shoreline.

enjoyment of the fire was a bottle of Paulaner Octoberfest beer, and a heavy coat, earmuffs and gloves, as the temperatures were dropping into the low forties that evening. Despite being so close to the fire pit, I could feel the chill on my backside, so I had to rotate back to front then sit down to warm up the chair.

Geez, what do people do out in the wilderness—build fires and sleep practically right next to it? They probably heated large rocks and put the heat-storing rocks next to their beds, I thought to myself.

I was no Bear Grylls. And I didn't think I would become one anytime soon. A friend, Robin Horwitz—a Deaf entrepreneur, co-founder of Convo Relay, and stock market trader who runs his own interpreting agency, Interpreter Now (www.interpreter-now.com), and lifts weights as a hobby—once told me, "You know… you have to expand your comfort zone by doing new things that literally make you uncomfortable. Once you do that, your comfort zone is bigger than before. And that's the secret to living a blissful life."

Wise advice. In a way, this RV life was stretching my comfort zone; I was trying new things, being outside when it was cold and not quite comfortable and going for weeks without a bathtub. Robin would probably roll his eyes at that, but hey, I'm expanding my comfort zone slowly and surely.

The time came to check out of the park and fly to Atlanta. Everything was stowed away, and she was ready to roll within an hour. My flight was at 3:50 p.m., so I headed for the airport. As I drove towards Salt Lake City International Airport, the approaching below-freezing temperatures forecast for the weekend bothered me. I would feel better if I had the RV hooked up to electricity, leave the 60-watt bulb on under a wet bay and the heat on fifty-five degrees. Then something clicked. Airport parking was nine dollars per day without hook-ups. The park I was staying in? Twenty dollars a night with a 50-amp hook-up, and water as well. (Sadly, they have increased the price since then.)

D'oh! Why didn't I just extend my stay there for another week and pay the eleven-dollar difference each day for electricity? This would give me tremendous peace of mind. I immediately turned her around and headed back to the park. I was racing against time. I called for Lyft while briefly pulled over on the shoulder (knowing it would take some time for the driver to arrive), then the Discovery and I rocketed back to the park. I ran inside the office and asked to book a week. The park ranger said he couldn't verify if the site was available because the Internet was down.

Oh, no. I typed on my phone, explaining my desperate situation and the need for the site. He graciously called the national reservations center and found out the site was available after all. I wrote a check for $140 and thanked him profusely.

My Lyft ride was already outside. I waved him down and told him to give me a few minutes as I backed our Discovery into the site, put her jacks down and leveled her, hooked her up, and locked down the expensive surge protector. I set the heat to fifty-five degrees. I turned off everything that wasn't necessary. I locked her up and jumped in the car to the airport, breathing a huge sigh of relief. Then I realized I would need to ask the park ranger for a favor—to check on the power pedestal each day to ensure the fuse wasn't tripped or to restore after any temporary power outage. I decided I could make that call when

I was in Atlanta the next day. At the airport, I flew through the security lines with TSA PreCheck and got to the gate just in time to board my flight.

Moments later, I was airborne. It was just then that I suddenly realized I hadn't turned on the hot water heater to help keep the Discovery warm.

Chapter 33
ATLANTA AND THE RETURN HOME

The Deafhood 201 course at Georgia Center for the Deaf and Hard of Hearing went quite well that weekend. I loved going to Le Petit Marche for their out-of-this-world breakfasts. I never knew you could cook eggs in a way that made your mouth water. Clearly, I had to rethink how I cooked my eggs. I returned to the restaurant every morning, to eat and to write this book. I loved the restaurant's ambiance and décor as much as the food.

Breakfasts, which I ate as I worked, at Le Petit Marche were sublime.

I kept on refining the 201 curriculum and I added a satirical work—a dinner menu at a fine restaurant serving the so-called "parental choice"—reflecting the absurdity of Deaf education as we know it today, which only obfuscates the epidemic of language deprivation, causing harm to so many Deaf and hard of hearing children.

choice de la Parenté

FINE DEAF EDUCATION MENU

Filet of Oralia with Sautéed Lipreading

A steak of beautiful dreams of independence through listening and speaking only, without any need for limiting sign languages which makes one independent from interpreters for a lifetime.* **Any contact with sign language or silly Deaf culture is forbidden.**

Pairs well with Delux de Cochlear Implante or
Club Hearing Aid Soda

Scrambled Languages with Light Deaf Culture sauce

A mishmash of artificial sign communication systems including SEE, LOVE, MCE and cued speech thrown together. Uncertified sign language interpreter serving as a teacher assistant is included. Sometimes.

Pairs well with Aloneé Mainstreamé cocktail,
Isolated Experience drink, or Club Hearing Aid Soda

Cued Speech with Speech Training

A visual feast of handmade hand-shapes and symbols to aid speechreading, enabling one to enjoy English more fully. There is no need for American Sign Language. After all, English is the only language that matters, right?

Pairs well with Separated Mainstreamé cocktail or
Isolated Experience drink

ƒƒ

Available upon request only: Deaf Schools

Residential school with animal-like and primitive American Sign Language. Despite rich social and role models, this approach is too limiting, isolating, and focuses on wrong priorities. This isn't recommended menu item, therefore available only upon request

The restaurant refuses to take responsibility for varied outcomes for this menu item due to family circumstances, class status, multiple languages and the factors at home. Consuming this is your full responsibility.

My satirical take on the current Deaf education system.

The class responded well to this poster. Some suggested that I publish it and sell it online. But for me, the real heartbreak is to stand by, feeling powerless as thousands and thousands of our Deaf siblings are deprived of their natural signed languages, Deaf cultural role models reflecting their intersectional identities, and their own identities. This has been going on for far too long in our communities, and I am determined to end this war of attrition, erasure, marginalization, and replacement of natural Deaf cultures and signed languages.

However, I knew that this task begins with convincing your own people to fight for our language and culture together. Together we can ensure language equality for all.

Campfires bring me serenity.

With hope and gratitude, I said goodbye to my Deafhood siblings in Atlanta and headed back to Salt Lake City. The worry crept in. Would I find everything dead inside the Discovery again? Or would I find something else? Frozen pipes? Leaky faucets or connectors?

The smokestack in the background is actually as tall as the Empire State Building in New York City.

The flight home was uneventful, and I picked up a pizza inside the airport, knowing that I didn't really have much food available in the Discovery. There weren't any food stores within walking distance of the state park, either.

Upon entering my home, I found everything in tip-top shape and relatively warm. I checked underneath the sinks and even under the shower, and everything looked perfect. I knew I had a couple more nights here at the park, so I bought more firewood from the office.

That night, I felt such a bliss, watching the fire roar. I texted my friend, Kelby Brick, and I told him, "There is something primal about fires, tending to them and watching them."

He agreed. "Yes, fires are oddly empowering."

The quiet moments like this were when I appreciated being alone and the solitude. Even so, I would have loved to have a friend magically pop in for a couple of hours, to share company and quiet moments of watching the fire. If only teleportation were possible.

The days at the park were serene. I also enjoyed walking around during the day, taking in the scenery. The huge smokestack for the metal refinery towered nearby, yet it was dwarfed by the mountains behind it. This smokestack is as nearly as tall as New York's Empire State Building, but the optics made it appear deceptively small.

The all-too-brief stay at the state park came to an end, it was time to head to Salt Lake City KOA so I could easily travel to the Robert G. Sanderson Deaf Community Center in Taylorsville for my final Deafhood 201 course of the year.

Before the jacks were pulled up, a halfhearted attempt to bike to the grocery store didn't pan out—the shortcut I wanted to take wasn't good, and it was far too cold to brave the long way. A mental note was made to buy warm tights or long johns as soon as possible. I figured I could bike from the campsite to the Deaf center as well. But for now, it was time to get moving.

Chapter 34
SALT LAKE CITY

The Salt Lake City KOA was nice, and I got a free upgrade to an end site with a fire pit and patio. The trees were already showing their fall colors, although as a Midwesterner, I thought this rather late in the season.

I met up with Ben Jarashow for lunch at Dog Haus in the Sandy area so he could give me a couple of packages that had been delivered for me. He invited me for Friendsgiving the following week, and I gladly accepted. Then I was off to buy food and clothes.

Back at the campsite, I picked up two bundles of firewood, and I settled in at Site 78 after performing some leveling magic with two-by-eight boards on the left tires to ensure they stayed in contact with the pad. I then biked the thirteen miles to the Robert G. Sanderson Deaf Community Center in Taylorsville. The map said biking would take seventy-five minutes. Since I had an electric bike, I assumed it would take less time, maybe forty-five minutes.

Well, I nearly froze.

The Jordan River trail zigzagged all over, and the temperatures were freezing. I barely made it to the center with five minutes to spare, and I still had to connect my MacBook and VGA adapter to the projector and set up the class. A friend, Stephanie Mathis, offered to drive me back to the campsite after the class. She was the executive director of Sego Lilly, a nonprofit serving Deaf people experiencing domestic violence. Her husband, Dan Mathis, had become director of the Sanderson Deaf Center six months earlier. Both are humble, Deaf, and active LDS members who have done a lot for the Utah Deaf community.

Unfortunately, my bike wouldn't fit in their SUV. Someone mentioned that there was a TRAX light rail station at Murray Central. It was a ride in warmth and comfort all way to downtown Salt Lake City, where I then rode the bike back to the Discovery.

The warmth didn't last, though. In the morning, I woke to find interior temperatures hovering at fifty-five degrees. The LP tank was empty. I had assumed she had two twenty-five-gallon LP tanks connected to each other, and I had only been using one tank. I wanted to run it down and then switch over to the second tank.

Nope, my Discovery model only had one twenty-five-gallon LP tank. Earlier models ran the generator off the dedicated fifty-gallon tank plus had another twenty-five-gallon tank for household heating and appliances. I had mixed these up, but something else also confused me. Above my driver's seat, the house dashboard with master and aux switches and level indicators had labels for LP#1 and LP#2.

This meant I had to stow away everything and pull up the jacks to get her tank filled up next to the KOA office. While I had the Discovery out and about, I decided to shop for a ladder, an additional space heater, and do some food shopping. I also stopped by a glass place to order a single pane replacement for my bedroom window. That cost forty-nine dollars; it would be ready by the next Tuesday, before Thanksgiving.

I also saw sights like the Salt Lake Temple, which took forty years to build. I had been inside the temple before. It was such a beautiful place, filled with warm spirit and the sense of peace.

Friday night I built another fire in the fire pit, yet the experience was a real chilly one—I longed for a slightly warmer temperature. My son Alec had booked a flight on Allegiant to Las Vegas on November 25 and I was looking forward to hugging him, spending time with him and doing all of this in a much warmer climate.

Stephanie picked me up and dropped me off for the rest of the weekend, and we caught up as much as we could while riding together. The Deafhood 201 class went well, and I continued to make refinements to the curriculum, updating several slides. I added an

A wall at the Robert G. Sanderson Deaf community center in Taylorsville, Utah.

idea that Paddy Ladd mentioned in his book: the idea of "newly recognizing" Deaf babies, rather than diagnosing them.

One of my friends, Judy Pratt, suggested that we should have trained Deaf technicians who could visit all parents during newborn hearing screening tests, introducing them to sign language, Deaf cultures and so forth—greatly reducing parents' fears if the baby were to be "newly recognized" as Deaf. The slide ends with the line, "Hat tip to Judy Pratt."

The days after the class were reserved for my recovery and self-care time. I also scheduled a mobile RV repair for Wednesday of that week, the day before Thanksgiving. Stew came out and he tried to diagnose why there was 1.1 amp draw on the chassis batteries when everything was "off"—and zero amps when the master and aux switches were off.

[4] Paddy Ladd, *Understanding Deaf Culture* (Clevedon, Multilingual Matters, 2003), 438.

We had a vampire drain somewhere in the system. After an hour, I told him to stop—it was clear we weren't getting anywhere. I paid him seventy-five dollars and thanked him for his time. I mentioned the need to replace the inverter and he suggested that I go back to the factory default, Xantrex Freedom 458 2000w inverter. I also ran the water pump so he could listen to it, and he said the pump sounded fine. We were all set. I had to increase the pressure on the water pump earlier because it would oscillate in pressure and keep turning on and off constantly.

I knew I might need to replace the pump soon, though.

Chapter 35
SOUTHWARD
TOWARDS ALEC

For Friendsgiving at the Jarashows', I slow-cooked a Quorn (vegetarian) roast with chopped onions, carrots and potatoes. I got the recipe from Nancy Kelly-Jones and her husband, Clyde, both former teachers at the Illinois School for the Deaf; they had participated in my Deafhood class in Atlanta. The dish was well received.

I ended up staying from two in the afternoon until around nine-thirty that night, a record for my introverted self. I gave tours of the Discovery to several friends, including retired California School for the Deaf, Riverside superintendent Mal Grossinger and his family, who oohed and ahhed at the interior of the Discovery. Mal was initially puzzled as to why I had spent so much on her, but after the tour he admitted, "This is really nice!"

My heart warm, I headed south to a Walmart in Payson, Utah for the night. The next morning, I had to head back to the Jarashows' house because I had forgotten a package there. I also grabbed this opportunity for a picture with Ben and Kat.

With that, I was off to Cedar City where I spent the night at a rest area before arriving in picturesque St. George. There, I shopped at Camping World and Target. I even hopped on a couple of used and new motorhomes at Camping World and a local RV dealership. None floated my boat. I realized I loved my Discovery more than ever.

I was really looking forward to picking up my son Alec and hugging him hard. I missed him; it had been nearly two months since I last saw him.

I arrived in Las Vegas at night, appreciating the huge expanse of glittering lights on the horizon as I drove down on Interstate 15. I had to pick up Alec at 8:00 a.m. so I wanted to park just for the night. I found an oversized parking lot at Main Street Casino for ten dollars a night, and I walked around Fremont Street to take in the sights and enjoy a flight of microbrews and a bowl of French onion soup.

In the morning, Alec made his way through the confusing maze of McCarran International Airport. I drove to the arrivals area to pick him up and realized the clearance was only eight feet; the Discovery was over twelve feet. I panicked.

I looked around, trying to get out of this situation without having to back up into the oncoming traffic. I spotted an exit to the taxi loading area that wasn't height-restricted and I pulled up. Alec was already on his way so we tried to figure out how he could find me. An attendant radioed his co-worker, who helped guide Alec to where I was parked. The attendant told me to use the departing flights area the next time.

Alec and I hugged for what seemed like an eternity. I was so glad he was with me. For all my self-care and solitude needs, I still missed my children. It is always hard to be thousands of miles away from them.

We drove through the strip to the Circus Circus RV Park but there was no one at the office, and the walk required to get anywhere we wanted to go was ridiculous. Instead, we parked and took a city bus to the Venetian, and then went to The VOID, a new virtual reality arcade with a Star Wars theme. We were disappointed there were no subtitles or captioning even on their introductory training video, and during the virtual reality session throughout. I asked for half off the admission price of seventy-five dollars for both of us, but the manager refused. She said even a person in a wheelchair

Alec at Red Rocks Canyon in Nevada.

would have to pay the full price. I pointed out that a wheelchair user could still hear and get full access to the audio information. She capitulated and offered a 10 percent discount, and we went ahead—though I told her we would be filing a complaint with Department of Justice for this violation of the Americans with Disabilities Act. We had the HTC Vive Virtual Reality system in the past, and many games had a subtitle option that could be toggled on or off with ease. Subtitles added so much to the experience for us.

Despite this initial frustration, Alec and I were impressed with the VOID experience, even more so because we could use ASL inside the simulation. We could move each of our fingers and do a thumbs up, fingerspell a little, and sign. It wasn't perfect, but we could understand each other maybe 60 percent of the time; other times, the tracking was off, and our arms would fly off in strange directions.

Still, a huge step forward. Just add the subtitles—it is not that hard, and should be automatically included.

Our Discovery rests on a quiet site at the Red Rocks campground.

We then spent the night at the Main Street Casino RV Park with full hook-ups for thirty-one dollars a night plus a hundred-dollar deposit. We did a couple loads of laundry and filled up the water tank to the max since we were headed to the Red Rocks Campground, which did not have hook-ups. We walked around, taking in the Fremont Street Experience and eating at a decent local sushi restaurant. The RV park's location made it highly walkable—something I wish more cities emulated, providing urban RV resorts with easy walking distance to shopping and dining.

The next day, we headed to Summerlin and shopped for food before we visited our old home where we lived for a few months, renting from our friends John and Mary Yeh. John T. C. Yeh is a renowned Deaf entrepreneur who founded a technology contracting company, Integrated Microsystems (IMS), with his brothers. The company was later sold to CACI International, Inc. Yeh then invested in my company, *DeafNation*, and helped merge DeafNation into WebbyNation with Joel and Jed Barish. The partnership lasted for a couple of years before I sold my shares to the Barish brothers. They transformed DeafNation

Alec stands overlooking the entire Las Vegas valley. His birthplace—Summerlin Hospital—is on his left.

from a monthly newspaper into an online video news outlet and began hosting community expos across the country.

I reminisced with my son about my days at *DeafNation*. I, along with my partners William "Billy" Schwall, Jr. and Jonathan H. Kovacs, had established the first Deaf community full-color cover monthly newspaper. I remember designing the distinctive *DeafNation* logo at Billy's home one night—the blue and red logo that remains in use to this day. Billy, a dear friend, and I have continued to stay in touch over the years.

The next exhilarating experience was the Red Rock Canyon campground for two nights where we headed out to Red Rocks National Park and went for a difficult hike up to Turtlehead Peak. I was not in great physical shape, yet, but we managed to make it all way to the top intact, where we quietly took in the amazing views.

The hike was strenuous, and it was cold and windy at the peak. But, oh man, was the climb worth the trip! The views were beautiful and expansive.

As we approached the top, I said to Alec, "Hell with this, let's eat at a Mexican restaurant after we make it down. I'm craving something hot, comforting, and tasty."

Alec replied, "That sounds so good. Yes, I'm game."

Visions of gooey Mexican dishes tantalized us as we began our climb down, carefully so we could arrive at the bottom with our bodies intact. There were a couple of really close calls, but we made it.

"Let's go straight to the restaurant. I'm famished!" Alec said.

"I feel you. Let's go," I happily agreed.

We started the RV up and drove the long one-way loop around the park, taking in the scenery. We had our meal at a fancy Mexican restaurant with great happy hour deals.

For our next stop we wanted something different. Mount Charleston was only a forty-minute drive from Las Vegas, but it was colder with bona fide pine trees. This area is considered a climate island with certain species of birds and other animals not found anywhere else as a result of being surrounded by hot deserts.

We had a couple more city stops to make first though: Planet Fitness, to sign up for the Black Card VIP membership and take advantage of their hydromassage session. Then we filled up on diesel and LP, before getting on the road in the dark of night. Our Discovery made the steep climb uphill, taking us from a two-thousand-feet elevation to eight thousand feet in only twelve miles.

We were stunned when the cool weather turned into cold weather… and snow.

Chapter 36
OUR DISCOVERY'S FIRST SNOWFALL

Nervous, jittery, and full of anticipation. I was mindful of Murphy's Law: anything that could go wrong, would. So I was expecting the unexpected.

We were facing our first snow, up to six inches with 15-18 mph winds. And all of these just minutes from warm and dry Las Vegas. We decided to climb up to Mount Charleston to camp at Fletcher View Campground for two nights.

The climb was steep. José at J R Diesel Repair had warned me that the Discovery's radiator wasn't in good condition and would have to be replaced soon. I had to keep a watchful eye on the engine temperature while climbing. To ensure optimal temps, I shifted to third gear for most of the climb, only shifting down to second gear for a brief stretch, and maintained a speed of 35 mph so the engine would stay at or above 2,500 rpm to keep the radiator cool. The furthest the indicator went was the halfway mark, which was better than my recent travels through Colorado where I didn't really downshift properly.

I wanted to be cautious, so I sent a message to the Discovery Owners group for advice, especially from those who winter-camped with their Discovery on a regular basis, on what we should do to prepare for the snow and wind.

Given all the challenges I've experienced with our Discovery 37U, I wanted to check in with you, especially those who are experienced with winter camping with their Discoverys, on what I should do to prepare for three to six inches of snow?

We are only forty minutes from dry, warm Las Vegas! We are here at Fletcher View Campground at 8,300 feet—it was such a thrill climbing here with our Discovery (and its iffy radiator)—and we forgot to check weather conditions. It will snow here all afternoon and night, three to six inches total with 15-18 mph winds in the afternoon.

- Both slide-outs are out—seal is good
- 60-watt light bulb is in the wet bay
- 50-amp shore power hooked up
- LP tank is full
- Two space heaters running inside to reduce the LP usage
- The awning is retracted
- Hot water tank is on
- Fresh water tank at 63 percent, gray at 45 percent, black at 20 percent

It is raining right now—switching to sleet, then rain, then full-blown snow, with temps dropping from thirty-six to twenty-eight in a couple of hours.

The has been covered up with the hitch and tied down good. Anything else in terms of preventive actions I should be doing? The slide-out toppers are in fair shape.

Snow will stop late tonight, and we are checking out tomorrow noon and need to make our way down to Vegas by 4:00-5:00 p.m. so I am confident that the roads will be okay by then.

Again, men make plans, God laughs—or so they say.

Marvin

At 10:21 a.m., the rain had turned into white snow and the road conditions were a mixture of sleet and slush. Alec and I were comfortably set up at our dining/work table, facing each other. He played Minecraft on our gaming laptop, and I wrote on my laptop.

Snow was coming down, wet and way ahead of schedule; according to the Dark Sky app, it was supposed to rain until around 1:00 p.m. before it became heavy snow.

With the slide-out extended, Alec and I were comfortable and warm.

Checking again, I noticed the forecast had been upgraded to as many as seven inches over the next twelve hours. The snow was supposed to stop at 6:00 the next morning. I was due to give a video presentation to the Alaska Deaf community Friday evening, so we planned to return to Las Vegas to ensure a good Internet connection, probably at Starbucks. My fingers were crossed. The replies began to pour in within minutes of my posting, the first from Al and Karin.

What is the expected low? If that is only down to twenty-eight then you should be alright.

With sleet in the forecast and your needing to leave tomorrow you could consider bringing in the slides while the conditions are good if that is an option you can live with. Otherwise, you will have to wait until the tops of the slide-outs and toppers are thawed off and clean before retracting.

Having to leave tomorrow with no alternative is not a good way to plan/drive in those conditions. If all is OK tomorrow then go, but otherwise I would consider waiting for better conditions. Leaving earlier in the wrong conditions could mean arriving later (or not at all). Take care!

Al was right; not having an alternative plan for the next day was asking for trouble. The T-Mobile signal was actually great, so if worse came to worse, we could stay put until we were sure the roads were clear, and I could give my presentation from here. That would kill my 50 GB "unlimited" data cap, but I would live.

The group had recently shared a new sixty-five-dollars-a-month prepaid Verizon hotspot service that was truly unlimited but managed and prioritized from the start rather than after a given cap, and the RVers reported really good experience with this service. I planned on stopping by the Verizon store in Las Vegas once we got down there.

No advice, you guys are prepared for the next twenty-four hours. We have gone through much more with much less prep. Real nice up there. We are now in Pahrump. Have a good time. Happy Holidays.
—
Dave & Linda Mayfield
2017/40e and 2017 Grand Cherokee 4x4

If I had a 2017 Discovery—a beautiful coach with far better insulation and more tech stuff—I would probably be less concerned. But it was good to know that Discovery coaches could endure winter conditions for the most part. And it was always a nice feeling to know there was a fellow Discovery owner nearby—well, within the same state.

When it starts snowing, I would pull the slides in. I made the mistake of letting snow get blown under the slide toppers and it is a lot easier for the wind to blow it in there than for you to dig it out.

Harry Spencer
2002 38D

This clinched it for us—we pulled in our slide-outs right after these messages, especially knowing it would be windy that afternoon. The outside seal for the main slide-out needed to be replaced because there was a leak letting some sprinkles of water and cold air, so we used towels to seal those up when slide-outs were fully in. We needed to replace the seals, and I asked the group for more advice about that.

A minute later, Teri Dykman emailed me directly:

Pull in your slides!!! Lot less space to heat and less places for the wind to catch! Been there, done that, and it surely helped to pull in the slides.

Teri Dykman
37V '99 and 05 PT Cruiser

The group's lived experiences were a real treasure to have, and with the Discovery Owners Association regarded as one of the best owners' associations out there, joining this group for only twenty dollars a year was really a no-brainer for me. I could easily save hundreds, if not thousands, with maintenance tips, diagnosis and troubleshooting, and years of accumulated collective wisdom. I replied:

Many thanks to all, including one who emailed me directly, for the recommendations to pull in our slides. We did just that now. We are cozy and comfortable inside, knowing that the winds will get up to 15-18 mph with gusts later in the afternoon.

We do not have a water connection—there are no water hook-ups here—and a heated hose is one thing I am considering buying… So we are operating on our internal water tank for now.

With gratitude.

PS: Oh, the seals on our main slide-out—when closed—aren't that good. Can anyone point me to ordering replacement seals for the outside slide-out frame? The interior seals seem to be in good condition.

As the day went by, the snow accumulated to about three inches and everything was sparkling clean and beautiful. The high winds didn't quite materialize, and the snow stopped early in the evening. We had dodged the worst of the potential snowfall and winds.

We were cozy inside, writing, watching television and movies, reading books, and talking and laughing with each other. Besides, our bodies were aching after the strenuous hike up to Turtlehead Peak.

During the night, as the temps dipped below freezing, we felt the chill in certain spots such as by the head of my bed, the mirrored closet area and floor around it, and the front cockpit area. But it was still comfortable.

In the morning, the entire area was clear, the mountainous landscape was completely covered in glittery snow against a clear blue sky. It was an enchanting view. We were grateful for our stay here. The only thing that would have been better was if we had a fireplace inside. Newer Discovery units have them; maybe someday.

Despite the beauty, we were ready to head south to Lake Havasu City and a warmer climate. The slide-outs were already retracted, so the preparations to leave were shorter this time. I scouted for a Starbucks and found at least four in the city, so I would be set for my presentation that evening.

As we left the campground, Alec shot a time-lapse video of us driving down the road. The snow cleared up relatively quickly as we rolled down the six-thousand-foot elevation. Then it was all desert again shortly after. The transformation dazzled us.

On the drive down, we experienced something I'd thought I'd only see in cartoons—a localized storm cloud raining over a depressed person. There was literally pouring rain all around the Discovery, yet nothing immediately beyond us as we drove the fifteen miles down and the temperature rose from thirty-one to fifty-eight degrees. The sight was something to behold.

We picked up a package at a local mailing station near Summerlin that charged only $2.50 per day to hold unlimited packages. We then did some quick food shopping and stopped by the Verizon Wireless store to look into the prepaid unlimited hotspot service. I picked one up. This hotspot would supplement our cell service and provide options when we were in areas with limited service.

We discussed our route and the fact that we needed to dump our tanks and fill up with fresh

Waking up to this winter wonderland, just hours after leaving a warmer climate, was awesome.

Alec and I built a campfire at Willow Beach under a gorgeous sky.

water. I suggested Camping World, which was sort of out of our way south of Vegas, but Alec wasn't interested in seeing other RVs while we were there. Instead, we headed to Willow

Willow Beach Campground just south of the Hoover Dam.

Campground just south of the Hoover Dam off the 93 in Arizona for the dump.

The place was a gem. Gorgeous setting, immaculate sites, and we got half-off rates with our Golden Access passport for two nights with 50-amp, fresh water, and sewer hook-ups along with a picnic table and a huge fire pit. We absolutely loved it.

The bonus? Excellent campground Wi-Fi coverage despite zero cell service for both Verizon and T-Mobile. Finding great Wi-Fi performance in RV parks was rare.

After this place, we wanted our next site to have the darkest possible sky so we could observe the Milky Way galaxy band and many other objects normally not seen due to light pollution. Even though the sky was clearer at Willow Campground than in the Vegas area, there was still light pollution from Las Vegas and Boulder City. After some searching with no luck, we found a Bureau of Land Management campground further south on U.S. Route 93 called Burro Creek Campground. We decided to head there on Sunday morning, December 2. The sites were first come, first served, and we were confident that we could get a site for at least two nights.

Chapter 37
DARK SKIES AND THE HUNT FOR GREMLINS

Alec had seen more than six shooting stars in his life, but I kept missing them, so on his sixth shooting star, he wished I would see one.

Within minutes, we both saw the same shooting star. I made my wish with gratitude. The clear skies were beautiful. We could see the Milky Way band though the display was subdued. Alec said the one he saw in Gore, Virginia was more colorful.

Phoenix was only ninety miles away, which could have been a factor in terms of light pollution.

We loved the two nights we stayed there. Alec was thrilled to find a small lizard given the colder temperatures. No scorpions. No rattlesnakes, thank goodness. Maybe we just didn't hear them nearby… but believe me when I say ignorance is bliss; until we get bitten, that is.

We were surrounded by Saguaro cacti. There was a

Alec is dwarfed by a giant Saguaro cactus at the remote but beautiful Burro Creek campground.

small desert garden at the entrance, and we were easily dwarfed by the cacti there. "These can be as old as three hundred years, and it takes eighty to one hundred years before they grow their first arm," Alec told me.

Wow.

Our next stop was Lake Havasu City, where we hoped to use our inflatable SeaEagle SE330 kayak for the first time. There is a remarkable difference between scouting a location online and actually driving to the location. You take in so much more: the elevation, the scenery, the surrounding areas, and so on. Your mental map of the place is exponentially expanded as you appreciate the vast size and sheer scale of the mountain ranges along with the stark, yet beautiful desert landscape.

Unfortunately, Lake Havasu City was a let-down. London Bridge was nice, but the shopping district surrounding it was so disappointing. So faux urban. The rest of the city was a big sprawlsville, filled with cookie-cutter development and suburban-style strip malls. If the person who bought London Bridge had pushed for a beautiful and walkable master plan for the city, this would have been a gem in the desert.

Temperatures for the entire southwest had been way below average this season. The cold dashed our plans to use the kayak. With no vehicle in tow, our options for unloading and loading the kayak were also limited. If we wanted to kayak, we would have to cough up thirty-five dollars a night at the state park right on the beach.

We headed south to Lone Pine and finally, for the first time, we boondocked on Bureau of Land Management land for free. The site was not level; we had to raise our Discovery, so her front tires didn't touch the ground—a bad idea in general because there is too much risk of something going wrong. Don't do this if you can avoid it. At least the rear tires were completely in touch with the ground, with the parking brake in place; we just

Try to avoid lifting the coach's tires off the ground if you can help it. And use wooden boards. You can cause damage to the jacks, tires, and chassis if things don't go right.

didn't have enough wooden boards to help the front tires stay in contact with the ground.

That night we had a campfire and watched an episode from the first season of *The West Wing* and an episode of the *Final Table*.

I went to bed, worried that we might not be able to successfully retract the leveling jacks and bring her back to ground safely. The next morning, I discussed my concerns with Alec. He was confident that the jacks would retract safely and easily. I checked the wooden blocks under the jacks, and I began to agree with Alec.

It turned out Alec was right. She lowered herself rock-steady, and we were back on the ground before we knew it. We moved to a higher point—actually, the highest point that was accessible to our big rig, easily acquiring cell signals for both of our T-Mobile iPhones and Verizon Mi-Fi. Leveling remained a challenge, but this time the front tires remained in contact with the help of wooden boards, and the jacks weren't maxed out.

During our time boondocking, we studied the battery situation. The four 6-volt Duracell AGM batteries with 380-amp hours provided 190 usable amp hours, because the batteries shouldn't have gone below 50 percent charge. Yet they seemed to struggle to keep our RV powered through the night with the heat on. In the morning, indicators would be green-yellow (meaning 70-81 percent capacity), and despite running the 7500-watt diesel generator for six to eight hours the next day, the batteries never fully charged. The next morning, indicators were red-yellow (meaning 41-60 percent charge remaining). The See Level II indicator showed 11.8 volts, but we weren't sure how accurate this was because the volts shown did not correspond to the green, green-yellow, yellow, and yellow-red indicators.

In other words, according to the indicators, the first night used about 40 amps (81 percent or more left). The next day generators charged maybe 20 amps back into the batteries. Then the second night, it drained 40 amps again, bringing batteries down to 50 percent or less.

To charge the batteries faster, we typically turn everything off except the heat when we run the generator. With the heat on, the blowers are the only thing running, and the control panel should show a 2-amp draw per hour. This would imply we use only about 20 amps per night.

I suspected the AGM batteries were either defective or seriously damaged, and the Tripp-Lite Work Truck Utility inverter was woefully underpowered to charge the batteries. I began considering replacing the AGM batteries with one or two Battle Born 100-amp hour Lithium Iron Phosphate (LiFePo4) batteries because they could be charged at a much faster rate, but I didn't know if the Tripp-Lite inverter could properly fast-charge lithium batteries. I wasn't sure if the factory default Xantrex Freedom 458 inverter could do it either. I needed to find out soon because running the generator the entire day and still not having a fully charged battery at night wasn't working for us. It also meant long-term boondocking for up to two weeks wasn't really an option, because running the generator for eight hours a day consumed about four gallons of diesel. At $3.25 a gallon, this was at least thirteen dollars per day in operating costs. I also had to consider the pollution and noise.

At a minimum, we needed a new inverter ($1,000-plus), a 400-watt solar system ($1,000 and install), and possibly new batteries—again ($950 for Battle Born 100-amp hour LiFePo4 or $740 for four AGM batteries). All of this added up to at least a $3,000 investment. I had bought these new AGM batteries on September 2 at Sam's Club in Traverse City, and it was possible they were damaged due to being depleted under 50 percent in November when I flew to Chicago. I could try and go back to Sam's Club and get them replaced or contact Duracell for warranty service. If all failed, then I would consider contacting my credit card company about accidental damage coverage.

A few days later, I was poring through the Tripp-Lite inverter manual and discovered a dip switch that would switch to high-charging mode; mine was set to low charging mode for smaller batteries to extend their life—no wonder!

After changing this dip switch, the Tripp-Lite indicators showed my batteries at 90 percent capacity, and within two hours the batteries were nearly fully charged. After that, it showed green lights after ten hours overnight with the heater on, and even with the Coway Mighty air filter running for four hours in the morning.

But the voltage shown on the SeeLevel II indicator told a different story: 12.7 at night, and 11.9-12.3 in the morning. I needed to independently verify these numbers with a voltmeter, but I was not yet sure how to do this. The voltage showed the batteries were at 30 to 50 percent in the morning, yet the Tripp-Lite control board was green (90 percent charge). Something was way off here. When I measured with my voltmeter, with the generator and the engine off and only the Tripp-Lite 1250-watt inverter on, I got a 13.45-volt reading. Something wasn't right.

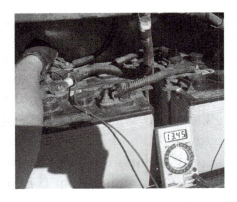

The voltmeter gave me a reading, but was it accurate?

According to the instructions I found online, I was supposed to wait up to twelve hours with everything turned off before taking the measurement. I couldn't do that. I was living in our Discovery full-time. People in the Discovery Owners group said I only needed twenty minutes of idle time before re-measuring and that if the meter showed 13 volts, the batteries were being charged.

I suspected that the relay switch between the chassis and the house batteries was stuck. Another possibility was that the chassis and house batteries were wired together by mistake. This would explain why the chassis batteries died if the Discovery was left without the generator running for more than three days. Again, they were new batteries. Plus I hadn't the foggiest what this relay looked like or where it was located. I asked for help from the Discovery owners group. And the help poured in.

Marve!

What are you trying to accomplish? The picture tells me your alternator, or inverter is charging. Anything above 12.6 is a full charge with everything off. This picture does not indicate if the batteries will sustain a charge.

Only a load test will do that, or a hydrometer reading. What does the battery show after two hours of no charging, and then checking at the same terminals? Shore power pulled, engine off.

This battery bank is in need of cleaning. I use lube grease on the terminals after removing all connectors and cleaning the posts. The terminals going to the fuse also need cleaning.

Gary Bogart
200037V

I quickly replied:

Um, the alternator and inverter weren't charging at all. It was inverting. The engine is off. The generator is off. I checked two hours after a nearly full charge, and it showed 13.62 volts. Even when I turn off the inverter. The chassis batteries are showing 13.68 volts. Sigh. Something isn't adding up here. The SeeLevel II monitor shows 12.4 volts. But the Tripp-Lite work truck utility 1250-watt inverter/charger indicator shows green, which means 91 percent or higher remaining charge. These are Duracell GC2 AGM batteries bought last September and they have higher voltage than the regular deep cycle, but not by that much.

The confusion remained and another response came.

We may be misunderstanding something. Is the coach plugged into shore power? The Freedom inverter (even if the inverter is turned off) is still a charger and will ALWAYS come on when you plug in shore power.

Al & Karin 99 34Q
Cummins ISB 5.9 275

I replied,

No shore power. I'm at Las Vegas Bay Campground and have been here since Thursday. No hook-ups at all. It took my generator five hours to fully charge my 400-amp hour AGM batteries—if the indicator was right, it took that much time to restore about 20 amps (10 percent used). Typical? I'm looking to buy a Renogy premium Eclipse solar panel kit 300 watts for $895 via amazon. com soon so I won't have to run the generator except when I need to run the microwave, vacuum cleaner, or ice machine.

This reminds me. I wanted the damn ice machine and vacuum cleaner to run off the inverter as well and I needed to find out if this was possible. The ice machine couldn't be using up so much energy; it just runs the water pump briefly then empties the ice, right?

Al's response was:

12.4 volts is probably about right. I would suspect your voltmeter is way off first. That the Tripp-Lite idiot light is green doesn't mean a lot. The control panel for the Freedom Inverter also stays "full" for a long time although the inverter/devices have been running. In fact, sometimes we still have the "full" light the next morning.

I was hoping the Tripp-Lite indicators were actually right, because otherwise, the new AGM batteries might be undergoing heavy abuse.

Marvin,

Although you are looking to buy a new solar panel, do you have any solar panels on the roof right now? I have a small 60-watt solar panel and in the daytime it does charge my batteries to about 13.5 volts, even when my coach is in storage. If you are seeing significantly different voltage readings using different readouts, get an accurate reading with a reliable multi-meter. Try checking with a multi-meter at the batteries with the battery disconnect switches activated.

If you are actually reading over 13 volts, SOMETHING is charging your batteries.

Frank M–2011 D 40X

Ah, good point! There was a small panel up there… but wait a minute! Another email came in.

One of the fallacies regarding batteries is you can fully charge them in an hour or two with the inverter running the generator. Truth be known, the bulk of the battery charge can be replaced in that time, but as a battery approaches 85 to 90 percent, it takes a long time to achieve 100 percent. That is because the charge is significantly reduced at that percentage or throttled back by the charger electronics.

It is a fact that solar panels can sustain this process, because of the physics of the process. The same can be accomplished with the inverter although the last 5 to 10 percent might take two hours. I tend to think you are getting erroneous readings with your meter. And... if you are actually reading higher than 12.6 volts disconnected, I would suspect that.

Gary Bogart
200037V

He then added in a separate post, "I just googled your AGM batteries, and the standing voltage is 12.8 to 12.9 volts."

I thought my meter was good, because when I measured other things, the numbers seemed spot-on. I replied to both Frank and Gary.

Good point about a small solar panel. There is one small panel on top of one of the AC units, I think. But the kicker is... I actually took these readings in pitch black evening. It gets dark at 4:45 p.m. here in Vegas and it absolutely throws me off. Grins.

But seriously. 13.62 volts in the dark?

The only thing I can think of is that... somehow the chassis batteries is charging the house batteries, and no wonder because the chassis batteries would go dead after few days of being parked. But again, I've been here since Friday night to Monday night and the chassis batteries seem to have voltage—oh wait. The generator will charge both chassis and house batteries, right? That's different than just leaving it parked for a few days without generator or shore power—then my chassis batteries will die.

Is it possible that they got tied up together by mistake?

I replied to Al.

This is why I'm trying to get an independent reading of the battery voltage because either can't be right, at least not entirely. But with my reading, I'm even more confused and so is everyone here.

My new AGM batteries were nearly completely drained (down to 9 volts) on November 5 and the stupid inverter didn't have auto shut off protection like the Xantrex 458 does. So, I was worried about the real capacity of my AGM batteries, hence my efforts to get to bottom of the conflicting voltage numbers/indicators.

Maybe chassis batteries and house batteries are somehow wired together by mistake. Sigh. This is a little beyond my skills. But again, even a mobile RV repairman in SLC was stumped and charged me seventy-five dollars for his visit.

Al responded:

Marvin—The chassis batteries are only two 12-volt batteries hooked up in parallel. So, they only have around 12.7 volts when not being charged too. The house batteries are two sets of two 6-volt batteries, each set of two being hooked up in series. Also, only around 12.7 volts when not being charged.

If someone tied the two banks together permanently, instead of that being controlled by the charging relay, then you could run the chassis batteries down at the same time you are running the house batteries down. You can check that because then both (coach and chassis) would always show the same voltage regardless of whether charging or being used to power the inverter/coach. Yes, even if not permanently tied together, using the engine alternator, shore or generator power the charge would normally charge both banks because the charging relay would close.

13.6 is not too high if being charged but is not normal when not being charged after twenty minutes or so. SeeLevel is actually a reputable gauge manufacturer. With your description (no shore power, no generator, no solar since it was dark and some usage) I would first think the SeeLevel reading is correct. Don't try to read too much into that voltage reading while the battery is being used (interior lights or whatever on). All charts of battery charge condition based on voltage assume that there is NO load for at least 20 minutes or more. Using the microwave for thirty seconds over the inverter I can pull the coach batteries down to around 11.5 volts easily while still on, but they will recover back to well over 12 immediately afterwards and all the way to 12.6 inside of several minutes when it is off again.

Did the RV tech have his own voltmeter and read the same as you did with yours (under the same conditions)?

Twenty minutes, no load or usage, okay. I could try and check for that.

Marv, checking your batteries for actual state of charge really can't be done with the batteries hooked up, nor with a voltmeter. Not trying to be disrespectful, but you're troubleshooting without enough knowledge about all the components, and how they work in the system. It will take several hours to "top off" batteries that are at 90 percent depending on your particular inverter. Heck, on my last unit, it took two days to fully charge four Trogen t145s. Also, 300 watts of output in solar is not going to make you "generator free." Not even close. If I can help I will be in Quartzsite in January and Laughlin or Vegas by late February. Be glad to walk you through it. Oh, if you prefer, drop me a line and I'll give you my phone number. Lots of confusion when you start trying to understand batteries, believe me, I know!
--
Bob & Jeanni Horvat
2007 Discovery 40x, 330 cat
2018 JLU Jeep Wrangler Rubicon
Full Time from Co.

I loved it when members offered to help in person. They were awesome. And if 300 watts wouldn't be enough, I'd bump it to 400 watts. With Renogy's Eclipse higher efficiency panels that handled shadows and shade better, I thought we would be good as long as I used the power conservatively.

As Al pointed out, check both battery banks and compare readings. If they are the same, suspect a problem with the relay. I have seen these relays become stuck from pitting and are easily replaced. Make sure it is a constant-on type. You can also remove the battery cable from the post to the relay and re-read the voltage. If you remove both cables to the relay, you can ohm out the relay.
Still have no answer how you can have charging voltage when not charging. Have you tried taking the ground off both battery banks therefore isolating them, and do a reading?

Scratching my bald head.

Gary Bogart
200037V

Which cable was ground? *Sigh.* I was still so new to this whole thing. I asked for what this relay looked like.

Quick question—what does this relay look like and where is it located?

I shut down the inverter, switched off the Aux button, and waited 20 minutes. I still show a 13.32-volt reading on the house and chassis batteries. I decided to switch off the master as well, so everything is OFF, and I took an immediate reading of both and they began to diverge—chassis 13.42 volts and house 13.32 volts. I am going to wait fifteen more minutes before I take another reading. Then I have to turn everything on and run the generator and engine block heater (you turn this on at what temperature outside?), and move out of this campground.

Al chimed in with an idea, but…

Marvin—I don't know for sure what the relay looks like on the CAT models. But it doesn't matter because you can test it without accessing it. Now that the master is OFF the readings are diverging so it appears the relay is still there, and the cables are not simply bridged (but may not be working as designed). We all have two battery disconnects (one for coach/aux and one for chassis). Is that what you mean by master?

HOWEVER, I have an idea (happens once in a while). Since your coach has been extensively rewired in the inverter area and has a separate charger and inverter, I wonder whether the charger is not hooked up to an inverter line???? Seems crazy but I think it would in fact "work" and would result in the battery voltages never being right (always high) and faster discharge of the batteries too when not on shore power/generator/alternator. Would not explain the lower reading of the SeeLevel gauge but I believe that can be possibly calibrated.

Or your meter is showing wrong. You have not indicated whether your RV technician used another meter and had the high readings.

You don't need the block heater at all to start but it does save some engine wear when the temps are under about thirty-five degrees and it has been on for several hours.

Al & Karin 99 34Q
Cummins ISB 5.9 275
Freightliner

I clarified:

Al—

My Tripp-Lite UT1250WUL Work Truck inverter/charger is a combined unit, both inverter and charger in one. And yes, master as in chassis, and aux as in coach/house. And you are correct that there was SOME re-wiring done professionally to offload the microwave line since the 1250-watt inverter couldn't handle that.

Gary Bogart sent me docs on the BIRD relay offline—many thanks! Now I need to locate that BIRD relay—it's not in the battery/inverter compartment. Hmm. Maybe under the front dash or in the front generator compartment? The docs say it's in the engine compartment, and I will try there. But I'm pulling out for today, so I'll put this on hold for now until tomorrow or the next two days.

Al had more ideas.

If a combined inverter/charger then it wouldn't be connected to the inverter output. It was just a crazy idea in trying to figure a reason for what you are seeing. Didn't really expect it to be that way.

If like the older coaches, then the BIRD relay can be behind the BCC box and not visible without dismounting the BCC. It will NOT be in the front of the coach anywhere but it will be close to the batteries. I think on the CATs it was a Trombetta relay.

If your aux start button works, then you can hear it clunk (you may want to get help) when someone presses and releases the aux start button on the dash as long as the voltage is below 12.7.

Al & Karin 99 34Q
Cummins ISB 5.9 275

I couldn't find the dang relay. Nothing remotely resembled the BIRD relay photo Gary Bogart sent.

Batteries can hold a head charge. Just flip the headlights on for a couple minutes and then back off, then read the voltage, after charging. That head voltage can get you, it has confused the heck out of me in the past.

Mel Price
2008 39R
Cummins ISB 6.7L
Freightliner Chassis

Ah, good to know! I was in a panic. I still couldn't find the BIRD relay in my Discovery. I decided to upload a full spread of pictures of my inverter compartment, hoping someone could help me identify my relay.

Al replied, calming me down.

No, you've got it in your pictures. Relax. It's the lower relay with the large leads to it (third picture—I deleted the others below). I'm not sure that it is bad though! I don't think I would order yet.

Oh, good. But if the relay was not bad, then what was the problem here? Al continued:

Marvin, Let's pull back and take a moment to think, maybe for a day or so. Maybe someone else has an idea too. Nothing you have described up to now indicates a problem with the BIRD relay. The only issue that we have at the moment is your voltage meter reading of 13.65 while not on shore, generator or solar charging. That has nothing to do with the BIRD relay.

We need a verification whether that reading is accurate (with another voltmeter or so) or whether the SeeLevel reading of 12.6 or less is accurate. It was my understanding that both were taken at about the same time under the same circumstances. Until we know what the voltage really is, we can't continue. But neither Gary B. or I can figure out at the moment WHY you should have any voltage higher than 12.6 or so when the batteries have not been charged for hours.

Please ask around for someone with a voltmeter and measure again, with all charging sources having been disconnected for at least thirty minutes. Mel's suggestion of turning on the headlights for five minutes is also good and should pull down the chassis batteries to or under 12.7 volts. That is what I use to force my BIRD relay to release (disconnect) when I want to do that quickly.

Gary Bogart asked for clarification about the BIRD relay, which didn't match the pictures he sent me.

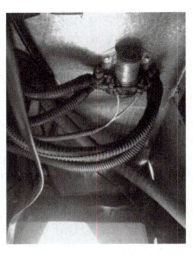

The Trombetta relay (the third photo Al referred to).

Al!

Now you have me confused. Are you saying the relay pictured contains the BIRD? My understanding of the BIRD is as described in this PDF I have included, and has an electronic board to determine charging voltage, and if and when the batteries are coupled. I know at some point this was upgraded, but not sure of the year. Since I only once got into this issue with a National Diesel coach which was a 2007, I have not laid eyes on the BIRD in my coach, or any others I have seen. We used a solenoid that looked like a starter solenoid but was a constant duty as the contacts had stuck keeping the batteries coupled all the time. I simply replaced it, and all was well. I have a post in the Bulletin board forum, asking for where this BIRD is located on my year coach (a 2000 37V). I just checked, and no one has responded. The description in the PDF listed below, says it is in a waterproof case, and might be in the engine compartment.

https://www.discoveryowners.com/BIRD.pdf

I sure would like to see a schematic of Marve's aftermarket Inverter charger and trace the direction of the cables. Obviously, the wiring has changed, but this should not impact our current dilemma regarding the high voltage of the batteries at rest. Hope we can get this figured out.

Gary Bogart

Another email startled me:

By the way, does your picture show a double male plug? From the inverter to a duplex outlet? That's a great way to get the blood flowing!! That should be removed immediately!

--

Doug
2006 Discovery 39V
330 CAT
Dallas, TX

Al replied to Gary's confusion, clearing things up about the different relays used for specific model years.

Hi Gary—That relay in the picture is the combined aux start and BIRD relay. On the CAT models it is often a Trombetta relay but that is only the manufacturer. It is a heavy-duty relay that is mounted outside of the BCC on all of the diesel coaches due to the heavy starting current when it is used as aux start. The white wires go to the BCC and are supplied with current by two separate circuits. One is the aux starting circuit with the switch up front which energizes the relay with 12 volts only as long as you are pressing the switch. The other circuit is the BIRD circuit which is built into the BCC circuit board. Both circuits run over the BCC board and are fused there (3 amp and/or 5 amp fuses) and use the same white wires to the relay. When the BIRD circuit energizes the relay then you have a momentary 12 volts for about 1 second and then it changes to a pulsed 12 volt which measures as about 6 volts as a holding voltage.

On my (and I assume your) coach, the BIRD relay is hidden behind the BCC. Look with a mirror there and you can find it.

On the much later coaches starting around 2010 or even later, they actually separated the BIRD relay from the aux start relay and use two relays, one for each purpose. That is so that the BIRD relay does not have to carry so much current. The battery cables to the BIRD are then also fused (about 200 or 300 amps). Very confusing!

Al then responded to Doug's alarm about the wiring (or re-wiring) in my RV.

Doug—No. Marv's coach was rewired in that area. The incoming power line for the original inverter (30 amp) was moved to a junction box with outlets (in the picture to the right of the inverter). The new, weaker inverter is plugged into the junction box with a black power cord, as is the old line out to the microwave, which the inverter can't carry anymore. So, the microwave hard wiring is one of the orange plugs you see. The other orange plug (stuck into the inverter) is the hardwiring of the second old line out of the original inverter and provides power to the outlets in the coach. It looks like a deadman cord (both orange plugs) but it isn't since they are actually two different circuits (although they look like the same one) and it is actually OK. Gary B. and I already had that discussion a couple of months ago.

That is partially what makes things a bit hard to fathom on Marvin's coach. But we will get to the bottom of it!

A different Gary chimed in. Being a master RV technician, he clearly knew many things.

Gary, I had a 2001.5 and the BIRD is actually a circuit built into the Battery Control Center on that year Discovery. It controls the big relay, often made by Trombetta, so the relay might say Trombetta on it.

I don't know if there was ever a free-standing BIRD used on some earlier Discoverys but I suspect so or nobody would have added that BIRD pdf to the Hints pages.

Gary Osburn
2012 Discovery 42M
osburnrvservice.net

I had a giddy reaction to Al's apparent spot-on summary of my replacement inverter/charger and the wiring.

Al, I'm impressed. I never could quite figure out the extensive modifications made by previous seller when he installed Tripp-Lite inverter/charger, and you pretty much nailed it by looking at the pictures. I think. I am going to copy and paste your summary so I can rewire when we install the Xantrex 458 later on.

I'll hold off on Affordable (cough, cough) RV Repair for now. Alban CAT Power charged $115 an hour for labor. EDCO Welding in Indianapolis $75 an hour. J R Diesel Repair $100 an hour. Michigan CAT in Kalkaska, Michigan $115 an hour. The only one I know that charged higher was $142 an hour at Johnson Freightliner in Maryland.

Measured again this morning with See Level II showing 12.2 volts, while Tripp-Lite indicator showing green (91 percent or more charge left). 13.32 volts on house, 13.36 volts on chassis. I've turned off the inverter. I have switched off the master (chassis) and aux (house) switches now. I am going to wait an hour before I measure both the chassis and house batteries again.

Things we know...
1. My chassis batteries go dead in three days when left alone (no generator, no driving, or anything). These are NAPA, brand-new as of last June. (House batteries are new as of September 2, 2018.)
2. Both batteries measure 13.3 volts or higher consistently.
3. Mobile RV repair in SLC had clamp multimeter that showed house batteries would be giving off 2.1 amps, and chassis batteries giving off 1.2 amps (except when the master switch is off then it goes to nearly zero). He couldn't make heads or tails of it.
4. I could go ahead and install 400-watt Renogy Eclipse (superior panels with 19 percent efficiency) for $1,100 and this probably will keep both batteries "topped off" or leave it with sufficient charge, BUT...
5. Still need to get bottom of this because AGM batteries may be taking a severe beating, if See Level II numbers are right, and I need to put a stop to this.
6. See Level II did show a volt reading of 9 volts that night in Salt Lake City when I got home from Chicago and everything was completely dead. According to a doc Gary Bogart shared with me, anything below 10.5 volts is considered unrecoverable or truly dead. Yet my batteries have recovered and they do hold a charge. How well is the question.

Question:

The inverter/charger would switch from bulk charging rate to absorption then to float based on some kind of resistance it receives from the batteries, right? In other words, the Tripp-Lite indicators should be more accurate than See Level II since it's charging based on feedback it receives from the batteries? This shouldn't be a situation like a battery monitoring kit where you manually input the total amp hour capacity and then it measures amps going to or leaving the batteries, adding/subtracting them—inverters don't operate that way, right?
I'll be posting in an hour or so with the readings. I've ordered the Etekcity Digital Clamp Multimeter MSR-C600 from Amazon. I will be picking it up later and I can verify again with this meter.

Further discussion on BIRD relay, and whether mine had that particular model or not, took place.

Al,

It was always my understanding that the BIRD was the circuit board which measured voltage and decided which battery bank was charged, or isolated. I never thought it was capable of carrying battery amperage and the physical characteristics (shown in the PDF I sent originally) show only low amperage connections to it. I thought once the issue of which battery bank, then the solenoid relay (pictured in the photo posted by Marv) was energized or not depending on what the BIRD authorized. You are now saying the BIRD in my coach is hidden behind the BCC which has the removable cover located on the back wall of the inverter compartment. Thanks for the edification. Even at my age, I am capable of learning a few new things. I have only owned this coach for nineteen-plus years.

Thanks,
Gary Bogart

He quickly followed up with:

Al,

I just re-read your post, and my comment regarding the BIRD location was wrong. I now understand that you were saying the BIRD is on the board in the BCC. Got it.

Gary Bogart

Still frustrated, I tried testing the batteries again and updated the group.

Over an hour with EVERYTHING OFF—master (chassis), aux (house), and inverter—chassis batteries measured 13.49 volts. House batteries measured 13.41 volts.

I double-checked by using my meter on AA and C and D batteries, and they were accurate within two decimal places. I will check again when I pick up my new digital clamp meter later today or tomorrow.

I'm stumped. Perhaps there's a secret fusion-powered reactor hidden somewhere inside my Discovery. Cold fusion, no? :-)

Should I keep my appointment with Affordable RV Repair tomorrow morning? My concern is that they would go on a fishing expedition, racking up labor hours. I would prefer to have this figured out myself.

Oh, here's a closer look at the possible Trombetta relay here just in case.

Al pointed out:

Marvin, the first "problem" or thing to solve is where is the higher voltage coming from (if it is indeed higher voltage). Anything over 12.7 is suspect.

Either you have a charge coming from somewhere or your meter is not reading correctly. The last time you measured you said it was dark. Now it is not. If you have a functioning solar panel on the AC unit (even the small ones) it COULD come from there, even with the battery disconnects off.

If you have a tow [vehicle] then measure the voltage on that battery with your meter, otherwise ask someone where you are at whether you can just measure the voltage on their car battery after it has stood for an hour or so and then let us know. That small voltages are OK on your meter does not really mean anything. I'm not aware of meters going off like that but your description is always that you have everything off....

Only when we can accurately measure the voltage, can we make a statement about the BIRD relay. Your prior descriptions seemed to indicate that it works but at the moment no one can tell. I feel you would be wasting money replacing the relay without knowing what is going on and I'm afraid your concern of them fishing could be valid. We can't even tell at the moment when or how well which batteries are charging if we can't get an accurate voltage reading.

Gary Bogart suggested a way to resolve this, which looked to be labor-intensive, and I really didn't want to do this.

Marv!

I would like to get this resolved as much as you. I spoke with a retired engineer friend of mine from Bell telephone. He suggests two things to attempt to iron out this problem.

Disconnect all cables from your batteries. I would photograph the current cable arrangement, and also make a drawing where each cable goes.

Measure the voltage of each battery, after the batteries have set unhooked for two hours. Record that information for each of your house and starting batteries. Make sure they are all not connected.

Using an alternate voltmeter, check the voltage and compare between the two meters.

This may sound like a pain in the butt to do this, but if we are to get to the bottom of the issue, this is the sure way.

Report this information on the forum so several of us can take a look.

I would do this if it came to that. What blew my mind was that Gary took the time to talk with a friend about this, and I was grateful. When I finally tested it with the brand-new digital clamp voltmeter that night, I was floored to find that the reading was very different from the old voltmeter. The old voltmeter was bad, clearly.

Al and Gary and everyone else,

Update—this is not a full update since I'm on shore power right now and have to run errands all day before I settle down at Lower Government Wash BLM land for the next few days so I can do further diagnostics (and install the soft close drawer rails and drill through the glass sliding mirror doors to install steel ball bearing wheels, and so on).

My new voltmeter with the clamp arrived yesterday, and I tested quickly. You know what? Al's suspicions were spot-on. My old voltmeter is way off. Last night, it showed 12.83 volts after I turned on the headlights for a few minutes then turned everything off. The chassis batteries showed 13v.

12.83 volts is nearly full for AGM battery—they need 12.9 volts for a 100 percent charge. And the Tripp-Lite indicator lights lined up with this reading pretty accurately.

This morning, while on shore power, the new voltmeter showed 13.65 volts and the old voltmeter showed 14.85 volts. So, off into the trash heap the old one goes.

Interesting note: See Level II shows 13.2 volts while on shore power, not 13.65 volts so See Level II is off by a margin. I will be doing further testing while boondocking this weekend and will post updates.

Unsolved:
1. Chassis batteries go bye-bye after three days of being left alone. Clamp shows 1.2 amp draw unless master (chassis) is switched off, then 0 amps.
2. Tripp-Lite inverter/charger indicator goes from green to red after a while on 50-amp shore power then back to green. Not green-yellow or yellow, but red for a good couple of hours before back to green again. I need to call Tripp-Lite and find out what's going on.

One day, we will get to the bottom of this, hopefully. My experience with my friends—who I hadn't met yet—in the Discovery Owners Association group clearly showed how helpful they could be, how generous they were with their time to sit down and type these posts. I couldn't go wrong with a group like this. My advice for any first-time RV owner is that the first thing to do after buying an RV is sign up for this group.

My kids. The Discovery Owners group. Mechanics like Dan Greer and Alan Spence. They all helped me tremendously on my journey.

Chapter 38
BOONDOCKING BEFORE PALM SPRINGS

DECEMBER 27, 2018

- Mileage: **120,752**
- Previous total: **$28,984.43**
- ProBrico soft-close drawer rails: **$179.95**
- Victron Battery Monitoring Kit BM-712 with Bluetooth: **$226.95**
- Inamax Wi-FI Adapter and USB extended cable: **$29.99**
- Shurflo water pump and accumulator: Gift from kids
- Current total: **$29,421.32**
- Credit score: **620**

After I dropped off Alec at the McCarran International Airport on December 7, I had a whole week to myself before the woman I was seeing would join me. I did some food shopping and other errands before heading back to Las Vegas Bay Campground for a few more nights. I was kind of forced to; I only had a twenty-dollar bill, so I paid for two nights instead of one. I ended up staying three more nights.

It was bliss.

Before I went back to the campground, I stopped at a local RV dealership and checked out the brand-new Winnebago Horizon. I had to admit that this was one of the few RVs that made me salivate. But with a price tag approaching $400,000, it was definitely pricey. The interior design was Euro-style with more expansive window views and a simply sleek design. This and the Newmar New Aire was near the top of my wish list, along with that crazy, stupid-expensive, yet gorgeous, Foretravel Luxury Villa Spa and custom-built Newell coaches.

Still, when the tour was done, I was happy to be back in the Discovery. My own *Chicago*.

At the campground, I was able to decompress, spend time alone, and enjoy the solitude. I did some light maintenance on the Discovery. After a few days, I headed back to Las Vegas and did more errands including picking up packages from Ship and More on Sahara Avenue.

I headed to check out the Kingman Wash site, but the signs said four-wheel drive was recommended. The dirt road was literally like a washboard, so I turned around and stayed a night in the Hoover Dam Casino truck parking lot before heading back into Las Vegas for even more errands.

The next night I spent at Clark County's Shooting Range RV Park. It was a nice place with great views. I washed my blankets and sheets at a laundromat the following day and then picked up an Impossible Burger burrito from a vegan taco shop next door. I also filled the LP gas tanks at a local U-Haul place before heading to the Lake Mead National Recreational camping area by Government Wash Road.

I was literally racing against the sun. The sky was getting darker by the minute, and I needed to find a site. I was glad I had been here before, so I knew the general layout of the land, but driving in the dark, trying to find a site… I could feel the stress creeping upon me.

I kept on driving past many RVs parked in various locations, and I stopped at a turnabout with a sign clearly saying no camping allowed here—which made sense because the RVs needed space to turn around.

But an alluring site downhill from this turnabout caught my eye. I got out and walked around. There were no signs

The view of Lake Mead from inside the RV. It was a dream come true.

posted forbidding camping beyond this point. This site was incredible, a miniature peninsula with Lake Mead surrounding the tiny site. I walked all the way down and made sure there was enough space to set up the Discovery for a few days.

The sunset was complete, and it was really dark out there. I could see a lone fisherman off to the right. I wondered: *Should I?* I didn't see anything that would prevent me from setting up on that spot. The views alone would be out of this world.

I walked back up to the RV and drove her slowly down the hill, threading her carefully to the site since the space was narrow with fairly steep hills on both sides. I would have to back her all the way up to the turnabout in order to leave.

I eased her into a spot that was actually fairly level and gave me enough space to exit our Discovery with ease. *There!* I spied a homemade rock fire pit just ahead. Perfect.

I got out and walked around in disbelief. I had done it. With such a prime spot I wondered why nobody else had claimed that spot. It was too good to be true, I thought—and I imagined a Bureau of Land Management official would ring my doorbell in middle of the night and kick me out.

I let her down and put the jacks down and got the slides out. Nervous, I got outside and walked around. I was really afraid she would shift and slide into the water.

She seemed solid, though. It was dark. I was tired. I was definitely staying put for the night.

Chicago atop a small peninsula, surrounded by Lake Mead. Sublime.

As I cleaned up inside, *Chicago* shifted suddenly to the left. I told myself it just a slight movement, most likely occurring as gravel rocks under the jacks shifted. *Crap.* My heart beat rapidly.

I got outside and took another walk around. She looked good and solid. *Okay*, I told myself, *it should be okay*. But it didn't help that my bedroom slide-out was out over the sharp slope to the water. I was afraid that my weight on my bed could cause her to shift suddenly, and not in a good way. That night I woke up a few times, worried about the RV teetering on the edge.

The sights the next morning were absolutely magnificent. I stopped worrying after that.

I loved writing my book while looking out to the lake, and this site really took the cake. It wasn't until later that I noticed people walking past my Discovery and setting up to fish— basically, invading my space. I looked on Google Maps and saw that the peninsula was clearly marked as a fishing pier.

No wonder. Oops.

I had to share this space with everyone else, but I didn't mind. I did not have a lot of outdoor space with a picnic table, grill or anything like that. Just a lawn chair and a fire pit. I was happy with the view while writing and working on projects inside my cozy home.

I stayed for three glorious nights, and I loved every minute. I wouldn't repeat my visit at this particular site, of course—I never intended to impose on those who came to fish. My bad.

One of my projects was replacing the cheap plastic sliding door hardware on my bedroom closet. Theo and my dad tried to make it work last summer but that didn't even last a month, so

Left: the damaged sliding door plastic wheel, barely a few months old. Right: All better! A steel wheel was put in its place.

into the trash the hardware went. I bought steel- bearing wheels and I drilled a hole through the metal frame and secured them. They slid perfectly, which was good riddance for an annoyance.

I needed to install a locking latch to prevent them from opening up while in motion. That was next on my to-do list. I had also ordered soft-close drawers made by Probrico from Amazon based on a Discovery owner's recommendation. They were heavy! I ordered five for the bedroom, four for the kitchen, and three for the bathroom. All together, they cost me over $180. The installation was a pain, requiring a lot of contortionist moves on my part to place them using spacers to make sure they aligned perfectly and worked flawlessly.

Well, nearly flawlessly. After spending a good five hours on these, they worked well enough. They were a vast improvement over the old simple drawer guides, at least. I donated the old drawers, still usable, to Goodwill. With proper oiling and installation, they could work pretty well for someone. I probably should have dropped these off at Habitat for Humanity given Habitat's mission to help house as many people as possible, though.

I decided to bike around to explore. I realized there was more potential sites I could have set up on, but my particular site turned out to be one of my favorite sites because of the short distance to shopping and one of the most affordable airports in Las Vegas—an unbeatable combination. In my line of work, teaching all over the country, access to a relatively affordable airport was always a huge asset.

A new oil leak mark next to the previous leak in the same spot. Sigh.

On December 16, my then-girlfriend Riley flew in and joined me for the week. The entire week was incredible. We stayed at Las Vegas Bay Campground, Red Rocks Campground, and Willow Beach Campground right on the Colorado River. We spent the final night at the Hoover Dam Casino truck parking lot before I dropped her off at the airport early in the morning.

What? You want details? No, sorry. But I can say the week went better than I hoped for. And the fact that we spent all of it within the Discovery, comfortable and relaxed, was icing on the cake.

At the Willow Beach campground, the incredible hosts there gave us the same site Alec and I had before. A day later, I was dumbfounded to find two nearly identical oil leaks—one from the previous stay and one from this stay.

I had to fix the engine leak. Damn it. I had spent way too much on this for it to still be leaking. Ugh. Most times the leak was much smaller—about the size of two phone chargers—but it seemed after the strenuous drive to the Willow Beach campground, the leak was bigger than usual. I felt awful for ruining the site's new concrete pad; I poured fine sand on the oil before we left.

On the night before Riley flew back home, we explored downtown Boulder City and ate at Momo's Sushi. They had extraordinarily good miso soup and their rolls were amazing. In fact, their miso soup was easily one of the top three in the nation for me, along with Nooshi in the Washington, DC Eastern Market area and Akebono in Sacramento.

After dropping Riley off, I did errands and picked up my TireTraker TT-500 tire pressure monitoring package and installed it. Bruce Plumb and others in the Discovery Owners group emphasized the need for a monitor for safety purposes. And guess what? They were right.

As soon as the monitoring system was installed, I discovered the right rear inside tire had lost much of its pressure due to a loose valve stem. I took the Discovery to the TruckAmerica truck stop because most places were closed (it was December 23), and they repaired the tire valve stem. They told me that the tire was off-rim, much to my disappointment.

After that, I headed to the Red Rocks Canyon campground and was perplexed to see a sign, "Due to the government shutdown, this campground is closed." I had read up on this and it seemed that some campgrounds would remain open, but it would be "camp at your own risk" and all facilities would be locked up. Not in this case. Instead, I headed to the Main Street Casino RV Park for two nights so I could join Russ and Melody Stein and their family on Christmas Day. We had a lot of fun together, and I was grateful for their kindness.

We all went to Wynn's Encore and checked out the colorful Christmas interior design and décor, which were incredible. With that, I said my goodbyes and headed south to Palm Springs to meet up with Theo and his now-girlfriend Brianna for the next two weeks. Before I drove south, I had to make another stop at TravelAmerica because the tire monitor was showing the same tire losing pressure again. They fixed that right away. The tire monitor had paid for itself already.

I drove through Searchlight, Nevada into the Joshua Tree National Park area, driving through Twenty-Nine Thousand Palms until I came to the RV park.

I had checked Passport America for good deals and discovered the Sky Valley Resort campground. I made a reservation and drove there. It turned out they had a hot springs-fed swimming pool and hot tubs that were heavenly. The place was immaculate with well-kept trailers and RVs laid out in a neat streetscape. The Wi-Fi was lacking, though. It was so bad that I couldn't even FaceTime or make video relay calls. The cellular services for T-Mobile and Verizon in that area were also spotty.

As soon as I parked at the site, Theo and Brianna arrived in her father's Land Rover and joined me. I had missed Theo and I was happy to see them both. We spent the next two weeks doing a lot of work on the Discovery. My four children also had pooled their money to buy me a new water

Theo took out the water bay and its connections so he could replace the water pump and paint over the rust.

pump along with a pre-filter and an accumulator to replace a slowly failing pump. I was thrilled—and even more thrilled that Theo would be doing the work of swapping out the pump instead of me.

Seriously. The compartment holding the pump was so cramped and complicated; even people in the Discovery Owners group complained of the difficulty in removing the metal cover to access the connectors and hoses behind them. Theo decided to tackle the rust first by sanding down the sides of the slide-out compartment next to the water connections bay. He then gave the compartment box three good coats of spray paint.

A new Shurflo pump with the accumulator and pre-filter in place.

I also had ordered a Victron Battery Monitoring Kit with Bluetooth so I could monitor my energy usage on my iPhone. We wanted to see what kind of amps we were drawing during the night with the heat on. But when time came to install it, we were a little stumped. We consulted Al from the Discovery Owners group and he was able to point out which cabling I needed to move to the new shunt. Al was a gem for me.

While stumped, I told Theo I wanted to check the air cleaner unit just to be sure the filter was still in good shape. I had worried that the previous filter had been blown by another issue within the air intake. Taking out the air filter took some doing, and I strained my back, but the piping and air cleaner looked good… this time. *Whew.*

Putting the cleaner back in proved to be a challenge for us, but after several tries, we got it back in, with a few choice swear words thrown in for good measure.

We also had the Renogy Eclipse Premium kit for a 400-watt solar panel and a 40-amp Rover solar controller, along with four tilt frame kits. We were wondering where to install the controller since there wasn't much space inside the battery compartment. We briefly entertained the idea of putting the controller in the black tank bay, but that would have required some tricky wiring behind the chassis.

Racing against the fading sunlight, Theo completes the install in time.

Al rescued us again (I told you he was a gem) by suggesting we put it in my bedroom closet and that we use the rear cap. The rear cap was hollow, so if the wiring from roof going in the rear cap leaked, it would just leak onto the ground harmlessly. Good idea.

We held off on the solar install for the time being, and Theo went ahead with the water pump replacement by removing the water connections plating. This took him an hour and half. He also sanded and spray-painted the rusted portions and replaced the pump. The new pump had rubber footings, but the manual said to mount the pump on a piece of wood or plywood to reduce the noise and vibrations.

"Hey, this says we gotta use a piece of wood to mount this," I said.

"I know… but we don't have any here. I looked for one in the area. I think we will be fine without it," Theo said.

"No, that's a bad idea. The paper here clearly says we need to have a wooden board!" I insisted.

"We only have a small piece for old pump, and it won't fit the accumulator—we need a longer piece. Trust me, Dad. We will be fine."

"You don't want to do all this work and have to redo this. It's easier to do this right the first time."

Theo waved my concerns away, and I figured he knew what he was doing, hopefully.

By the time everything was assembled, the sun was setting. Theo rushed to finish everything up. I had worried that we were replacing too many parts all at once, making it harder to diagnose any problems that might pop up.

The sky was getting darker with each passing second. When Theo tried to turn on the pump, it was completely dark. That didn't faze him, though, and he said, "Here we go!"

The pump switch light didn't come on. *Crap.*

We groaned. We had to figure out why the pump wouldn't turn on. Theo had to do some soldering on the wiring, so it was possible that the problem was there.

"Let me try again," he said optimistically. No luck.

We then both looked at each other at the same time. Theo said, "Fuse! I must have shorted it while installing the pump." We ran inside and found a blown 10-amp fuse. We chuckled, and quickly replaced it with a 15-amp fuse.

We went back outside in the dark, flashlights on. Theo tried again with bated breath. The water pump's lighting up was a welcome sight.

"Yes!" We pumped air into the accumulator to the specified 30 psi. Everything was running well, to our relief. There was a small leak from the pre-filter and Theo had to remove it for later replacement.

Next up, the air brake system air dryer cartridge needed to be changed out since we didn't know when it was last changed. The cartridge looked kind of rough. I had picked up a new air dryer cartridge while in Missouri, but I never had time to

The air brake dryer cartridge looking quite nasty.

replace it. Theo was happy to do it.

I had bought a large ratcheting rubber grip tool from Harbor Freight earlier that came in handy; Theo used it to loosen the cartridge. As soon as it came out, *whoa...* It was pretty disgusting: rusted, and the filter inside was filled with goop. Theo cleaned it out and installed the new interior filter before screwing the cartridge on. We started her up, ran the air pressure, and braked.

Everything worked great. Another task crossed off our to-do list.

While Theo worked on the water pump, Brianna worked on reorganizing my cabinets. She put all the shot glasses and liquors in one place. She found a piece of scrap wood that looked good as a shot glass holder and went to work on it, using drills and Dremel tools. The result was really satisfying and holds my four-piece shot glass set in place to this day.

After doing some reading and getting more helpful advice from Al in the Discovery Owners group, Theo and I were ready to tackle the Victron Battery Monitoring kit. Al's guidance really made things easy for us as we installed the shunt and rewired things a bit. Everything worked beautifully. Theo and I made bets on how many amp hours would be consumed in one night with both heat zones set to sixty-five degrees. He guessed 100 to 125 amps, while I guessed 60 to 70 amps.

The result: 68 Ah consumed in one night. I won. So, basically my 390 Ah AGM batteries had enough capacity to see us through the night with heat blowers on. We discovered the typical usage over the next few weeks showed a range from 55 to 110 Ah usage, depending on what we did that night such as watching television or working late into the night.

Victron also showed an astonishing difference between LED light bulbs and the old-fashioned ones. When the LED bulbs were switched on, Victron showed an increase of 0.1 or 0.2 amp for each bulb; old-style bulbs used 3 to 4 amps each. A huge difference.

With that installed, we wrapped up our stay in the Sky Valley Resort. We would miss the hot spring-fed tubs, but it was time to move onto boondocking west of Salton City. We

The Victron Smart Battery Monitoring kit shows information on my iPhone.

went into the Palm Springs area to shop for food and firewood. We also fueled up our Discovery and the Land Rover at Red Earth Casino, which had the lowest diesel and gas prices we'd seen so far.

We left a little later that morning and were running out of daylight. We wouldn't make it by night to the Rockhouse Campground, a free, privately-owned RV boondocking site at an abandoned mine. I found a free RV lot by the Salton Sea in Salton City that used to be a city RV park. This made it easy for us to set up even in the dark, and we settled for the evening.

The next day, we explored the seafront, which despite being smelly, dead, and desolate, was oddly beautiful, if not stark.

That evening we finally turned on the water pump and used the water… and the floor roared to life, shaking the floor with high pitched vibrations.

"What?! What the hell was that?" I exclaimed.

Theo looked at me, realization dawning on his face, "Uh oh, the water pump…"

The vibrations were bone-chatteringly loud—louder than ever before.

I glared at Theo, "No more taking short cuts, son." I sighed. If the instruction sheet clearly states something for a quieter operation, just do it. No exceptions.

The pump continued to roar as we filled the kitchen sink to wash the dishes. Our hearts dropped.

Chapter 39
SOLAR PANELS

DECEMBER 30, 2018

- Mileage: **120,902**
- Previous total: **$29,421.32**
- Renogy LiFePo4 170 Ah 12V battery: **$1,420.24**
- Renogy 400-watt premium eclipse solar panels with 40-amp Rover MPPT controller: **$1,437.41**
- Thermostatic mixing valve wall mount for shower (Pro tip: Skip this cheap one, go for a Grohe thermostatic shower valve at $250 on Amazon. We went through the cheap valve twice, the handles kept wearing down after six months: **$39.99**
- Current total: **$32,318.96**
- Credit score: **620**

After one night by the Salton Sea, we drove through Salton City with a brief stop-over by Ray's Motel where I had spent the previous February with Russ Stein, Barry Solomon, and Butch Zein for a weekend of ATVing. I was surprised by how often I would return to places I didn't expect to return to—as if there were a rhythm to life.

We stopped for lunch at the same Mexican place I had eaten at the year before, and it was decent. We then checked out ATV and RZR rental rates before we decided to just enjoy the nature

Brianna atop her dad's Land Rover at the Rockhouse campground.

and scenery. We picked up a fourteen-gauge wire from local hardware store, a full twenty feet long just in case we needed longer wiring. We did end up using twelve feet.

From Salton City, we headed westward towards the town of Borrego Springs, turning off at the Rockhouse Campground to boondock at no charge for the next few days before Theo and Brianna dropped me off at the Palm Springs airport on Saturday for a business trip.

As soon as we turned onto the dirt pavement, we looked for a site. After a few tries, we found the perfect spot, the rear end facing south, the windshield taking in the expansive and gorgeous mountains and valley before us. There were more RVs behind us and to our sides but nothing in front of us.

Sweet!

The place was simply gorgeous. An existing fire pit surrounded by rocks was already set up next to our Discovery. We settled in and were comfortable. We were ready to tackle the solar installation after receiving suggestions from the Discovery Owners group.

We built a fire that evening and had s'mores, enjoying the dark sky and expansive space as we huddled up next to the Discovery. I watched the fire cast its lights and shadows on the white wall of our motorhome, the "Discovery" logo emblazoned on the side wall, and I was filled with gratitude. I reflected on the months prior, the roller coaster of joys and disappointments. Despite all the setbacks, the experience of driving, camping, boondocking, and living full time with our beloved *Chicago* was worth it.

The model name of *Discovery* felt so fitting, so apt. We were discovering

Sitting by campfires is good for your soul.

I stayed busy taking pictures as Theo did the real work. I did help... a bit.

ourselves in the process. Our ability to adapt was much greater than I initially thought. Sure, my finances weren't looking good, but at that moment, I felt confident that we would find a way through this.

I handed off responsibility for the fire to Theo and went inside to climb into bed. It didn't matter where we were or how cold or windy it was outside, I was home and comfortable.

I showered the next morning, with the water pump roaring, annoying the heck out of Brianna and Theo. Our next project was to install the solar panels, and we were ready with a plan. We mounted the Rover 40-amp solar controller in the closet, which took two tries to secure properly. Afterwards, we took

Four 100-watt Renogy Eclipse panels all lined up and ready to be installed on the roof.

out the solar panels and tried to get a better sense of the panel sizes, and how long the cabling would extend between the panels. We started to assemble the panels on the tilting frames we had bought for forty dollars each.

We mounted the tilting frames on all four panels inside, avoiding sand and dust from outside. No, I wasn't just taking pictures. I swear I was helping.

The plan was to carry the panels and the frames out with cardboard covering the top of panels to ensure we didn't get shocked when hooking them up. We would lay them on the side of the Discovery in preparation of bringing them up on the roof. In the process of assembling the tilt frames, the significance of sheer number of bolts required to adjust the tilt dawned on me. We realized there was a lot involved to tilt the panels every time we needed them tilted, and we would need to go up on the roof any time we needed to adjust the tilt. I wished there was a way to tilt them electronically, but at the time there were not any. (Pro tip: According to *Gone with the Wynns* on YouTube, tilting panels are not worth it. You are better off installing more solar panels closer to each other.)

Before bringing the panels and frames up on the roof, we needed to decide how we would lay out the panels. Most RVs have four panels

Panels in their final configuration. They were set to tilt without shadow interference.

tilted towards the front. We did not want to do that because the windows would be where my office space was, which would make my workspace hot with the sun beating down all day.

We did not have windows on the rear end. It seemed better if we parked our Discovery's rear end facing the winter sun southward. This would produce less heat inside

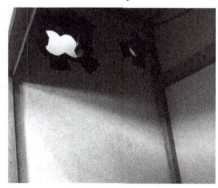

Yup, we drilled through the air intake chute in the rear. We had to use duct tape to seal the breach.

on sunny days and we could keep our windows open to enjoy the scenery. This meant we would need to place the panels tilted towards the rear end, but we also needed to space them out so we could walk between them.

In our first layout, we placed the panels all on the driver's side to see what it looked like, still intending to tilt and point them towards the rear. We ended up placing them closer to the rear end side by side.

With the panels set up, we did not drill the screws on the roof just yet. We wanted to see how well they worked in that

A sheet metal plate with adhesive backing now covers the holes.

configuration first. We drilled a hole in the rear cap, removing the broken radio antenna and using that as second hole for solar panel wiring. Theo went down to my bedroom closet to drill a two-inch hole through the wall, while I stayed on the roof to feed the cable down, jiggering it around so he could catch it and bring it in.

Theo and I FaceTimed during the whole process, since we obviously couldn't holler to each other.

"Dad, I can feel the cable clicking around—it's so close but I don't see it."

I pulled the cable out and tried again. No dice. Third try—again, no luck.

"You'll have to drill another hole—maybe a bit further left," I suggested.

Theo agreed. He drilled further left from the initial hole. Theo looked puzzled on FaceTime as an additional piece of black plastic fell out when he pulled out a bore that wasn't present in the first hole. I snaked the cable down again, but after multiple tries Theo still couldn't see the cable. He drilled three more holes, making one big opening.

"Dad, oh crap… I just realized something…"

I froze. "What? Don't keep me in suspense!"

"Come down. You got to see this."

Uh-oh. I climbed down the ladders and walked inside.

The newly installed panels tilt towards the sun.

Theo neatly installed and tied up the wiring and then stuffed in a paper towel to cover the hole.

Theo looked at me, apologetically, "We drilled through the air intake chute."

"We did what?" I asked.

"Yes, we drilled through the air intake plastic chute. I couldn't see the cable you threaded to me. The first hole was just outside of that chute but on the other side, and now we created a huge opening in the air intake chute."

We should have gone underneath and lined up where the two holes on the roof were—which we did right after this. We identified a space further left of this huge hole. Theo used Gorilla duct tape to seal the edges to prevent insulation foam from being sucked into the air filter.

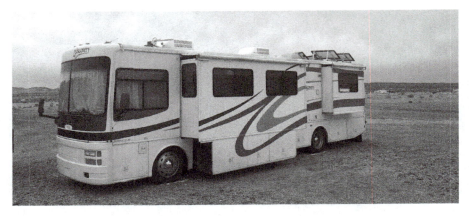

Of course, as soon as we installed solar panels, the clouds came. A conspiracy, I'm telling you.

We took turns looking underneath, trying to identify the exact spot where Theo should drill the fifth—and hopefully last—hole. After a few tries, we felt confident that we had the right location.

Theo kept drilling through, grimacing a bit. We were nervous about hitting the air chute again. He finally broke through.

He felt his way, and turned to me. "We missed the side wall by just a fraction of an inch!"

I let out a huge sigh of relief before I climbed back up on the roof and fed the cables. Theo caught them and pulled them inside easily. A sense of victory came over us.

I wasn't sure what we would do about that huge opening going into the air intake chute. Would we need to replace the chute? This would require removing the rear cap—a labor intensive process, I was sure.

Theo turned to me, "I got this. I have an idea."

By now, I had learned to trust him despite our setbacks. He does come up with good solutions, and sure enough, he did just that the next day. He took a piece of metal plate we had used to cover the front radiator fan (it turned out we didn't need to do that, so that sheet metal came in handy for this fix). He put sealant around the opening before screwing the sheet metal on, securing it nicely.

We then hooked up the solar panels to the controller (holding off on the final wire cuts for later) and we saw the controller start charging the batteries with about 4 amps. This was with the sun already beginning to set. We had huge smiles on our faces and were feeling pretty good. We managed to pull this off in one day, thanks in part to helpful advice from Al and the Discovery Owners group.

The weather forecast showed no winds expected that night, but I duct-taped the panels frames on the roof to secure them. We would do the final install and clean up the next morning.

We settled down for the evening, building another fire. After cooking a delicious dinner, we had s'mores. I felt content. We now had a way to generate energy without having to rely on the smelly and noisy generator.

Theo filled up the kitchen sink so he could wash the dishes, and the water pump roared to life. He paused, turned halfway to Brianna and me, and signed emphatically, "I. Hate. That. Water. Pump."

The next day, after suffering through the loud vibrating pump during showers, we tackled the clean-up: bolting down the frames and cutting the wires to the correct length, and then reattaching them to the Rover controller. Theo finished up the bedroom closet area. Everything was looking nice and neat.

The roof looked nice with the panels tilted towards the sun, and the Renogy app on my iPhone showed the panels were producing 24 amps of energy, easily charging the batteries.

The day after that, however, the skies were really cloudy. The amps generated hovered between 6 to 8 amps. Though this was enough to cover the idle energy use inside the Discovery of 4 to 5 amps and still charge the batteries in a small way, we had to run the generator for a couple of hours to top her off. Still, this was better than a full five and half hours of generator time.

The Rover 40-amp controller could handle up to 500 watts, so I was considering eventually adding one more panel to give us some cushion for less sunny days.

Everything was looking good when Theo and Brianna drove me to the Palm Springs airport to catch my flight to Kansas City. As I said goodbye to Theo and Brianna, I was feeling pretty good about the Discovery.

The water pump was another story, though.

Chapter 40
LOW-HANGING TREES WREAK HAVOC

I was off to Olathe, Kansas for a week-long Deafhood train-the-trainers program (our first ever) and the Deafhood Institute team meeting, led by coordinator Chriz Dally and Deafhood Foundation board organizing chair. They had screened over thirty applicants and selected nine finalists for this opportunity. I had butterflies in my stomach as I contemplated how the training should go because I knew that we would be learning as we went along during that week.

During that week, there was multicultural and diversity training provided by SooHyun Tak, a gifted facilitator from Gallaudet University who is also a licensed counselor and teacher. She was born in Seoul, South Korea and her family emigrated to the United States for SooHyun's education. She went to Lexington School for the Deaf in New York City. She uses the racial/cultural identity development

Having a good time with SooHyun Tak, Star Grieser, and David Cowan in Kansas.

framework by Derald Wing Sue as a part of her training to illustrate how people in marginalized groups process and evolve with their identities, and she challenged us to really dig deep, to unpack and examine our privileges within the Deaf world and become more aware.

For me, unpacking my white, male, straight, cisgender, and able-bodied privileges was both difficult and rewarding work. This is a journey that continues throughout my life. We must constantly be aware of what we don't know, since lack of awareness may hurt others, whether deliberately or not.

The importance of awareness, on a more superficial level, could be found in driving *Chicago* around. I easily forget how tall and long she is. This point hit home with great force when Theo and Brianna dropped *Chicago* off at the Palm Springs Airport parking lot so I could easily get in and drive away when I flew back.

Theo was driving around the parking lot, trying to thread through some tricky situations—a lot of low hanging trees, tight curb cuts, and tight turns. I was on FaceTime with him because he wanted to tell me something. As I waited for him to park, I was startled when something hit the RV with such a force that it knocked out the two-by-four stud bracing the slide-out towards him, narrowly missing his head.

I frantically signed to Theo, "What happened?!"

He quickly responded, "Hit a curb, I think. Too tight here."

A minute later, he pulled into two parking spots, and he was done. We talked for a minute before signing off. I wanted him to be sure everything was turned off—the water pump, the water heater, the heat. All other devices were to be unplugged. Only the refrigerator would remain on; he needed to ensure she was fairly level so the refrigerator would run properly on LP gas.

A few minutes later, my heart fell into my stomach when Theo texted me: "I am so, so sorry."

I stared at the iPhone's three blinking dots as he wrote his next message.

"I damaged the roof from the tree."

I texted back, "How bad?"

He repeated, "So, so sorry. And solar panels. It is bad."

Crap! The panels were only a week and half old. I was at that moment driving a rental car to a restaurant with my friend and Deafhood colleague Butch Zein.

"Do you want me to drive so you can text?" Butch offered, seeing the distress on my face.

I declined, saying I would put down my phone until we got to the restaurant. My heart was pounding. I was freaking out, to be honest. As soon as we pulled into the restaurant parking lot, I texted Theo back. But before I could hit send, Theo texted, "I don't know what to say."

I steeled myself, "Take pictures. Eternabond any holes."

"I don't want to take pictures. I am in shock, honestly."

Shit! I pleaded, "Take pictures please. Assess the damage." I followed up quickly with, "I love you and I always will forgive you. We will get through this. Take pictures. Identify all damage to avoid further damages from leaks, etc."

The pictures came, and I was sickened. Theo FaceTimed me, aghast. I told him I was

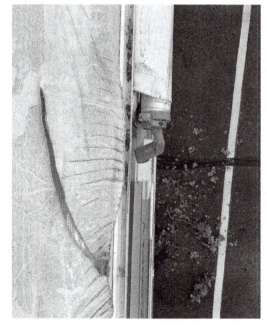

The gash on the roof and the damaged slide topper.

glad he and Brianna were safe and unhurt. After some talking, Theo got up and went to work in repairing as much as he possibly could.

I stared at the pictures of the damage for a good few minutes, digesting and worrying. The roof damage seemed cosmetic and the Eternabond would take care of that.

The week-old panels badly damaged.

The slide-out topper was another story, though. The frame holding the rollers was completely bent out of shape. I knew I shouldn't dare to bring out the slide-out until this was replaced—approximately $350 for the smaller one, and more for the main one.

The solar panel damage was more painful for me because we had just installed them a week and half ago. The panels cost $185 each. I wished there was insurance for such bad luck—my insurance had a $500 comprehensive deductible, so

Theo did his magic and the panels were nearly restored to their original condition.

that wouldn't cover the panels. I recalled that some of my credit cards would offer accidental damage coverage for purchases within the first ninety days. I checked, but it wasn't the credit card I had used to buy the panels. *Damn.*

An hour or so later, Theo texted me back that he had done the repairs to the best of his ability. He sent me pictures of the repairs, and where *Chicago* was parked so I would know where to look for her when I got back to Palm Springs. They had a fairly small parking lot so finding her wasn't a major concern.

I was impressed with Theo's work. The roof shear was Eternabonded cleanly, and the repair on the solar panels had restored them to like-new condition. However, one of the panels had to be replaced. It had actually arrived somewhat damaged; someone at the factory apparently scratched an "S W" on the diodes below the glass cover and I sent pictures to Renogy and they agreed to replace it.

I was confident that Renogy would do right by us and replace the panel even with this additional damage. As for the second panel, I would have to silicone caulk the corners to ensure rain did not get under the glass, onto the solar panel diodes themselves.

Theo anxiously FaceTimed me when I arrived in Palm Springs as I walked up to *Chicago*.

"Dad, so...?"

Standing outside, I said, "Hold on—let me pull up the Renogy app and see how many amps were generated these past few days."

I looked and was happy to report back to Theo. "All is good. Highest amps generated one day was 143 amps. Her batteries are in good condition. She started just fine."

Theo was visibly relieved. So was I.

I walked around her, inspecting for any

It actually was the bedroom slide toppers that had been damaged, not the main living room slide-out.

blockages and making sure the air bags were fully inflated. Suddenly I noticed something. My heart sank.

"Theo, I didn't realize the bedroom slide topper was also damaged!"

He replied, "Say what?!" I told him to hold on as I inspected the main slide-out toppers and saw they were fine.

"Oh," I said. "Never mind. I thought it was the main slide topper that was damaged, and I was disappointed to find the bedroom slide topper damaged on top of this. But I realize I misunderstood you."

Theo rolled his eyes. "Thanks for scaring me... for nothing."

Since it was the smaller topper that was damaged, it should be cheaper to replace. This was a relief.

Butch had flown back with me, so I dropped him off at his home, then went food shopping before heading back to Sky Valley Resort for two nights. I needed to wash clothes, so I wanted full hook-ups, and I liked the resort and the natural hot springs spa. I checked in after hours and found I was assigned to #916. But there was someone else on that site, so I used the same site I had before, #912.

As soon as I backed up the Discovery, put down her jacks, leveled her, and expanded the slide-out, I realized I was sick with a fever. Body aches. Chills. Everything. I crawled into bed. I struggled to sleep that night, waking up sweaty and in horrible pain. I took a pain reliever, which helped a bit.

The morning didn't bring relief; it was raining nonstop, and I felt even worse. I had a hard time moving around. Thank goodness for the excellent Berkey water filter system. The water was delicious, and I drank lots of it. I had to go to the Sky Valley Resort office, a good fifteen-minute walk, in the rain to pay for the site and notify them that I was staying at a different site. I pulled myself together, despite still running a fever, and grabbed my umbrella. The slow walk was wet and miserable.

As soon as I arrived, the sign in the window proclaimed the office was... closed. For lunch. It was 12:15 p.m.

Groaning, I turned and shuffled back to my RV and climbed back into bed. I slept soundly for the next few hours. When I woke up, I was concerned because I did not want them to think I was squatting or avoiding payment. The frustrating process of making a reservation started the previous day at the Denver International Airport, where I had a short layover on the way to Palm Springs.

I tried to make a reservation via the Sky Valley Resort website. I couldn't because there was some kind of mobile web site error. So, I tried to call via Convo Relay, but the signal inside the airport was bad. I decided to email them through their website. No reply.

As soon as I landed, I called again but the office was already closed, and the answering machine mentioned an after-hours box, which I took advantage of. The envelope they left for me clearly stated I had to come in the next day to settle my payment.

It was still raining outside. The clock surged towards the end of the day. I wasn't going to shuffle all way back to the office. To add insult to the injury, the park Wi-Fi was so bad that it couldn't support a simple FaceTime or video call. The cell signals for both Verizon and T-Mobile in this area were also bad.

Despite that, I tried to call via Convo Relay. I felt sorry for the interpreter, who struggled to understand me, saying, "You're breaking up. All pixelated. I can't see you." I had to use of the built-in text feature, typing messages to the interpreter. The person working in the front office was confused.

The video broke up and I lost the connection. I growled. Why didn't they reply to my email? That would have made things a whole lot easier.

Video relay services and LTE cell phone services are a huge blessing for the Deaf community, putting us nearly on par with hearing people's access through voice calls, but "nearly" in this situation was clearly not enough.

Five o'clock came and went, and I gave up. I went back to bed. I was doubled over on my bed, moaning—definitely not one of my best moments. I worried that security would ring my doorbell and demand that I vacate the spot. I knew that wasn't likely; they would probably just note that I was sick and tell me to come in the next day.

On top of this, during the garbled video call, I was also informed for the first time that the Passport America fifty-percent discount wasn't available in January and February. That made my stay a whole lot more expensive than initially expected. I wasn't too thrilled.

The next day and a lot of water later, I began to feel better. I received an email from the front office telling me to stay in so they wouldn't be exposed to whatever I had, and they happily extended the Passport America rate for me, allowing me to stay in for another day. I was very relieved.

I did point out in my response that they should look at their Wi-Fi system because this had become an Americans with Disabilities Act accessibility issue. They had been nice about my previous and current stay, and I wanted to work with them rather than filing a complaint with the U.S. Department of Justice. I hope they have somehow fixed this by now.

Later that day, Mel Carter, a legend in the Deaf community, stopped by for a visit. Mel was a teacher, advocate, performer and a comedian who lived in the area after retiring from the California State University, Northridge Deaf Studies department. I was so thrilled to have his company. I had served with him on the board of the Deafhood Foundation for many years, and we often roomed together during the board retreats. He graciously brought over a vegan sandwich from the Native Foods Cafe in Palm Desert, and I was happy for something delicious and substantial after consuming only soup while I was sick. We chatted and caught up.

I had missed working with him because he knew how to lighten the mood during tense discussions, and he shared his wisdom and insights in a profound way at times. I was glad to see him again.

Mel Carter visits me in Palm Spring.

After he left, I rested for the remainder of the evening. I planned to head out the next day, but I wasn't sure if I should head for Rockhouse Campground again and start making my way to Phoenix via Yuma and Los Algodones, Mexico, or drive to Ontario, California where the Renogy solar company was located and replace the damaged panel.

I texted Theo, "Since I am so close to Ontario, California where Renogy is… should I make the trip and replace the panel? Get this over with?"

Theo replied, "I don't know. What would it cost you in diesel fuel to get there and back?"

I did a quick calculation. The drive would be about seventy miles one way, so one hundred and forty miles round trip divided by seven miles per gallon average resulting in twenty gallons consumed. The going rate for diesel in California was about $3.30, so it would be about sixty-six dollars in diesel.

"Sixty-six dollars, round trip. But the hassle of packing up the defective panel and shipping it back, and waiting for the replacement… This trip is definitely worth the drive," I told Theo. He agreed.

I drove to the Renogy headquarters. I went through the metropolitan Los Angeles area to Riverside, California where California School for the Deaf, Riverside (CSDR) is. It also happened that the school was hosting the Clerc Classic basketball and cheerleading tournaments, hosting Deaf schools from all over the nation.

Both my kids Theo and Stefania had participated in Clerc Classic basketball and cheerleading tournaments

Stefania, a four-year-straight cheerleading Clerc Classic champion.

during their high school years. In fact, Stefania holds the distinction of being the only person to capture four straight championships, and on top of this remarkable accomplishment, she did it while attending two schools—Indiana School for the Deaf in her first two years and Model Secondary School for the Deaf in her final two years. She pulled this off despite struggling with the transition to MSSD; she had transferred to MSSD so I could go back to Gallaudet to finish my bachelor's degree.

I don't know how she did it, but she did it with such grace and resilience. At the end of her final competition, I saw her break down and cry. She knew that her time as a cheerleader had come to an end. I remember tearing up when I saw her, sitting on the bleachers among her teammates, awaiting the competition results.

I thought of Don Cochran as I drove. One of my best friends, who was also the best man in my wedding years ago, Don teaches high school math at CSDR. The son of Deaf parents with both hearing and Deaf siblings, Don grew up in Roy, Utah, attending Utah Schools for the Deaf and the Blind before transferring to MSSD. That's where we met.

I decided to video-message him, letting him know I was in the area. I knew that with Clerc Classic he might be busy, but I thought I would check anyway. Luckily, he

Don Cochran and me inside the Discovery.

happened to be available that day. He drove to Ontario to meet me in the Renogy's narrow parking lot.

Upon arrival, I was on the roof in the rain, disconnecting the solar panel from the roof mount. I planned on removing the remaining tilt frame mount from the comfort of their front lobby, indoors, dry and clean. Soon after, I entered the headquarters. Don arrived, and we bear-hugged.

"So good to see you again! I wanted to let you know that I was literally in your backyard in the Palm Springs area, but I was so busy with doing the upgrades to our RV and spending time with my son Theo and his girlfriend," I said.

"Yeah, I was surprised. At the same time, I understand. You really do have a huge RV outside. That seems to be a handful," Don smiled.

"Definitely. You don't know the half of it," I grinned.

The solar panel was exchanged for a new one. When I opened the new panel, there were scratches on that one as well. I sighed, and I called the employee over and pointed out the scratches. She looked surprised. She had someone take it away and said they would check the next panel before bringing it out.

As we waited, Don and I continued catching up. The rain continued to come down, soaking everything outside. They eventually brought out a pristine solar panel and I mounted the brackets, carefully lining up the same holes as before so the bracket would then fit onto the roof brackets. They did line up—somewhat; I had to make some adjustments before they were good to go. Don helped me hoist the panel up on roof and we worked together securing the panel. After plug-in, the panels were producing around 1.6 amps despite it being a very cloudy, gray and rainy day. Not too bad.

Don and I went out for dinner, and I gave him a ride in our Discovery. We continued chatting until he had to leave for the Ontario airport to pick up his sister and her son from Texas for the tournament. We hugged and said our goodbyes.

Sometime during our conversation, I mentioned to Don that the Discovery already had been to the Atlantic Ocean and was now so close to the Pacific. After dropping Don off, I thought to myself: Why don't I find an oceanside campground and complete her journey from sea to shining sea?

Chapter 41
FROM SEA TO SHINING SEA

Before the Discovery could make its way to Bolsa Chica State Park, a beachfront location on the Pacific Ocean just north of Huntington Beach, the day was slipping away fast. I needed a place to park overnight. The AllStays app on my iPhone showed only one Walmart in the area allowing overnight stays, just north of Ontario off I-15 in Rancho Cucamonga. Even then I wasn't sure because the reviews showed conflicting reports whether the store allowed overnight parking.

I drove there anyway. As I pulled into the parking lot, I saw a huge sign screaming that there was no RV parking allowed. This was discouraging. I parked and went inside and asked the manager where I should park for the night. She radioed security and came back to me apologetically: there was definitely no overnight parking allowed.

I took a deep sigh. It was 9:00 p.m., and it was raining and foggy. I cursed the sheer lack of a nationwide RV park reservation system akin to Hotels.com where I could enter dates and see what park was available. Sure, KOA had a nationwide reservation system, but they wanted seventy-five dollars a night at a fairgrounds parking lot. No, thanks. ReserveAmerica didn't allow for last-minute, same-day searches. RVonthego.com doesn't search for sites by dates and is terribly cumbersome.

Too bad. I think a lot of RV parks would fill their sites easily if there was such a unified booking site.

I frantically searched around for nearby campgrounds, muttering about how hostile the metro Los Angeles area was to RVers. I came across Bonita Ranch RV Park, which had a site available with electrical and water hook-ups for thirty dollars a night. And it was only a twenty-two-minute drive from where I was, up in the San Bernardino mountains.

Should have been an easy drive, you'd think.

I drove north on Interstate 15 towards the exit that would take me up into the mountains. As I made my way to the Sierra Avenue exit, the fog was piling on rather thick. I downshifted to ensure the engine stayed at a higher rpm, keeping the radiator cool for the uphill climb. I stayed in the fifth gear, sometimes downshifting into fourth gear.

The visibility was awful. I could only see about sixty to a hundred feet ahead of me, and the rain continued to come down. The first sign sent the hairs on the back of my neck upright: "Rockslide Area." I could barely see the rocky walls to my right as I threaded her through.

Another sign came up, "Mud Slide Area." I had seen these signs before so I should be okay, right? Then a temporary large construction-type LED sign flashed, "High Risk of Mudslide Due to Recent Wildfires."

Uh-oh.

I crossed a couple of roads that had water running over them. Fortunately, it was not difficult. I drove on over a twisty road with sheer rock faces on my right side, being mindful to stay clear of any obstacles.

My heart was pounding. "Only a twenty-two-minute drive. Nothing to it, right?!" I muttered to myself. That seventy-five dollars for a night at KOA was beginning to look like a vastly smarter move.

There were some small rocks, fresh on the road, and I gently nudged the Discovery to avoid these. I really couldn't see the mountains or the surrounding area. I had no idea what I was driving into.

After what seemed like a heart-wrenching eternity, I finally came to an intersection taking me into the Bonita Ranch RV Park. I pulled up to their main office and parked, hopped out in the rain and into the office.

The first thing I did was to type on Cardzilla, "Boy, the drive up here was scary." The manager laughed and gave me a knowing nod.

The site was paid for, and he pointed out the first site that seemed a tight fit and told me I could have a couple of other pull-throughs if I wanted. The site he gave me had 30-amp power. The pull-throughs had only an 110-volt outlet.

I drove around trying to find the site but got lost. The campground was packed tightly with a lot of mature trees in the way. I worried about hitting the Discovery's solar panels and the roof like Theo did. The pull-throughs were a bad idea; the site was muddy and sloped downwards with rainwater coursing through the site. Forget it. I had to carefully drive through between the trees, which was stressful and frustrating.

I gave up and went back to the original 30-amp site. I had to carefully thread her between two thick trees standing by each other before I could back her up onto the site. It was a good thing that the site was more level than others. I set her down and leveled her fairly easy. I didn't bother with the slide-out. I ran outside and plugged her in for the night. I had plenty of water, so I didn't need to hook that up.

I was soaked, cold, and miserable. I hopped in my shower for a good long, hot shower. I then dropped into bed from sheer exhaustion. When I awoke the next morning and looked out, I saw that I was surrounded by the mountains, which were shrouded in a layer of fog. The trees were soaked, dripping water everywhere. The ground was black, rich-looking, and very wet. I got in my writing session for the morning. After breakfast, I

A raging river, swollen by heavy rains.

got out of the campground, headed for Bolsa Chica State Park. I would have to wait until the Rancho Cucamonga area before I could call the state park to see if they had a site available; the signal in the mountains was pretty much non-existent.

For now, I was worried the amount of rain overnight would have formed raging waters right next to the roads. Would the roads be impassable, leaving me trapped in the mountains?

As I drove out, the river was raging. I braced myself and guided the Discovery down the mountain. Luckily, the roads were clear all the way down.

I found a Whole Foods store I could pick up some food for the next few days and call the state park. They confirmed that they had a site available for me, but for only one night since it was a Thursday night. All other sites were booked for the weekend. The cost? Sixty-five dollars. I happily paid since it meant I would finally be by the Pacific Ocean.

I stopped for lunch at Mendocinco Farms to try the newest Impossible Burger 2.0. Though it was tasty, the special sauce—though so good—was so overpowering that I couldn't really appreciate the burger itself.

She made it. The Discovery by the Pacific Ocean at Bolsa Chica State Park.

By then, the rush hour traffic had dispersed, and I happily made my way to the western edge of the United States. I pulled into Bolsa Chica State Park and set up for the evening.

I had made it. From the Atlantic Ocean in April 2018 to the Pacific Ocean in January 2019, a journey of over 12,000 miles in about eight and half months. I was elated and also relieved. I wanted to share the moment with my family, so I texted them, "From sea to shining sea, our Discovery made it all way across the country."

The weather wasn't that great—it was still rainy and wet—but I didn't care. I set her up, leveled her, opened the slide-outs, and hooked her up. I went for a walk on the beach where I was surprised by the amount of oil rigs visible from the shore. It really hit home for me how we need to eliminate fossil fuels in a major way soon.

Soaking up the scenery, I watched the waves crashing onto the precariously-sloping beach, and felt the wind steadily weep over me. The feeling was incredible. Never mind the fact that the state park campground was a simple and cramped parking lot with hook-ups; the beach was right behind my Discovery.

Ahhh, the beach. The Pacific Ocean was a welcome sight after so many setbacks and surprises along the way.

I wished I had parked her facing the beach so I could see through the huge windshield and enjoy the view while writing, but the parking spaces weren't designed to allow that without the major hassle of turning around and going against the flow. This would have raised hackles from the campground host. So I was content with the view out of my bedroom window, watching the ocean waves crash in the distance.

I settled in for the evening, foregoing the fire pit because of the rain, and I took a moment to consider what my family and I had gone through with *Chicago* these past eight and a half months. Naturally, I wished we didn't have to spend so much money on repairs. I wished the inspector had done his job and accurately warned me of serious issues. I wished I had gone with a certified RV inspector, instead. I wished I had taken extra time in the buying process.

Yet, for all the pain she inflicted, she also brought me indescribable joy, beauty, serenity, solitude, shared experiences with my kids, and more. Without the challenges, Theo would not have had a chance to show his brilliance and inventiveness. Without the pain, I wouldn't have grown as much as a man and a father, taking bad news in stride yet continuing to be grateful for what I had. I wouldn't have learned to see money as simply a tool (clearly, I haven't had a chance to become a master of money... yet). My experiences had continued to teach me lessons in life, love, laughter and being appreciative.

Without these obstacles, we wouldn't have worked together as a family—Theo, Stefania, Alec, Warrick, my father, my stepmother, my mother, my aunt and her friend, and a few others—to improve the Discovery, making her an even more meaningful place.

Even as I write this, I strongly believe that each experience brought me lessons I really needed in my life, and a gift that I had wanted for a long time: the luxury and habit to write every day. An astounding achievement for me.

All of this made possible because I was trapped in a world of betrayal, anger, and sheer frustration. I couldn't sue the inspector. I couldn't recover any of my costs so far. I saw myself heading for a second bankruptcy. I had nowhere else to turn to, except to write what I experienced. And that was a cathartic outlet for me.

Chapter 42
ONWARDS TO MEXICO AND EASTWARD

The Discovery did not actually go into Mexico. I did, with the Discovery parked on the United States side. Even so, I hope to travel through Mexico and Central America with the Discovery one day.

After reaching the Pacific Ocean, I made my way south towards San Diego, with an eastward detour to the San Marcos Camping World store. I needed to replace the faulty LED bulbs in my dining table lamp, which the store agreed to exchange without a receipt. I also picked up an estimate to replace the damaged bedroom slide topper. The drive was so scenic. I was driving to the Bureau of Land Management Blair Valley area, just southeast of Julian, California where I would boondock for the next couple of days. I wanted to arrive before the sun set (spoiler: I didn't make it).

The roads were memorable: twisty, narrow, and downright exhilarating. Highway 78 passing through Santa Ysabel was pretty hair-raising until Google Maps directed me to turn onto Wynola Road. Now, that was a real spine-tingling, hair-standing-absolutely-on-end driving. The turns were so tight that I was amazed that the thirty-eight-foot behemoth made it through without a scratch.

When I arrived at Blair Valley, the sky was completely dark. The Saddle Ranch campground was a few miles away and accepted Passport America, but since they required a two-night stay, I passed on it.

As I drove in, I quickly realized how tricky navigation would be. The dirt roads had patches of standing muddy water and some of the

Driving on BLM land in the dark is stupid. Don't be like me and do that.

ground was soft from the recent rain. I had to drive around hardy bushes and huge rocks and plants in the dark. To my dismay, I discovered the next day there were a lot of paint scratches on the RV. I got stuck at one point, and my brakes made a horrific screeching vibration noise when backing up. Crap. I needed to get this checked.

After a few failed attempts, a kind neighbor came out and helped me settle into an area that was fairly level. But the damage was done. I had run her aground, damaging the bottom rail and cargo bay compartment. A tree branch had caught underneath one of the bay doors and broken off.

A good thing she wasn't new, or I would be apoplectic.

I sighed. I learned yet another lesson, though: Don't drive onto Bureau of Land Management land in the dark. Or at least,

The Blair Valley BLM site in California.

don't go too far onto the land; try to find an acceptable site closest to the main road for the night until you can see better the next day and move to a better site.

, I was shaken after damaging her, but I was happy to settle in for the night. I thought the site I was on was decent.

The view was unbeatable. I had the barest of a Wi-Fi connection through my Verizon hotspot, but it was enough that I could watch Netflix and even

Tire marks show where I stupidly damaged the Discovery.

FaceTime with my kids. I went biking around the next morning and found where I had run aground. I was horrified by what I saw: I really had done some serious damage.

I also found a broken-off piece from the Discovery. As I rode around, my bike's electric motor seized. I couldn't even roll it down the road and I had to drag it backwards for a while before the bike finally worked again. I made a mental note to contact FLX support about this issue. I decided it was best to avoid biking long distances until it was fixed, lest I get stranded.

The day before my planned departure for Los Algodones, Mexico, I checked the weather and discovered the risk of rain and actual winds of 25 mph with gusts of up to 60 mph. I didn't want to risk staying another night in that environment.

I checked the Octillo Wells State Recreational Vehicle Area and saw the forecast winds were considerably less, about 10

MARVIN T. MILLER   343

The ground was too soft. I had to use four-by-four wood beams.

mph, and no rain was expected there at all. One of the perks of being Deaf was that the off-road vehicle noise wouldn't bother me at all. I pulled up the jacks and headed out there just in time for the historic blood moon eclipse.

After stopping at the welcome center and asking for advice on where to set up for the night I learned that I could pretty much park anywhere in the area. So I picked a site and put down her jacks, which went right through the ground.

Crap. I had to pull up the jacks and move her to a slightly different area and add wooden boards which then held up better. I finally could settle down, appreciating the location and the vast desert landscape. I decided to sit outside and read on my Kindle Oasis, taking in the scenery while the sun set. The views around me were expansive, with mountains in the far distance and sculpted desert hills and landscape.

The weather was crisp and chilly that night, so I enjoyed the eclipse in the warmth of the campfire. The night sky darkened gradually as the moon disappeared in the total eclipse. I stayed up until the moon began to reemerge, and I was good for the night. I went to bed.

One of the many things on my to-do list was to install the brand-new lithium iron phosphate battery from Renogy. This needed to be done before I traveled to Yuma and Los Algodones.

The next morning, after writing and making breakfast, I noticed the Discovery was swaying. The winds had picked up to about twelve to fifteen miles an hour. After showering and getting dressed, I was intent on

Reading on my Kindle by a campfire is my idea of a good time.

tackling the battery swap. I also planned to rewire so I could monitor the voltage on the chassis batteries, instead of the temperature it currently monitors.

I opened my front door, and it slammed wide open. I panicked a bit, hoping the door was okay; closing it was a struggle. The wind gusts had picked up considerably, and dust and sand swirled everywhere.

I realized there was no way I could do the battery swap. The conditions were too dangerous for that kind of work. The cargo bay doors may be damaged in high winds if left open. Or I might get a good conk on my head once again. No, thanks.

I decided to head to Yuma.

The drive to the casino overnight parking lot near the border crossing at Los Algodones was an easy one, with occasional steering against high winds. I drove through the Imperial Dunes area. There was a dispersed camping site in that area but with the high winds, I didn't want to risk staying there in case I awoke to find myself knee deep in dangerously shifting dunes.

At the casino I had to sign up for their player's club and pay ten dollars for the night to park in their lot. I saw a few

RVs parked in dispersed sites half a mile south, but I wasn't sure if it was okay to camp there. Apparently, nobody asked these RVs to leave the next day, so I could have saved money and parked there.

Um, no... I'm good, thanks.

The next morning, I drove south to the parking lot at the border and paid another twelve dollars to the Quechan Indian Tribe to park for the day. Passport, cash, and credit cards in hand, I walked into Mexico with many other people, mostly white-haired senior citizens. I had expected to show my passport to Mexican officials, but there was nobody at the border.

I was immediately struck by the awesome deals on eyeglasses, dentistry, clothing, haircuts, shoe shining, alcohol, and souvenirs. People were friendly, although a bit assertive in offering their services or wares. A friendly shake of my head sufficed as I navigated to a memorable Mexican breakfast for five dollars plus the tip. I then walked to the SaniDental Group office. Though I did not have an appointment, I only waited a little over an hour before being seen by a dentist. Their facilities were state-of-the-art. They had everything they needed to serve patients. The dentist disagreed with my American dentist for a need to do three fillings, writing, "The fillings can wait—there are only beginning signs of a possible cavity." I paid thirty-five dollars for a complete cleaning service that was done professionally. I was impressed.

The line to enter the United States was ridiculously long.

During my visit to the dentist there was a power outage affecting more than half of the town. I needed a haircut and found a place offering haircut for five dollars, but the location had no power. No problem. A competent lady cut my hair by hand, and she did an amazing job. I gave her a five-dollar tip and thanked her. I wanted to eat lunch, but all the restaurants were without power except for a couple of food trucks. They served mostly meat-laden meals, so I passed.

I didn't want anything else, although I briefly considered buying Losartan blood pressure medication on the cheap but decided not to—something I regretted later on. I also saw a sign advertising free Viagra, and I had to chuckle at that. I headed back to the border. I was surprised there was a long, long line waiting to go through customs. I waited over an hour and half just so a border official could swipe my passport on a computer and ask if I had anything to declare. I was waved through. All the wait for just that? The only emergency is the collective lunacy that has shaped our perceptions of Mexico.

I definitely recommend visiting Los Algodones for dental, vision, medical, and other needs. The place is safe and clean, and

Chapter 43
SURPRISES

JANUARY 28, 2019

- Mileage: **122,600**
- Previous total: **$32,318.96**
- Transmission service and brake adjustment: **$375.18**
- Collision deductible (groan): **$500.00**
- Slide topper replacement (covered by Theo and not included in total): **$500.00**
- Current total: **$33,694.14**
- Credit score: **620**

Driving through Quartzsite in Arizona was a revelation for me. This reiterated an earlier point I had made: reading about and seeing photos cannot do justice to what you can see in real life. Quartzite's huge annual RV show was being held right then, but I had a flight to Boston to catch the next morning from Phoenix, so I couldn't stop over.

My curiosity was piqued by the huge tentpoles for their RV show as well as thousands upon thousands of RVs boondocking as far as I could see on the adjacent Bureau of Land Management lands. I was fascinated, and I drove around hoping to find parking and sprint into the show even for an hour, but I realized I arrived a few minutes after the show closed for the day.

Dang. Next year, maybe.

I stopped for the night at a rest area in the Tonopah area, then I dropped the RV off at Quality Truck Repair shop the next morning for a transmission drain and filter replacement as well as a brake adjustment while I flew to Boston.

My return flight from Boston was a long six-and-a-half-hour non-stop flight. I was cranky and weary. Quality Truck Repair had my Discovery parked on the street so I could get in

Lesson learned: don't take unnecessary risks with a huge motorcoach.

and sleep when I arrived. I settled my bill with them the next morning. I only had two nights before I had to fly out to Austin, Texas for the next Deafhood 101 class. After running a couple of other errands, I decided to stop at Planet Fitness to resolve a strange thirty-nine-dollar charge on my bill. It turned out that was an annual fee in addition to the twenty-one-dollars-a-month Black Card membership.

Back at the Discovery, the Planet Fitness assistant manager and a woman came up to my door. I stepped out and they informed me that I had unknowingly sideswiped the woman's car when I drove my Discovery through a narrow opening in the parking lot.

That was a stupid risk I took: the lot was full, and cars were parked next to each other just like any full parking lot. There was a single parking spots where I thought I could thread her between two cars parked adjacent to the space. I didn't feel anything while driving slowly between them on my way to a larger empty space a few rows down.

I was mortified and apologized to the woman. We exchanged insurance information, and I took photos of her car and the damage I had inflicted.

I knew I would be out the $500 deductible for this repair on the Discovery, if not a little more due to some prior damage to the rear right bumper—I had no idea if that would be covered as well. After that exchange, I was shaken, finding it somewhat difficult to drive. I was even more cautious in making turns. I couldn't shake this awful feeling even as I constantly checked my mirrors and made sure I had an extra margin for safety wherever I drove. I decided to head for the Lost Dutchman State Park, hoping they might have a site open since it was the middle of the week. It was a risk; the drive was further out eastward.

To my relief, they did have a space, although it was only in the overflow area with no hook-ups. I paid twenty dollars a night for two nights, and I headed to their dump station and emptied the gray water and filled up her freshwater tank.

As soon as I was done, a car backed in, blocking my exit.

What the hell is he doing? I was irritated. A gentleman got out of the car and calmly walked towards the Discovery. I was officially annoyed. *What is this? He's not even waving or anything. What does he want?*

I cautiously watched as he made his way to my front door, and realized, *Wait a minute... that guy looks familiar.* I squinted at him, getting out of my seat. It was Dick Booth, who I had met in Kansas.

I hopped out, and Dick smiled at me. We shook hands heartily. I typed on Cardzilla, "What?! What are the odds of you and me crossing paths again here in Arizona?"

He laughed and told me that they were also staying for three nights in the overflow parking lot. Claudia invited me over for dinner that night. Even though I was looking forward to a quiet evening alone that night being in between two classes and heavy travel, I couldn't say no to them—especially after crossing paths twice in only a few months.

I brought over my vegetarian food and they had theirs, and we chatted using Cardzilla and Siri. They asked me about

I played dominoes with Dick and Claudia Booth, all smiles before I wiped the floor with them.

my family, being Deaf, and my travels. I thoroughly enjoyed their neat 1999 Discovery 36T with a curved ceiling, which was unlike my flat ceiling, and I was mentally noting similarities and differences. My inverter switch was under my master bed, and theirs was right above the refrigerator—a better placement, in my opinion, although it makes for more challenging wiring work.

They then introduced me to the Mexican Domino Train game, and after several tries at communicating the rules to me, I caught on. I loved the game, probably because I beat them. Dick wasn't too happy about that, but he was a great sport. Claudia made sure I knew that I was welcome to stay at their place in Minnesota if I ever passed through there. I'll take them up on that offer.

As I walked back home, I realized my rattled feeling from the accident earlier had dissipated. I silently said a word of gratitude for the Booths and their hospitality.

The next day I wanted to tackle a few minor projects, including replacing the slow leaking toilet seal; I often lost all the water in the bowl within an hour, and concluded that the seal was bad. I picked up a new seal from the Camping World for forty-four dollars, and I looked up YouTube videos for the replacement process. I found one with a toilet like mine, and that helped a great deal. The replacement process was a breeze, and it only took me about twenty minutes.

Then, with the help of a friendly neighbor, Steve, I tackled the bent cargo bay wall and door with the broken door latch. I took a similarly-sized latch from the smaller water bay since that bay still had one good latch holding it shut. I put the latch in the front left side bay and tried to figure out how to straighten the badly bent wall/corner that kept hitting a bolt whenever the slide came out or in.

Dick stopped by and graciously lent us the tools I didn't have. With that, Steve figured out a way to straighten the cargo wall by using an adjustable wrench with pliers filling the gap so he could bend the wall straight.

Next, I tried to replace the broken sliding lock on the right-side front bay door, but the trim wouldn't come off. I chickened out, not wanting to damage the white trim by trying to pry it off. I figured I'd ask around for advice later. I also decided against swapping out the batteries for LiFePo4 because I didn't want to risk something going wrong while the Discovery was in storage. I wanted to be around to be sure the battery was functioning properly for at least a week.

With the battery swap delayed again, I would be past the return window and locked into keeping this battery. I don't recommend that because batteries are expensive.

My to-do list completed for the time being, I went out for a nice bike ride on the bike path in Lost Dutchman State Park. It was a unique scene with the cacti and desert landscape. At one point, I rode between two tall Saguaro cacti by accident.

Had I fallen at that juncture, that would have been painful; that generated some adrenaline right there. I didn't go far because I still hadn't resolved why the bike's electric motor seized up the last time.

Having dinner with the Booths by a campfire.

I set up a campfire, brought out food, and the Booths came over with their food and drinks as well. We chatted, swapping iPhones to read our conversations. The conversation included polite questions like, "Why don't you consider getting surgery to restore your hearing?"

I understand why hearing folks scratch their heads and wonder why we are fine the way we are. For us, sounds have little or no relevance in our lives. A good number of us were born Deaf, and we grew up without relying on sounds. Our language emerged and evolved to suit our visual and tactile way of being.

We do sometimes tire of being asked this question, but in this case, given that my conversations with the Booths had run across many topics, I appreciated their honesty and willingness to ask. And I was happy for the chance to answer.

I had an idea. I typed to Dick, "Imagine if an alien race came down and looked at you funny, 'What? You can't pick up Wi-Fi, cell, and GPS signals in your head? Wow. You are missing out!' But you have lived your lives without them so there has never been any need."

Dick replied, "Right on."

Truthfully, I don't know if I convinced them that night. I know I wouldn't be that convinced if DeafBlind people told me

The amazing panoramic view from the top of the Discovery at the beautiful Lost Dutchman State Park.

they felt they were our equals in every respect. That's a distortion within my subconscious, something I am continually working on. The DeafBlind community has been undergoing transformation these past few years. They have developed ProTactile ASL, which provides a lot of backchanneling information through touch, and they are innovating how DeafBlind education occurs in their own classrooms. These developments are affirming the DeafBlind way of existence.

I recognize that my thinking is hypocritical if I say, "Oh, those DeafBlind people—poor them" and then turn around and say to hearing folks, "Hey, we are both equals!"

A brilliant DeafBlind author and publisher John Lee Clark of Minnesota has written a mind-blowing piece introducing the idea of distantism. He argues how spoken and visual languages distance people from each other physically. This contributes to a serious lack, a sense of separateness that pervades our everyday lives. Be sure to Google John Lee Clark and distantism.[4]

As the evening came to a close, I invited both Dick and Claudia inside my Discovery for a tour. I enjoyed showing off, and it occurred to me right then that I could use their help getting the jammed laminate board out from under the main slide. The previous owner had installed the laminate flooring, and to prevent the slides from scratching them up he inserted scraps of the flooring under the slide tray.

[4] https://johnleeclark.tumblr.com/post/163762970913/distantism

Well, one of the boards had gotten stuck inside, and I struggled for some time to get the board out. I didn't want to cause additional strain for the slide-out motor. Dick and Claudia helped bring the slide in and out while I struggled to get the board out. No dice. Dick got his tools and lights, and even enlisted Steve for some help. We went outside under the slide-out, and we all struggled to get the board out.

We tried a pry bar to no avail. I was ready to throw in the towel. I told Dick and Steve to forget it, and that I was grateful for their help. Dick shook his head and went under the slide-out, and he powered through shifting the board back and forth. Suddenly, it was out.

I was stunned. The board was stuck inside something fierce, and he had simply done it. I typed to him, "I would have never believed that the board could come out. You reminded me that when there is a will, there is a way. Thank you."

Dick and Claudia came out as huge winners that evening, and I was grateful for that.

The final surprise—at least for this chapter—came at the tail end of my series of flights (Kansas, Boston, Austin, Chicago, then DC). I was wiped out by the end of my trip in DC. After visiting my boys at Gallaudet and participating in Gallaudet's General Studies program review as one of three outside reviewers.

I sat down at the airport in DC, looking out the large windows in the American Airlines terminal as I read my emails and messages. I decided to send a video message to Riley. I signed to her with one hand while the other was holding my iPhone. I did not realize the woman sitting next to me was watching me.

As soon as I finished the video message, she got my attention and asked how I could sign so quickly with only one hand. I laughed. Using the Cardzilla app I told her, "I grew up signing all the time, so I am used to it."

She spoke through Siri into Cardzilla, asking me if sign language was universal.

"Nope. All sign languages are different in each country, and it's pretty amazing to see."

We talked with each other, including about my Deaf kids and the Deaf community. I asked her where they were going. She said they were going to Miami for a week-long cruise. I told her I was headed back to Phoenix where my RV was located to continue my travels in the west.

Flooded? Or lightly watered?

She lit up. "What?! We own a campground in Maine. I am a third-generation campground owner. My grandfather came here from Sweden, and he opened this campground." She handed me a business card.

With a big grin, I told her, "I will definitely stop by when I am in your backyard one day—probably next year or so."

We shook hands and wished each other well.

I have been surprised often on my Deafhood and my RV journey, and I know I have a lot more to look forward to.

After spending a few days in the parking lot of Bass Pro Shops in Mesa, Arizona, I headed out to a Tortilla Flats dispersed camping site. I went back to Lost Dutchman State Park and paid fifteen dollars for an RV dump, emptying both the black and gray water tanks and refilling the fresh water tank. Although fifteen dollars was pricey, I was racing against diminishing daylight. Besides, their water was good, so I was okay with paying the premium.

A lone camper van on the right, and the Discovery on the left.

The Discovery powered through a stunningly gorgeous vista on twisty roads all the way past Tortilla Campground. Two portions of the road were covered with about an inch or two of water, and that gave me pause. There had been a sign earlier on the road saying, "Do not cross if flooded." Did one or two inches of water constitute a flood? I figured my Discovery could drive through safely, and she did. Twice.

After about 45 minutes, I pulled into what *Frugal Shunpiker's Guide to Boondocking in Arizona*[5] calls the "preferred entrance." What I overlooked in their guide was that there is nearly no signal for Verizon, and a barely one bar for T-Mobile's roaming cell partner. It took twenty minutes to send out a text message. I could only receive messages all at once every thirty minutes.

Sigh.

I needed the signal. I had calls to make. I wanted to do some research on the Internet. I thought to myself, *Oh, well… I'll settle in for maybe two days signal-free then head back to civilization and try again with a different site.*

I set up camp on a firm ground next to an existing stone-circled fire pit. The Discovery was set up in between two sites, one with a van way in back, seemingly stuck in muddy rut. The other was a tent and a car. I had waved to the woman while passing by.

The scenery was just exquisite. The sun was setting. I put on a heavy coat, earmuffs, and gloves, and I set up a campfire

[5] https://www.frugal-rv-travel.com/RV-Travel-Guide.html

Boondocking at the Tortilla Flat U.S. Forest Service site. No cell reception here, though.

for the evening. I even took out the cast iron pan and cooked Beyond Beef hamburgers on the open fire. I cut two slices of my family's favorite buffalo mozzarella cheese from Trader Joe's and put it on the burgers. I had fresh sourdough bread I bought from Whole Foods.

The burger was delicious. I had a Spaten Octoberfest beer I bought from Total Wine in Mesa, and a new Kindle Paperwhite was in my hands as I read *The IO Encounter* by Brandon Morris. The sun slowly slipped into the mountain range to the west, and after a while, the full moon arose, bathing the dark scene with otherworldly light.

Without cell reception I couldn't check my iPhone for temperatures. Instead, I did it the old-fashioned way: I brought out the thermostat on the Discovery's steps. After thirty minutes, the display showed thirty-six degrees at 8:00 p.m.

I freaked out. At this rate, the temperature would end up around twenty-five to twenty-eight degrees by the early morning hours. Would that cause Discovery's plumbing to freeze? I did not think so; I thought it would take more than a full day or so of below freezing temps to affect the plumbing.

But I had no Internet. I couldn't find out for sure. I wasn't hooked up to a shore power source, so I couldn't leave a 60-watt bulb on in the water bay. I began to panic slowly.

I wasn't sure what I should do. I did not really want to drive back to Bass Pro Shops in the dark.

As my mind debated the pros and cons of staying the night, my body was already stowing away gear inside the RV. I had to stop for a second. *That's it. If my body is doing this without my being aware of it, I am leaving,* I thought.

I walked around the RV before bringing in her main slide-out, and as I turned the key to bring it in, it struggled. It moved slowly before stopping.

"Oh, crap. Of all times and places to break down," I swore. I couldn't even call for a mobile RV service. I tried to bring the slide in again and again without any luck. Most hearing people could probably still place a voice call with the roaming cell service. Not me without the necessary high-speed data for video calls.

I remembered Dick Booth had warned me, "The slide sounds like it is really struggling—better have it checked out soon." I had scheduled the slide-out maintenance at Camping World for March 5, but this was happening right now. Damn it.

I paused for a while, thinking. *Okay, what if I were to move some heavy stuff away from the slide area?* I did just that: moving my office chair, a dining chair, a dehumidifier, and three drawers of stuff. I turned the key again.

The slide moved!

I started breathing. "Thank goodness. I am so getting out of here." I remembered that I left my lawn chair and cast-iron pan outside, so I went back out, put away the chair and mat, and turned around and walked towards the cast iron pan sitting on some rocks, cooling off. The night was dark yet moonlit so I could see the surrounding areas fairly well.

As I bent over to pick up the pan, I caught a dark silhouette of a human figure standing, frozen, about seventy-five feet away. This silhouette did not move. The hair on the back of my neck stood up. I picked up the pan and turned around, walking normally and I got inside. I locked the hell out of the door, turning both the regular and deadbolt locks.

After I calmed down, I tried to rationalize the situation: *Maybe this person was trying to call out to me, offering some help after hearing my struggle with the slide?*

But this figure had frozen, as if not wanting to be seen. Something was off about this whole thing, and I couldn't call 911 in this situation. I was getting the hell out of there.

I started her up, pulled up her jacks, and inflated her airbags. I waited a few minutes to let her airbags fully set up, but skipped the customary walk-around. I certainly wasn't going back out there.

I drove out, through the twisty roads in the dark. After about 50 minutes, I was back in the Bass Pro Shops parking lot. Even so, I still was on edge.

After doing some research online, I learned I could stay the night if the freezing temps dipped below for only a few hours. And the silhouette? It probably was nothing sinister, maybe even a tree stump or cactus. If this was a neighbor wanting to help, the person would have kept moving towards me or even waved to get my attention. So perhaps my gut instinct was right. Either way, I felt safer in my new spot.

The episode left me hoping for better surprises. More importantly, I continued to listen to my intuition. While boondocking is generally safe, this doesn't mean you can be oblivious to whatever is happening around you at each site.

Chapter 44
LET ME PUT IT THIS WAY...

This book has detailed how I felt about dealing with the Discovery from April until November of 2018, but the stories don't quite capture the sheer volume of punches I withstood in such a short time. I put together all my invoices and counted the days between each time I had to hand over my credit card. Just take a look at the list below.

Date	Service	Cost	Days in Between
April 19	Alban CAT Power	$2,464.51	
April 19	SimpleTire (four tires)	$1,286.92	12
May 1	Rice Tire Installation	$275.00	14
May 15	Air filter unit replacement	$80.00	7
May 22	Western Branch Diesel (brake repair)	$522.29	1
May 23	Western Branch Diesel (coolant hose)	$628.93	19
June 11	NAPA (two chassis batteries)	$282.18	35
July 16	East Coast Repair (jacks, gaskets, belts, and pulleys)	$4,492.64	8
July 24	REV Group (A/C and heat thermostat)	$148.34	8
July 24	MX awning repair kit	$414.94	

Date	Service	Cost	Days in Between
July 30	MaxxAir Vent and Warranty (Dicor)	$475.00	16
August 15	Michigan CAT Engine Repair	$6,051.91	12
Later	Refund	-$700.00	
August 27	MacAllister CAT (injector harness)	$2,200.26	5

I did not list the optional upgrades, even though I considered them necessary to continue full-time and boondocking. All in all, I averaged only thirteen days in between hits.

No wonder I was off-kilter the entire time.

The longest respite was thirty-five days. I was looking forward to much longer stretches in between maintenance on this Discovery going forward. The engine oil had been changed three times in less than four months. Each change cost approximately $350 so I easily spent $700 I wouldn't have to pay had I fixed all the gaskets at once. But with the $13,000 estimate in the first month, I just couldn't do it.

The labor costs totaled $12,591.79 alone, and the parts amounted to about $10,110.25, not including sales taxes and miscellaneous fees. I did not include every new part I bought.

I must admit that I was surprised; I had expected the labor costs to easily surpass the parts costs. However, we saved some money by doing some of the labor ourselves. Even so, the engine oil unfortunately was still leaking. About three to five quarter-sized drops for every two to three days of sitting still, despite Michigan Cat, MacAllister CAT and J R Diesel Repair's best efforts.

Thankfully, on my second visit to J R Diesel Repair, the last of the leaks was fixed. All the repairs after this one were mostly reasonable in cost, unlike the first eight months of ownership.

Chapter 45
ACCESSIBILITY AND
A DANGEROUS DRIVE

Leveled high off her front end, the Discovery rests at the Crown King dispersed site near Mayer, Arizona for a record eleven days. It was blissful, especially with a good Verizon signal.

My travels took me from Roosevelt Lake, Arizona to one of my favorite sites, the Crown King Road Bureau of Land Management site for eleven days of boondocking (my longest stay anywhere) and then to Prescott Valley and carefully navigating stunning Highway 89A through historic Jerome, nested on a mountain cliff. Other Arizona spots included Sedona, Flagstaff, and Kingman, before I went back to Las Vegas. That was where Stefania joined me for a week, and we discovered a waterfront dispersed site at Boxcar Cove on Lake Mead. We kayaked out in deep and clear waters and jumped from the cliffs.

Stefania flew back home the same day Theo and Brianna flew in. They joined me to Red Rocks Canyon and back to Boxcar Cove before going up to Salt Lake City where we stumbled across a spectacular dispersed site at Petroglyph Gap

The waterfront-dispersed site at Boxcar Cove on Lake Mead, an amazing find after driving two miles on a washboard gravel road. Stefania can be seen setting up a telescope that didn't pan out for us.

near Parowan. We stayed there for a night, and I came back to the same area two years later with Alec and his friend.

When we arrived in the Salt Lake City metro area, I stayed at Stansbury Island for nine nights after driving six miles of washboard gravel road. The site was great but teeming with bug life, much to my dismay. This was one of the times I wished I had a four-by-four vehicle to drive up to the mountaintop.

I loved staying at the Great Salt Lake State Park campground. It was only twenty dollars a night with electric and water hook-ups, and the dump site was about a hundred feet away. I stayed here for laundry days, and usually got a lot done on these days. Sometimes there was a funky smell coming from the Great Salt Lake, yet it was never anything I couldn't handle. I loved watching thunderstorms from a good twenty to forty miles away in the Tooele area and even as far as Ogden, an easy hour's drive away. I had to bring in my slide-outs several times due to high winds and rain.

My next trip took me through Idaho and Oregon where I presented a Deafhood workshop at the legendary National

Association of the Deaf Youth Leadership Camp (YLC) for Deaf high school teens. I initially hoped to head up to Washington and Vancouver, British Columbia, but decided to stay out west in the United States instead because of the plethora of free boondocking sites. I then returned to Arizona.

There, I drove through the scariest, narrow—not even two lanes wide—bumpy gravel road pass along steep mountain edges on the route between Tortilla Flats to Roosevelt Lake. I had already driven on smoothly paved roads twisting through the Tonto National Forest to the Tortilla campground area and the Tortilla Flats Bureau of Land Management dispersed camping sites. I assumed that the paved route would continue all the way to Roosevelt Lake, and I couldn't understand why Google, Apple Maps, and even Waze kept trying to route me the long way around via Payson, adding ninety miles. After the road suddenly turned into a wide gravel road, I understood why.

I did not want to turn back and take the long way back around. Warrick, who was visiting, and I saw a sign saying no trucks longer than forty feet were allowed due to hairpin turns. I took a deep breath and said to Warrick, "Okay, our Discovery is only thirty-eight feet long. We should be fine. Guess we will drive for about thirty miles on this gravel road." I wasn't thrilled, but this route was by far the shortest one and the most direct one.

As we drove on, another car passed us, the driver shaking his head in disbelief at us. I was offended, and I huffed under my breath. "I can drive this rig anywhere if I need to!" I signed to Warrick. "The sign said forty feet long, and we're just under that. So there."

Another car passed us, and the driver was even more animated, shaking his head. My heart sank a bit. The gravel road was wide at this point and a little bumpy, but nothing to worry about. We drove past the scenic lookout parking lot—basically, our last chance to turn around—and I committed ourselves to the route ahead.

As we drove up the mountain pass, another sign warned, "One-lane Road."

Holy hell.

Okay. We already had come this far, so we might as well press on.

That was a heart-stopping mistake.

The road narrowed, with a treacherously steep cliff drop off on my side, and another steep cliff wall on the passenger side. We barely had enough space to pull aside and allow a car or two to pass us. The area had record heavy rains in past few weeks, so the road was channeled with water run-off—all dry by now, but the road was incredibly bumpy, and I had to slow to a crawl to cross many of these mini-ditches.

The twists and turns high in the mountains, with steep cliffs on both sides, were stressful enough. Swearing and saying at one point, "This is nuts. Nuts. Nuts," I ran my hand through my hair, trying to find a semblance of inner peace I needed to thread our huge diesel pusher through a narrow space one could only charitably call a road.

I spotted a bridge all way down at the bottom, and I nearly had a heart attack. What if the bridge wasn't rated for a vehicle as heavy as ours? What if there was a low clearance? We would have had no choice but to drive her all the way back in reverse, which would be an incredibly difficult task, to say the least. I cursed myself for not checking the AllStays app for height or weight restrictions.

Fortunately, the bridge had no restrictions. I blew out a huge sigh of relief. The bridge was still a narrow, one-lane deal, though, so I had to carefully thread her through. Once we got over that bridge, the worst was over. We still had to drive for about twenty-five more miles on gravel before we finally reached Roosevelt Lake.

Never again, I swore to myself.

This route made some of the other hairy highways like 89A seem tame in comparison. However, miles of gravel road kicking up dirt and sand wasn't doing our compromised radiator any favors. After that experience, I became much more selective about on how far we went on gravel roads, and I bought a four-gallon hand pump water sprayer so I could at least wash off the radiator while boondocking.

Another potentially life-threatening situation brought an accessibility issue to the forefront. Riley was with me when the refrigerator gas burner went out, causing a propane leak inside the RV. We had no visual alarms installed. After struggling with what to do, I decided we would stay in a hotel for that night. Though I was able to fix the burner the next day, it was stressful for both of us. After she flew back home, I went into research mode, looking for the best accessibility devices for my RV. It turned out there were none that were a good fit. I even consulted with the Deaf RVers group on Facebook, and they agreed we were stuck without any good options.

There was the SafeAwake system that would flash and shake the bed if it detects the T-3 alarm pattern of a smoke alarm. This device costs $249. Ouch. This device successfully ignores all other sounds that could cause false alarms. However, it also ignores the T-4 alarm pattern from carbon monoxide alarms. So that was out for me.

I decided on a hard-wired BRK smoke and carbon monoxide flasher alarm, but after receiving the unit, reading the tiny four-point fine print in the enclosed folded-up manual, I discovered the flasher wouldn't operate on battery power. The alarm would be worthless if the inverter lost power in the middle of night; my life would be in danger then.

I tried Krown Research's alarm detector and signaler with a flasher and bed shaker, but the units gave off too many false alarms as I drove. I sent it back. Harris Communications (now

Diglo), an online retailer specializing in accessibility devices, suggested I look at Serene Innovations. Apparently, their devices listen for both T-3 and T-4 alarm patterns, but unfortunately, they also listen for other things, resulting in constant false alarms. As frustrating as this could get, it was okay for the time being.

Making safety accessible for all continues to be an area of concern for me. Deaf people used to have to buy an expensive separate box to decode closed captions, costing us about three hundred dollars per box. A decade later, a federal law was passed requiring all television sets to have closed captioning built in. The average cost of the chip needed to decode captions? Ten bucks. Now there are studies and reports on the benefits of increased use of closed captioning among many hearing people.

Universal design can benefit us all. Include Deaf people in the accessibility design process from the get-go, and you will have superior products. By including not only the auditory, but also visual and tactile feedback for all products—which often costs literally pennies on the dollar—and you gain more grateful customers.

Smoke and carbon monoxide alarm manufacturers should be able to easily include LED strobe lights that run on battery power. If my cheap and powerful LED flashlight could literally blind someone using only two AA batteries, manufacturers sure as hell can make battery powered safety devices that include an LED alert.

Sadly, this might not ever happen without legislation.

Chapter 46
THE ROAD TRIP
FROM HELL

JULY 21, 2019

- Mileage: **126,454**
- Previous total: **$33,694.14**
- 2002 Grand Cherokee Jeep 4WD: **$3,500.00**
- Failed AC repair: **$310.00**
- NSA ReadyBrake tow bar system and installation fee: **$2,913.00**
- Radiator for Jeep: **$780.00**
- Water pump for Jeep: **$275.00**
- Wheel seal and brake pads: **$321.34**
- Current total: **$41,793.48**
- Credit score: **599**

We made it.

We pulled into Camp Taloali in *Chicago*, with the 2002 Jeep Grand Cherokee in tow, right into the heart of campers and staff staring at us. The camp was home to the well-loved Youth Leadership Camp, founded fifty years ago by Frank R. Turk, Gary W. Olsen, and the late Donald Padden.

It was touch-and-go for a while. Relief washed over us as we set up for two nights. I was to give a Deafhood workshop the next morning for an hour and half. The workshop went well, and we played host to a scavenger hunt that afternoon. Their clue? "Where did our guest Marvin Miller sleep?" The teams found Riley and me lounging in front of the Discovery, sipping water. We asked them for five things they learned from the workshop (they answered with ease). We then handed them a new clue, and off they went.

After the hunt, I crashed. I went to bed around 5:00 p.m. and slept for an hour and half. I was depleted. Riley worked on her coursework. Sleep came as a welcome relief, though, because for a moment or two, I really believed we wouldn't make the trip to Oregon.

All the pain began when I decided I needed a towable vehicle. I had agreed to give a workshop at the camp on July 22. In early June, I decided I needed a towable vehicle—or as RVers call them, a toad. This meant towing a vehicle four wheels down with the Discovery, without a separate trailer or tow dolly.

The state of Indiana is fussy about registering and titling out of state vehicles. So, buying a car out of state? Forget it. I had to fly back to Indianapolis to do this. I needed to see my doctor for my annual checkup anyway, and I could visit with my family. I could then drive up to Chicago and spend some time with Riley. She and I were to attend her friend's wedding, then she would join me on the drive back west in the new vehicle. We would stop at Chriz Dally's and Nancy Frazier's home in Kansas for one night, then drive to NSA RV Products in Iola, Kansas. They would install the tow baseplate and brake cabling system.

It would be a nice drive all way back to Syracuse, Utah, where my Discovery was waiting at Dan and Stephanie Mathis's home in the suburbs. After hooking up the tow bar and the new vehicle, Riley and I would make our way northwest at a leisurely pace. We would stay a few nights at the "Caribbean of the Rockies" Bear Lake, then boondock for a few nights in Idaho and eastern Oregon, before arriving at the leadership camp.

This plan had us arriving a good couple days early, giving us time to adjust to the environs. I could work on my book as well. It was a great plan, right?

I contacted my friend John Steinberger, who was Deaf and had a dealer license. He had worked on several of my vehicles, and I trusted his judgment on used cars. I told him I was looking for a car, preferably a Jeep Cherokee or Honda CRV, for $3,000. He had one mint red Honda CRV but the asking price was too high at $4,800. I had to take a pass on that one.

Within two weeks, he found a 2002 Jeep Grand Cherokee Limited with four-wheel drive. The Jeep had a transfer case that could shift into neutral, which completely disconnected the axles. This was perfect for four-wheel flat towing behind the Discovery.

"Everything checks out good here. Even the radiator and axles," He texted me. I had told him about my run of bad luck with defective radiators. My previous red Honda had a blown radiator that had to be replaced for $1,000 in Colorado. My Discovery's radiator was in not-great shape, and she struggled to stay cool while uphill climbing. As you might have figured out by now, I was particular about radiators.

"Nope, all looks good. I will have the oil changed out. No leaks. Nothing. I would drive her anywhere in the United States," he texted back.

Okay, great. The day before my flight to Indianapolis, John texted me, "The air conditioning isn't blowing. There is an issue with the blend door or something. I will lower the price by $300. This should take about $200 to fix."

Damn. Air conditioning not working in the middle of July? Not good. John told me he would understand if I didn't take the Jeep. I decided to go and see the Jeep for myself with my daughter Stefania. We took it out for a drive and the Jeep was great. I bought it on the spot for $3,500.

The air conditioner fan was weak. I could feel the cold air coming out, but the blower wasn't working. I texted Riley, telling her that the trip could be rough with a non-working AC. She put on a brave front and said she would be happy to travel anywhere with me, even if we had to keep the windows down, the wind in our hair.

I wasn't convinced. What if we got stuck in traffic, something that Chicago was notorious for? Things could get unbearable, and fast.

I decided to take the Jeep to a shop near Aunt Laura's home. The shop took my Jeep the next day and replaced the actuator and evaporator. They had to take out the entire dashboard and took about a day and half.

The total bill was over $750.

The kicker was that the AC wasn't any better. The mechanic was stumped. But I was livid.

They deducted over $400 from my bill, and I paid $310 for the two new parts. This wasn't what I hoped for. But we had to head to Chicago for a friend's wedding on July 4.

The weather was hot. As long as my Jeep kept moving, things were comfortable inside. Riley and I were thrilled to be together, and we had a great time at the wedding. We visited her parents and hung out with her friends.

The time came for us to head west. Our first stop: Olathe, Kansas for an overnight stay before heading to Iola. I chose the mechanical-based ReadyBrake.com Elite tow bar system to tow the Jeep. It was supposedly more durable and less prone to failures compared to other electronic-based braking solutions. It was also the most affordable system by $500 to $1,000: I paid $1,899, plus $1,014 for the labor to install the baseplate and the braking cable inside the Jeep.

Theo FaceTimed me while I waited for the installation. "Dad, I found a possible solution to the air conditioning problem. The manufacturer misstated how to replace the blower unit in their guidelines. As a result, many mechanics install the unit with the wiring switched the wrong way. This causes the blower to run in reverse."

I was skeptical and said, "Switch the wiring around? No way. Really?"

He was insistent. "Yes, go to the Jeep and look under the glove compartment now."

I was hesitant because my Jeep was literally being worked on at the moment, but Theo insisted. The glove compartment was separate from the front baseplate where Phil was, so it should be okay, I figured.

"Okay, okay, let me get in there." I crouched down, holding my iPhone with Theo looking on via FaceTime. "Where the heck do I even look?"

"You should be able to find wiring leading up to the blower unit." After a couple of false starts, I pulled the wire. Theo then asked me, "Is that the wire with the right color on one side?"

I looked again and confirmed that it was the right one. "Now what?"

He said, "Okay, unplug the wiring." I did. "See the plastic covering the wires? You need to take that clip out and then switch the wire connectors around."

I struggled to release the plastic locking mechanism. I needed something like a tiny screwdriver to insert into the lock and unlock it. I looked around the Jeep and I found a piece of plastic with a sturdy tip. I went back and started fiddling.

"Yes!" I said to Theo. "I got it out! Whoa. The wire connectors fell out... Wait a second," I said, fumbling with the wires; I wanted to be sure I knew which side was which. After a few seconds, I managed to switch the line connectors around. I placed it back into the plastic housing. I felt a satisfying snap as it clicked into place.

"Done. What else do I need to do?"

Theo smiled. "Plug them together and start her up. If this doesn't work, then we need to look at the second item."

I sighed. I hoped it was that simple. Theo looked at me, "So, start her up, Dad."

"I can't. Phil is working on the front end. I'm going to have to wait until they finish with the install."

Theo made a face and groaned, "Come on. Ask!"

I wouldn't do it. I already was in their space—in their shop—so I decided to wait.

Riley and I took a nap in the waiting room in the chairs. After a few hours, the boss Tod Westervelt came to me. He said, "The installation is taking longer than we expected. We won't finish until tomorrow."

Well, crap. We had already booked a nice hotel room with great reviews in El Dorado, Kansas. With the delay, we would have to cancel. We contacted Hotels.com and they were able to change the booking to a local motel.

The local motel wasn't as nice as we would have liked. We had to request another set of sheets because the ones on the bed looked funky. But the bathtub was the best feature, spotless and comfortable. We only had to grin and bear it for one night. At least we were able to walk to downtown Iola for meals.

We woke up tired the next morning from sleeping on an uncomfortable mattress. Frustrated and hangry, I had to go through an overview of the tow bar system with Phil. He also showed me how to run the wiring under my Discovery. He then showed me where to install the brake dash light. I would also have to install the emergency breakaway wiring. So, I still had some work to do on my RV's end. I wished I could have brought the Discovery to them and had them set up everything.

Theo FaceTimed me, "Be sure to have me on FaceTime when you start the Jeep."

"Geez, okay, okay," I said, irritated. "I'm busy. They are showing me a lot of stuff here." Frowning, I motioned to Phil to continue showing me what I would need to do on my end. After a good twenty minutes, we loaded up the tow bar equipment in the Jeep. I called Riley over and we loaded our things in.

My iPhone rang. I answered.

"Well?" Theo's face looking at me, expectantly.

"Geez! I was about to FaceTime you, I swear," I grinned. We got in the Jeep, with our fingers mentally crossed. Would the blower finally blow cold air through the dash? Or would we need to look to see if the blend doors in the vent system were damaged? If that was the case, the fix would have been painful, requiring disassembly of the dashboard.

As Theo looked on nervously, I started it up. The Jeep was humming. "Ready? I'm about to turn on the AC," I said. Theo nodded. I hit the AC button and turned on the fan.

The cold air whooshed at us.

Our jaws dropped. "It works! It fricking works!" I signed to Theo. He broke out in a huge smile.

"This is unbelievable. All that time and expense, and it turns out be the crossed wiring," I said. "How the hell did you learn about this?"

Theo said, "I searched on the Internet for about ten minutes, and I found a discussion thread about this issue. A lot of people were having problems when they had their blower replaced. They didn't realize the unit was running in reverse."

Moral of the story? Mechanics do not know everything, and the Internet can be a valuable resource. Well, sometimes.

With the AC running strong, Riley and I thanked Phil and pulled out. We were starved. Sue, who worked at NSA RV Products, had recommended a local B&B country café, so we headed there. Her recommendation was perfect. The breakfast scramble with hash browns was heavenly. Sue passed away in 2021, and I am forever grateful for her compassion and help with my towing issues.

No longer hangry, we headed for Denver, where we would stay for a night with Rob and Wendy Koch and their kids, Will, Andor, and Sooah. We drove all day in comfort, thanks to Theo and the working AC, and we pulled in at around nine that night. Rob works as a programmer at a local technology company, and he is a certified Amazon Web Services developer. Wendy is a full-time homemaker who homeschools their kids.

Their kids blew us away. Polite, inquisitive, and entertaining, they took care of us nicely. We had a great time with the Kochs. As we said our goodbyes the next morning, we decided to check out the new Rocky Mountain Deaf School campus and take pictures.

The Jeep's radiator leaks—again.

As we returned to our Jeep, I noticed a huge leak right under the hood. What the heck was the leak? I knelt beside the Jeep and touched the fluid, which turned out to be from the coolant.

I groaned. Now what? We found a nearby highly-rated shop, and they quickly determined that I needed a brand-new radiator. What was it with me and radiators?! The estimate was around $780 and would take only a few hours. Wendy retrieved us so we could spend time at their home while we waited.

We weren't sure if we would have to stay another night. We wanted to be in Glenwood Springs and spend some time at Iron Mountain Hot Springs resort. We decided we would press westward as soon as the Jeep was done.

The Jeep was ready a few hours later. Wendy dropped us off and we again said our goodbyes and hugged. The new radiator looked sparkly. I had asked the shop for a professional opinion on how likely the baseplate installation had inadvertently damaged the radiator. The mechanics said they did not think it was a factor.

So I had to eat the cost myself. We made our way to Glenwood Springs, and stayed at a nice hotel for the night. The drive was beautiful and uneventful, except for a couple of times when other vehicles flashed their headlights at us.

"Maybe it is because I am driving carefully and safely," Riley said.

I agreed. "To hell with them. They're all in such a rush."

The next day we luxuriated in the hot springs, and we loved every minute of it. We wanted to stay longer, but we needed to make our way back to Utah and Chicago.

We drove all day through western Colorado and Utah. We stopped in Middle, Utah, to pick up my kayak I had lent to our friends. We then dined at the best restaurant in Salt Lake City—Takashi. The wait was about an hour and we were both tired, but we loved the sushi. If you are in Salt Lake City, stop at Takashi. Seriously. Just go.

After that, we drove to the Mathis home in Syracuse, Utah as the evening turned into a dark night. As I was driving on the interstate, several cars again flashed their headlights at us.

"I'm not driving that slow. What's their problem?" I growled.

As soon as I headed for the exit ramp, a car pulled ahead of us, and someone was pointing at the back of Jeep. I knew something was up. When the light turned red, I parked, got out, and ran to the back.

The taillights and brake lights were completely dark. No wonder people were flashing their headlights at us. They were trying to warn us of the problem. I felt dejected.

I thought NSA RV Products must have screwed up the installation when they put in the bulb and socket kit in our taillights. I sent off an angry email to Tod Westervelt at NSA RV Products. He was puzzled, and pointed out that the socket and bulb kit was wired separately from the Jeep's system.

Hmm. First the radiator leaking in the same area where the Demco baseplate was installed, and now this? I was skeptical. I discovered Tod was right when I later took out the taillights and the lights worked. Apparently, I had loose wiring somewhere in the Jeep. That meant I would have to check the lights from time to time.

On Friday night, we pulled up to *Chicago*, and a sense of relief came over me. We were home again. Unfortunately, this feeling was short-lived.

The next day we spent time visiting with the Mathis family. I held off on doing the wiring underneath the chassis until Sunday morning. The heat was brutal during the daytime. We kept running one of two rooftop air conditioning units to its max, and the unit struggled to keep the interior comfortable during afternoons and evenings. We could only run one unit because we were relying on a 15-amp connection to their house.

Riley and I both were uncomfortable and started to get a bit cranky. Sunday morning, I went outside and installed the hitch. The hitch riser wouldn't fit in my two-inch receiver. There was rust build-up inside. I had to use a screwdriver and hammer to get the rust out. This took some doing, but then the hitch riser went in snugly.

I then attached the ReadyBrake tow bar so I could properly size the wiring for the front dash brake light. I started to snake the wiring through the chassis, but noticed something wrong. The rear right wheel seal had broken on the Discovery, and fluid was leaking on the inside of the tire. Our plans to hook up the Jeep and head out to the Bear Lake campground promptly flew out of the window.

"We can't go anywhere until I schedule an appointment with a local diesel truck shop," I told Riley. She didn't take the news well. Hell, I didn't take the news well, either. We were uncomfortably hot, stuck in the suburbs. Worse, after calling several shops, the earliest we could get in was Wednesday morning, two days later. We had to stick around for three more nights in the brutal heat.

Fluid can be seen leaking out of the passenger rear wheel from a broken seal.

We finally found a way to cope on the last night; we were slow learners, all right? We set up on the Mathis family's driveway with our zero-gravity and lawn chairs, reading our books and drinking water.

On Wednesday morning, Riley drove the Jeep, following me in my RV to dump the overflowing gray tanks at a city RV dump. I rushed through the dumping process because we were already late for the repair shop. Riley looked on since she wasn't familiar with the process, and I did not have time to explain how things worked. I felt bad, and I knew I had to make it up to her. I felt we were in a hurry-up-and-wait mode, which frustrated the hell out of me.

We made it to Utah Truck and Trailer shop, and they quickly confirmed that my wheel seal had broken and contaminated the brake shoes, which had to be replaced. We went food shopping and had a sushi lunch in the meantime. They texted me that our RV was ready. We headed back, and I made yet another rookie mistake.

It was afternoon. The sun was beating down on us. I went ahead and hooked up the Jeep to the tow bar and adjusted the brake line with two- to three-inch slack, as instructed. This took some doing, adjusting the nuts and bolts repeatedly. The

All set! The brake line had the required two- to three-inch slack. The sun brutal, we were ready to go. But there was a problem: the tow bar arms weren't fully extended…

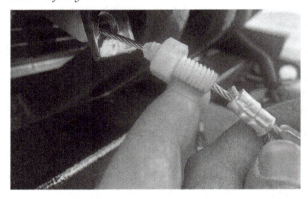

The unfortunate result of forgetting to fully extend the tow bar arms before installing the brake cable line.

sun and the heat were brutal. I was rushing through the process without double-checking the instruction manual. When I finished, I said, "Everything looks good. Let me pull the RV forward to lock in the telescoping arms of the tow bar."

It was only when I pulled forward that I realized I had screwed up. When the tow bar was fully extended, the brake line snapped tight, breaking the plastic tube connector right under the Jeep. This made extension and retraction of the brake line much more difficult.

I frantically readjusted the brake line, which took me about ten minutes of fumbling around with tools. The black Dewalt tool set burned in my hands because the sun was beating down on it. I had to find shade for the tool set while I worked on the brake line.

"I think we are good now. Let's tow her forward and see how it works," I tentatively said to Riley. She would drive *Chicago* forward a few hundred feet so I could assess whether the towing set up was done properly.

I shifted the four-by-four wheel transfer case and transmission into neutral. Riley then pulled the Jeep forward, and the Jeep complied. Everything looked good. I wasn't sure if the Jeep was truly towable, so I looked at the Jeep manual. After searching the pages for a good while, I realized the entire second half of the manual was simply gone. And the RV towing instructions were in the second half.

I groaned. "I gotta call Jeep and get the RV towing instructions," I said to Riley. I had her pull around on the street and park there. I then called the Jeep customer service line. After ten minutes, the representative apologized and said they didn't have access to manuals older than 2011; my Jeep was a 2002. They gave me a number to a company that sold manuals. When I called the company, they apologized, saying that they only sold printed copy of manuals. They didn't have electronic access to them.

"I'm so ready to break something," I growled to Riley. She was sympathetic and supportive, but I just wanted things to go right or at least easy for once.

Riley suggested we look for a local Jeep dealership. "Maybe they could help you out?"

Good idea.

We towed the Jeep to Heritage Jeep in Brigham City, about a sixteen-mile drive. Our Discovery did seem to struggle in towing the Jeep. As soon as we pulled in the dealership, we got out and we both smelled brake burn on the Jeep.

"Oh no, it looks like we pulled her with the brakes stuck in place," I said to Riley. A salesperson came out and he helped us find the missing pages of manual somewhere in his dealership computer network. The instructions clearly were different from what I did. The instructions stated that I had to leave the transmission in park, rather than neutral. I worried that I might have damaged the axles or transmission, but the procedure was in place to double check that the driveshaft was indeed completely disconnected when I placed the transfer case in neutral.

Whew.

The salesperson helped me adjust the tow brake line, and then I drove the RV while towing the Jeep around the parking lot. He confirmed that the brakes were disengaged. With an electronic copy of the three missing pages of the manual safely stored in my phone, we thanked him for his help and were, at long last, on our way to Bear Lake.

Climbing through the mountain pass between Brigham City and the Cache Valley, home of Logan, Utah proved a little tricky because *Chicago*'s radiator was not in the best shape. The temperature did climb, and we had to pull over for a little bit. I checked the Jeep again, and everything seemed okay. No burning smells this time.

Finally, as we pulled into Logan, I told Riley that I thought it was a good idea to stop for a night at a local Walmart store before we headed over the mountains to Bear Lake. I wanted to be sure that Jeep's brakes were working properly.

And they were—sort of. I wasn't quite sure if the brakes were fully disengaged after braking. I felt that the kink in the brake cabling prevented full retraction.

In the morning, after checking everything around the RV, we headed out to fill up on liquid propane, then backtracked a few miles back to the Maverik gas station for its free RV dump station. As soon as we began the dumping process, I noticed a large fluid leak underneath the Jeep.

"Shit. There's another leak under the Jeep!" I said to Riley. She gave me an exasperated look. I checked the fluid and the location of the leak. I FaceTimed Theo, "Man, another hit here… a leak."

Theo directed my iPhone to point at certain parts of the engine and said, "I got a good feeling that it's the water pump."

Shit. I Googled for highly rated auto mechanic shops, and it turned out there was a place right across from Maverik's. We made our way across, and within minutes, the mechanic confirmed Theo's diagnosis. The water pump had to be replaced, which set me back a couple of hours wait and $225.

As we waited, I could see Riley was upset. "Is this really what the RV life is all about? Being stuck at repair shops and waiting?" she asked.

"Honestly, no. This has been a tough string of problems. I have had months of problem-free traveling and relaxation. I want you to have a taste of that," I said.

"The last time I was with you, the refrigerator gas leaked inside the RV, and we had to cut our stay short and ended up in a hotel. Now this series of problems, stuck in waiting rooms in service shops instead of being in nature. I just feel like *Chicago* doesn't like me," she said.

Ouch. She was right, though; the hits kept on coming. The last time we had a peaceful time together was in December 2018 in Las Vegas. I hadn't mastered boondocking at that time, so we stayed at a campground. We enjoyed an entire week of sightseeing and relaxing in nature without any hassle.

"We will get through this, and we will make it to Bear Lake. We will enjoy nature soon," I reassured her, desperate to show Riley that RV life could be amazing.

With the repair done, we hooked the Jeep to *Chicago* and after checking the tow bars were locked in place, the axle in neutral, the transmission in park, it appeared all was good. I pulled out of the auto shop onto the state highway, and—

"What the hell?!"

My steering wheel was turned halfway to the left, as if the wheels had been knocked out of alignment.

There were some big potholes near the auto repair shop, so I thought maybe my Discovery had hit one and threw off the alignment. I pulled over to the shoulder and checked the front wheels. Everything looked fine.

I got Theo on FaceTime and yelled, "Now the steering wheel is way off! I must fight it in order to keep it straight! Damn. Damn it! Yet another repair issue!" Riley was horrified at my outburst but tried her best to comfort me.

I found a nearby diesel truck repair shop about two miles away. I hopped back in and headed there, the steering wheel still wildly out of whack. As I drove, angry and frustrated, two women in a school bus pulled up alongside, frantically waving us down.

"Now what?!" I pulled over again. They hopped out of the bus and started talking. I told them I was Deaf, and they pointed to the Jeep.

What? The Jeep? I walked to the front of Jeep, and there it was—the wheels had locked up and were slightly pointed to the left. *Chicago* had dragged the Jeep for a couple of miles. Riley talked to the women, and they told her, "We could hear the tires screaming all the way. It was horrifying."

I bent over and broke down in tears. The front tires were badly damaged. I hadn't realized that the ignition key needed to be in the proper unlocked position. I had accidentally left it in the locked and off position, which locked up the steering wheel.

Riley suggested, "Maybe that's why the steering wheel was way off."

We disconnected the Jeep and inspected the tires. They were intact enough to drive, and sure enough, the steering wheel had returned to its normal position.

I figured there was no need to stop at the diesel truck shop. I drove *Chicago*, and Riley followed me in the Jeep to Discount

Tire: Jeep had a road hazard warranty on the tires so they would replace them at a lower cost for me.

It turned out that the Discount Tire shop in Logan wasn't a part of the national chain. Their best offer was to replace both front tires for $166 each. Yikes, no. I despaired for a couple of minutes. Then I remembered that I had a full-sized spare tire in the back. They easily switched the front right tire with the spare, since the left front tire was not as badly damaged as the right one. We were good for at least a

The Jeep's tire treads were obliterated. There was no way we could tow her any further.

couple of thousand miles, at least until we got to Oregon. They didn't even charge me, and for that I was grateful.

Happier and hungry, we parked at a nearby Dollar Tree to eat lunch and do some shopping before we went up into the mountains to Bear Lake. I pulled into the parking lot, taking up five parking spaces. Riley drove the Jeep and pulled up behind me, and at the last minute, she pulled the Jeep around to park in front of me.

I parked *Chicago*. Sighing—I was frazzled from the recent chain of events of that day—I headed to the refrigerator, thinking about what to have for lunch.

Wait a minute. Are we moving? I sensed a gentle swaying motion. I looked out and saw the parking lot moving forward through the window.

What the hell? The situation dawned on me. I hadn't set the parking brake, and *Chicago* was sliding backwards in the parking lot!

I darted to the front and slammed the brakes; she screeched to a halt. I was rattled.

Riley got out of the Jeep, frantically waving, "Is everything okay?"

She was much further away from me now. There was nobody behind the RV, much to our relief. "Shit. That could have been catastrophic," I said.

"Yes, I was planning to park behind you, but for some reason, I decided to park in front of you. I'm so glad I did," Riley said.

Oh, yes. That makes two of us.

I had to sit down. Riley held me. I kept shaking my head, thinking, *what if we hit a car or worse yet, someone walking by?*

As we had dinner, I began to calm down. After shopping at the Dollar Tree, I drove as Riley followed behind in the Jeep into the Bear Lake valley. The view was striking, finally lifting our spirits. We were finally getting back to nature. We found a state park campground but no campground host. As we walked around the campground, we met a lady walking down the gravel road.

"Are you the campground host?" I asked using Cardzilla.

She smiled and shook her head, before speaking into my phone using the speech-to-text feature, "I don't know where they are. I had reserved all those sites for a family reunion, but I canceled the top-level sites as we didn't need them. They are available but they didn't bother to free them up."

Score! I thanked the lady, and we went ahead and set up in one of the empty sites. I paid for the campsite and placed the envelope in the box.

We brought over our folding chairs right by the water and with beers in our hands, we watched the sunset. Finally, after a few weeks of hell, we were finally getting to bask in nature, our feet and legs soaking in the water.

The next morning, Riley wanted to go out kayaking. I was preparing the RV for check out, and I stopped myself. I said, "You know what? Who cares if we check out late? Let's go kayaking."

It was simply sublime: the serene gliding over the calm waters. The shades of blue getting deeper as we paddled further away from the shore. The picturesque expanse around us. Riley leaned back into me, and I held her. We loved every minute of it.

When we finally left, we headed north following Google Maps for the most direct route. I reacted a bit too late when we ended up on a gravel road. I turned to Riley and said, "I've driven her for more than thirty miles on a gravel road and I swore I would never do it again. It's way too slow and it clogs up the radiator."

The problem was that I couldn't just back her up with the Jeep in tow. I tried, and the Discovery rebelled, turning all pear-shaped. We had to disconnect the Jeep because there wasn't enough room to turn around. Riley drove the Jeep as I backed up *Chicago* to the blacktop portion. We turned westward where the blacktop continued edging the northern end of Bear Lake onto the other side. Next, we hitched the Jeep back up and drove for hours until we reached a Flying J Plaza off Interstate 15 in McCammon, Idaho.

I pulled into the left turn lane, waiting to turn into the plaza. The driveway entrance was scratched up with deep grooves, the angle too steep. *That doesn't look too good*, I thought. I went ahead anyway, forgetting about the newly-installed six-inch drop hitch adapter with the tow bar. Sure enough, there was a loud scrape as we continued.

"Did you feel that?" Riley asked.

"Crap, yes. The hitch…" I said.

As soon as we parked her, I ran out to the back. The tow bar was badly scratched on the bottom, and the trailer light wiring was destroyed because I had snaked the cable on the underside. We had to get new trailer light wiring. The Flying J store didn't have it in stock, but a Harbor Freight in Pocatello, Idaho did. We pulled out of their lot from a different exit.

I sent a mental memo to Flying J: You serve trucks, RVs, buses, and more, and your entrance is something you need to fix soon. However, I also wished I didn't need a six-inch drop adapter. This would make driving on boondocking sites a bit more challenging.

After Harbor Freight I continued to worry about the Jeep wheel running hot. I FaceTimed Theo and shared, "I'm concerned about the brake lines breaking and dragging on the brakes. I am not 100 percent sure, though. The wheels are hot."

Theo nodded. "I've been looking that up, and you know what? You can just disengage the brake line from the tow bar. The RV has plenty of stopping power to handle the Jeep, according to many discussions on the forums."

"Are you sure?" I asked.

"Dad, the PVC cabling into the Jeep is broken and bent, causing all the friction. Forget it for now until we replace that cabling and it runs properly, then we can reattach the brakes."

I was skeptical. "But what about the damage to the brakes right now? I'm thinking of taking her to the Les Schwab tire center and have them check for free."

Theo agreed. Riley groaned at the idea of making yet another service stop, but it had to be done. After a night at the rest area on Interstate 84 west of Pocatello, we stopped in Rupert. The brakes checked out okay, but they warned me about the tire damage from dragging the Jeep.

The wheels still ran hot so I removed the brake line. The wheels cooled off considerably after that. It became clear that the tow bar brake line had been dragging on the brake pedal for quite a while. This meant the brakes would have to be replaced. They needed to be replaced anyway because the brakes pulsated when I pushed down on the brake—which meant all four rotors would have to go as well as the pads.

As I was ready to pull out of the gas station lot, I noticed that the angle of entrance was somewhat steep. Riley was in the bathroom, and I thought I could carefully pull *Chicago* onto the road. The front wheels gently shifted sideways as I pulled her out. Not too bad. I pulled her further out on the road, turning left. As soon as the rear axle hit the bump, the RV rocked hard sideways. *Uh-oh. I hope Riley is okay back there.*

Nope. She came out crying in pain. She had banged her head on the wall while getting up at the wrong moment. I was dejected. Riley was already fed up with *Chicago* and the Jeep after all the mechanical problems, and now I did this?

I fumed for a while during the drive westward towards Oregon. I turned to Riley and apologized for rushing to leave, saying I should have waited until she was safely seated.

She looked at me, "You know… Both *Chicago* and the Jeep kept giving us hell day after day. Maybe we should call the Jeep Hellfire."

I broke out in a wide grin. "Yeah, I like that. *Chicago* and *Hellfire*. Yes, let's make that official."

After an overnight stop at a nice rest area in Oregon, we made our way to Youth Leadership Camp without any further problems. The wheels remained cool. The drive along the Columbia River was calming.

We had made it. With *Chicago* and *Hellfire*.

Still, we were emotionally spent from all the hits we took in just sixteen days.

A bright spot was that the engine leak had finally stopped. Earlier in May 2019, J R Diesel Repair in Salt Lake City replaced an oil sensor O ring and that apparently was the fix that did the trick. They also replaced the air cleaner, the rusted-out metal pipe that Theo and Stefania helped clean out last year and replaced brake drums and shoes on the front passenger wheel. The final bill? $540. This was one of the rare times when I was pleasantly surprised by such a reasonable repair cost.

Chapter 47
THE WORLD CHANGES

FEBRUARY 2022

- Mileage: **150,218**
- Previous total: **$41,793.48**
- Xantrex 458 inverter/charger: **$1,576.88**
- Domestic toilet 510: **$312.76**
- MCD shades from Bontrager's RV Surplus: **$450.00**
- Magnum MS2812 2800W pure sine wave inverter (I sold the Xantrex 458): **$1,480.27**
- First attempt at replacement exhaust and manifold gaskets: **$423.47**
- Second attempt at replacement exhaust and manifold gaskets: **$150.00**
- Rear brake shoes, slack adjusters, brake chambers, axle differential fluid drainage and replacement: **$2,289.48**
- Yokohama front tires replacement: **$1,300.00**
- Radiator and charged air cooler, idle pulley, water pump, hoses, thermostats, fan belt, etc.: **$7,975.25**
- Borg Warner turbo and third attempt at exhaust manifold, and gaskets (third time's a charm): **$1,876.00**
- Koni FSD shocks for front/rear: **$665.11**
- Final total (not including other maintenance/repair costs): **$60,292.70**
- Credit score: **595**

n mid-January 2020, I began to take notice of warnings put out by Chris Martenson of www.peakprosperity.com about a new virus in Wuhan, China.

My kids and I had traveled to Austin, Texas, where Stefania, Alec and Warrick lived, from the Sky Valley Resort in Desert Hot Springs, California. Back in California, we had to deal with a broken inverter, damaged by a power pedestal that was not grounded at all and had 60-amp breakers instead of the usual 50. I found a brand-new, factory OEM Xantrex 458 single in, dual output inverter for the Discovery from Sunbird RV in the metro Palm Springs area, and had it installed on New Year's Eve.

I tried to get Sky Valley Resort to reimburse me for this damage, but they refused. They insisted that there was no evidence that it was their fault despite a statement from an RV mobile technician pointing to the pedestal problem.

Even so, I love Sky Valley Resort and I highly recommend them for their pristine hot springs pools and tubs. The resort is clean and well-kept. Just be sure to check the power pedestal for proper grounding and ensure 50-amp breakers are in place.

Having done some research, I wanted to go with a Magnum MS2812 inverter or an MS2012 dual output unit. The Magnum model was pure sine wave, while the Xantrex 458 was a modified sine wave. On a modified sine wave inverter, sensitive electronics may not work properly. But I was told by a customer service agent at Xantrex that I absolutely had to use the original 458, nothing else.

The agent was wrong. We should have gone with the Magnum. In our case, it would make a life-saving difference by enabling us to install a wired visual strobe smoke and carbon monoxide alarm. So, two months later, we replaced the Xantrex with Magnum following the recommendation of Chris Bayus from M&M RV Electronics in Ohio City, Ohio.

I made a mistake, though. To save about four hundred dollars, I ordered the inverter via Amazon rather than through

M&M RV Electronics. By doing so, I lost the tech support I would have from M&M. It was a struggle, but Alec and I managed to install the new inverter ourselves. We literally shoehorned that damn thing inside the battery compartment.

Theo and I also replaced the failing AGM batteries with two BattleBorn 100-amp hour LiFePo4 ones in February. We then installed the lithium isolation manager unit to replace the older Trombetta relay.

Our Discovery guardian angel, Al, came through with the workaround of adding a relay to make the unit operate properly, switching on and off to prevent engine alternator burn out.

We were mooch-docking on our friend's driveway when the virus I'd heard about arrived in the United States and the shutdowns began. We stayed in place for a few months in Austin, wondering when it would be safe to travel again and if this COVID-19 virus was temporary or permanent.

It wasn't until late May 2020 that I felt it was safe to travel to Indiana before going to my father's place in Roscommon, Michigan for a second round of renovations and maintenance on the Discovery. By this time, the Discovery's Onan Generator one-thousand-hour maintenance was due, and I needed to do extensive maintenance work, including fixing the main slide-out leaks, taking out the generator from underneath, and replacing the drive belt, coolant hoses, and a couple of other things.

Theo and I also replaced the furnace blower motor, fan, and heating element. On top of that, we replaced the frayed shore power cord with a brand new one from Bontrager's Surplus store in White Pigeon, Michigan. I replaced the worn-down Irvine double blinds with vastly superior MCD double shades, also available in limited sizes at Bontragers. All but four windows on the main slide-out were swapped out, and wow, what a difference—making for an incredibly dark bedroom.

Shortly after we pulled in at my father's, we took the RV to Michigan CAT again. They found her exhaust manifold was leaking badly and quoted us $3,700. I was nearing the maximum of my credit line once again, so I didn't want to spend that much, especially because the radiator and quite possibly the charged air cooler would need attention soon.

Theo shook his head. "No, we will do it ourselves."

So, we did. To be precise, Theo did it. With $400-plus in parts, Theo disassembled the turbo, which checked out just fine, and replaced the manifold gaskets all in an afternoon. He had blown me away with his ingenuity once again.

We also were successful in dropping the generator using Harbor Freight's one-hundred-dollar motorcycle lift. We even painted and primed the rusted areas.

However, odd electrical issues cropped up after we put the generator back in. Sometimes, when the generator shut off, the inverter would also shut down. This hadn't happened often enough to warrant us digging further to track the problem yet, and the problem eventually went away. Gremlins, probably. Much later, I learned from Al we were supposed to shut down our coach's electrical system and disconnect house batteries first before removing the generator. *Oh.* That made sense. Oops.

The engine oil analysis came back after I successfully changed the oil myself for the first time, and it was easier than I thought. But during that process, I discovered that we had a fuel filter in addition to the fuel/water separator filter—something we didn't change for over two years. I never knew about this filter, and none of the oil change places at RV shops alerted me to the fact we needed to change the fuel filter with every oil change. As a result, the oil analysis showed significant number of metals, pointing to a possible scuffing in the pistons.

I nearly gave up at one point on trying to continue with the RV life. Too many hits kept on coming, as my credit card balances continued to rise. The constant worry was getting to me. Yet deep down inside me, I knew I wasn't ready to let go of this wonderful life.

I sat down with myself, facing the anxieties that threatened to overwhelm me. I asked myself why I was traveling and living full-time in our Discovery. What was I doing these past two and half years? Was it because I wanted to be outdoors? Not really, although I certainly enjoyed going out for a hike from time to time. Was it because I wanted to learn new skills such as mountain climbing or kayaking? No. Did I do this to join many of the Deaf community on their camping trips and RV gatherings? No.

Then why did I love boondocking off-grid for weeks, absorbing invigorating scenery through my expansive windows from my office desk and chair? Spending my time writing. Just being.

Solitude. I realized I had been chasing solitude all this time. But why?

I grew up as an only child. I often took out my Honda 70cc three-wheeler and spent hours and hours riding around my grandparents' farm, dreaming while riding with constant, comforting vibrations underneath my feet and hands and feeling the wind in my hair. I loved my time alone. Having four children—though they are out-of-this-world amazing kids who I love very, very much—I struggled to find pockets of peace and quiet here and there for years. Especially being a single father for long stretches of time... I so badly needed this solitude.

I found that with my Discovery, but the solitude came and went due to my busy schedule flying out and teaching Deafhood classes, and with my kids joining me from time to time. Solitude came in between those times, and it took me days to recover, to regain the energy I gave away teaching or being with my kids and my friends. Yet I was sick of being constantly bombarded with repairs and unexpected costs. It was like a never-ending game of whack-a-mole.

I knew something had to change. Could I flick a magic wand and make my RV problems go away? No. What could I change? Over time, I came to realize that the only thing I had control over was… myself.

After my time with my father and my stepmother in February, I stayed for a while with Aunt Laura in Indianapolis. She offered me to stay with her and her roommate, Dari, on a permanent basis. I gratefully told her I appreciated the offer, but I wasn't sure what I wanted to do next.

If I were to continue my travels and living full time in the Discovery, I had to change my mindset and my attitude. But how? I looked around for guidance, and I found one approach that helped me tremendously: *Zero Limits* by Joe Vitale. In his book, he refers to the Hawaiian practice of *ho'oponopono* and shares the story of a psychologist who apparently cured a wing filled with criminally insane patients without ever holding one-on-one sessions with them. The psychologist sat down with each patient's folder, reviewing their history and information. He then would say, "I love you. I am sorry. Please forgive me. Thank you." And he would repeat that process as often as he could. Over the course of few months, the patients began doing better. The staff turnovers reduced to the point of having too much staff. All except two patients were released.

The point of *ho'oponopono* is the idea that the problems and the challenges you see in your life reflects what is happening inside of yourself. By doing the "I am sorry. Please forgive me. I love you. Thank you," exercise, Vitale was taking responsibility for what was happening in front of him and cleansing his spirit/being as well as everyone else's. As a result, the problems around you fade away. Each one of us reacts from a place of memory—whether it's from childhood upbringing or something that happened in the past, we react with frustration, anger, and pain.

As soon as I began to practice this, I found greater inner peace. I found serenity. I began seeing the Discovery in a new light, full of gratitude. I became even more grateful for the solitude, the sights, the time to recover and to write.

I found myself less fearful. Less anxious.

The ancient practice of *ho'oponopono* says when we cleanse, it is like cleaning a cluttered desktop screen full of old and no longer useful files. We are creating room. A space for inspiration. Truth be told, I find myself inspired more often. Bright ideas, insights and actions pop up more and more as I practice cleansing.

I held on to this book I wrote for over a year after I finished, afraid of… exactly what? I wasn't sure. I didn't want to begin the editing and publishing process. But by practicing *ho'oponopono*, I released my fears and anxieties about taking the next step with this book.

As a result, you now have this book in your hands.

Taking responsibility for what happens inside me and altering my perception of the world has made a huge difference for me. As I write this, I am on a site at Isla Blanca RV Park in South Padre Island, Texas, the Discovery swaying in high winds and the slide topper flapping noisily at times. Alec and Stefania are with me, and we are about to witness a history-making event tomorrow: the first flight of Starship Serial Number 8 by SpaceX. We can see the rocket standing on the launchpad across the bay.

I am living a rich, abundant life right now. And I am grateful for that.

Read Vitale's book, and whatever other book you feel is valuable. Read the scriptures. Read the classic literature. The wisdom is in there, yours for taking and sharing. More importantly, go out there and see the world for yourself. I love books, photos and videos, but they can only do so much. *Be there. Be present.*

OCTOBER 2020

A year later as I write this, my life has changed for the better... dramatically. SpaceX successfully launched and stuck the landing with the Starship SN15, and the company managed to stack the full booster with Starship SN20 on top in preparation for its maiden orbital voyage later this year. The pandemic peaked with the Delta variant and then with Omicron. We'll see where the pandemic takes us next.

Chicago is at her strongest ever. A few months ago, Alec and his friend Max Skjeveland met up with me at the Grand Canyon south entrance, and we traveled together for a few months working our way up to Salt Lake City. I wanted José Gutierrez of J R Diesel Repair to replace her radiator and charged air cooler because he did honest work, and his prices were fair. On the way there, I saw my son transformed by the experience of setting out on his own in a Toyota Prius bought from Raychelle Harris (the same one who I went to that not-so-haunted house with). Alec and Max camped as they made their way from Indiana to Texas then to New Mexico and Arizona. Alec matured quickly during this time and became more helpful, more considerate, and had a sense of adventure I hadn't seen before. He did not complete high school, but he embarked on this journey, he took the GED test without studying much and passed on his first try. Currently, he's a freshman at Gallaudet University and considering majoring in accounting. I am so proud of Alec.

I found myself thoroughly enjoying my time with a renewed Alec and his friends. But as always, during the trip to Salt Lake City, we experienced setbacks. The brakes were not working well, and the RV would slide back slowly if parked on sloped surfaces. I knew this had to be addressed. I figured maybe she needed new pads, which would cost a few hundred dollars at least. The shops in St. George, Utah were busy. I found one on the way in a small town near Parowan, Utah called RoadRunner

Truck Repair service. Mick, an energetic, grandfatherly figure agreed to work on the Discovery.

It turned out she needed more than just pads. Both wheel seals were leaking on the rear axles. The pads were contaminated. The joints were badly rusted. The differential axle fluid was low, most likely causing the wheel seals to break often. We stayed at his shop for the weekend as Mick worked nonstop for two days. I had to drive from Parowan to St. George to pick up brake parts for him to finish the job. The total repair bill was $2,250. Yet I was grateful because I knew Mick had given me a break by not charging me the weekend surcharge. And he worked incredibly hard throughout our entire stay. I even gave him Clif energy bars to snack on and water as he went full-on repairing the Discovery.

A word of advice based on my hard lessons learned: Don't release the parking brake while the RV is raised off her rear tires on her own leveling jacks. Mick had asked me to do that, forgetting that if you release the parking brakes, the leveling jacks will automatically retract. We were terrified when our Discovery juddered and tilted over precipitously, nearly hitting the wall. Mick scrambled out from under the exposed rear axle just in time. The cargo bay compartments were bent but Mick helped us straighten them out.

All was good after that. I was just thankful nothing bad happened. I asked him, as we settled the bill, how long he had been a diesel truck mechanic.

"Since I was seventeen years old." Wow. I was in awe of his knowledge and skills. If you ever need service in that area, go to him. You won't regret it.

MAY 2021

We pulled up at J R Diesel Repair in Salt Lake City in late May 2021. It was finally time for us to replace what was a huge impediment to *Chicago*'s performance: the radiator and charged air cooler. I shared this with the Discovery Owner's Group on June 6, 2021:

Hi,

I thought I would share what has been happening with my beloved *Chicago*, our Discovery 37U (2001.5). When we first bought her three years ago, the inspector who was NOT NRVIA certified inspected her for $450. He texted me after I asked him about how serious the rust was. His reply: "Not severe. It's from a northern state, normal."

Well, not.

One mechanic told me to return her. I could not. It was too late. Even Alan Spence of Michigan CAT showed me a million-mile truck they were overhauling, and he turned to me, "That truck has way, way less rust than yours."

The radiator was already in bad shape from the first day we bought her. Lots of busted fins and bent ones. We tried our best to wash and clean her—at first after three cycles of washing, we got bubbles all around. But never again after that. Only in parts here and there. Her performance was fast degrading. Turbo psi— after we installed VMSPC last March—showed 4 to 17 psi at its highest. Black smoke was coming out every time we accelerated or went uphill. From St. George, Utah to Cedar City, the uphill portion on I-15 was so challenging for *Chicago*. We had to pull her over three times to let her cool down on the shoulder.

It was time to replace them. Thankfully, somehow my crypto investments began to pay off and I was able to get a loan against them to pay off a small portion of my credit card debt—I knew the only shop I would trust with this work was J R Diesel Repair in South Salt Lake City. José Gutierrez came through for me twice in the past three years, finally fixing her oil leaks and coming well under my feared estimates. A pleasant surprise that I still can't find anywhere else, except for EDCO Welding & Truck Repair in Indianapolis.

So, we brought her to the shop, thinking maybe it'll take a week. I was hoping that our CAC could be taken out and repaired for a few hundred dollars.

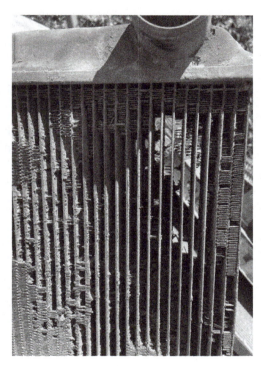

Well, as of today, our Chicago has been in shop for two weeks. Last Friday, José showed us our radiator which was...

Let's put it this way—we must have had a legion of guardian angels holding her together these past three years. José says the radiator was the worst he ever saw in his life, and he has been working in truck repair for a long time. He showed us other radiators that were replaced, and wow, they were practically pristine in comparison.

CAC was completely shot. José told me there was no way it could be repaired. He found a new one in Illinois for $1,450, and we had to wait for it to arrive.

As José dove into the backend further, he texted me back from his ancient flip phone: "Looking at your fan belt idler pulley is due for replace...and your a/c compressor is no good the clutch bearing is dry am looking for compressor I will text you in one hour."

Uh-oh. I had asked him to look at everything on the back end. And to replace thermostats, water pump (turned out my Discovery had the wrong model of water pump all along!), and anything else that needed replacing including the steel tube from turbo to CAC unit—he is having that custom made as well.

"Hi, reporting an update. I found an AC compressor in Phoenix AZ... will be here Monday if you want to come and I walk you through or text me reason to replace compressor cause pulley about to break."

So, we had to stay in the hotel a bit longer. Now aiming for—realistically—a Tuesday completion. We also bought four Koni FSD shocks and asked José to replace them and to flush the steering fluid and fill with new ones as well. And he has been unable to give me an estimate—I'm praying and hoping for something less than an $8,000 job right now. It could be likely more, but with José, I am hopeful.

José says he had to use torch to cut through many rusted bolts—they kept rounding off—then drill them out. The rust is just unimaginably bad. So, Mr. Inspector... (@#$%& you, sir.) Even the fan belt drive mount had one bolt broken in half. José drilled that out and its ready for new bolt.

If I had taken her to a Freightliner or CAT shop for this work, I would be in so much trouble.

Yet, I have learned so much and grown so much—I'm forty-nine years old—and I'm just grateful that I can pay for this work, and with my books soon to be published, I am confident things will work out fine. In the end, I am at peace, and I am excited to have her back soon, in better shape than ever. The house frames are rusted through in places, and one day, I will need to take her to a body shop and replace those frame pieces to ensure her house frame does not bend too much while leveling or traveling down the road.

And more importantly, all your support and help has been incredibly valuable. Thank you.

I will keep you updated on the final cost and how she drives after—I never had her at full strength before. José says the CAT 3126b engine is still running strong. But if I had not brought her in now, the engine would have been in trouble shortly down the road. It simply did not have enough air coming in.

Up next after earnings from the book sales: Bigger lithium battery (800+ amp hour EVE battery packs), 3000-watt sliding out solar panels on rooftop (youtu.be/cM5s4F-7AOk) and two mini-split AC/heat units. Then I will be able to boondock in high heat with ease.

Also, any advice in protecting the new radiator and CAC going forward? I boondock a lot, which means driving her over dirt and gravel roads often. I saw this metal screen installed. I'm thinking of doing this: www.irv2.com/forums/f258/protecting-a-rear-radiator-dp-317164.html

By the way, if one of my books ever hit the New York Times best-selling list, I'm looking at a Newell Coach (one can always dream big!) or a good Newmar side radiator coach. But we will be keeping our beloved Discovery for my family members and friends to join me from time to time, or even find a piece of land and set her up for HipCamp or Airbnb.

With gratitude,
Marvin

The first response came in from Kerry Pinkerton: "WOW! That radiator is beyond shot. WAY beyond."

Clay chimed in, "Was the coach, or at least the rear end, under water? I'll go with Kerry but add HOLY WOW! That much corrosion on so much begs the question, what caused this."

I was happy to see a reply from Bruce Plumb:

Marvin,

First, shame on that inspector.

If you get all of that done for $8K you have done well! Owning one of these things is not for the faint-hearted. Hopefully you get the book published and it does well!

I am in agreement with Clay and Kerry, WOW!

In the upper Midwest they use a lot of salt (other corrosive chemicals?) on the roads in the winter. When a vehicle is used frequently, such as several times during the winter season, it further accelerates the corrosion. Automobiles have taken extensive steps to deal with this and HAVE made improvement, but you still see a lot of "rust buckets" in that region. Much harder to accomplish on a DP. I suspect this is the core problem. Unlike an over the road truck with the radiator in the front, a diesel pusher has an amazing amount of turbulence in the area of the rear of the motor home. First the rear tires kick up a constant mist of water and anything contained therein, and a lot of this gets sucked up by the fan and pushed through the radiator.

Hopefully once you get this BIG (and expensive) issue corrected, you can systematically, starting with the worst remaining area, start cleaning, treating, and repainting the other metal areas. Time-consuming but possible.

Just like my $30K engine last year, I hated it happened to me. While I hated spending $30K in that manner, it did not ruin us. The frustration part is there was nothing I could have done, just luck of the draw. When you pay the bill and get back on the road, you WILL feel good about having taken care of those items. I feel that way about my new engine.

BTW, when we bought our 2003 D in 2008 and paid cash (sold a quarter of land), it was a real financial stretch. I hated turning an appreciating asset into one that depreciates. I immediately started doing the maintenance and in so doing was learning about filter and fluid changes and frequencies. I spoke both with CAT and Allison dealers. While doing so I asked them what the cost would be to replace and engine and tranny. I was appalled at the answers. Nearly $7,000 on the Allison and close to $20K on the engine! This was nearly unbelievable to me. I wrote the following next to each of these numbers: TAKE CARE OF IT!!!

Keep us posted.

Bruce and Nancy Plumb (aka Mrs. Plumb). Est. 1972

A few days later, I posted an update:

After two and a half weeks—the original estimate was three or four days—I finally got the beloved Discovery back.

New radiator, new CAC, new water pump, new AC compressor, new idle pulley, new belt, many new bolts, and many had to be drilled out. Lots of hours on dealing with rust. Oil changed, replaced fuel filter and new air cleaner unit. New turbo pipe to CAC. Some other stuff as well including replacing the four shocks with Koni FSD ones (José also struggled with the bolts due to rust). He cut out some shop labor hours to help me out, and the final bill was...

$7,975.25.

Not too bad, considering the rust and degree of difficulty involved. If I had done this at Freightliner, it would be $12,000 easy.

It was like driving a new RV. New shock absorbers in place, and not worrying about the temperature was stunning. Refreshing.

I took her up to Parley's Summit and onwards to Jordanelle State Park in Utah. The climb was brutal. I passed two semis chugging up hill. I maintained 40-45 mph speed, and the temps held, staying at 204-208 before briefly hitting 215 degrees and quickly climbing down. Ever since that, I've driven her to Winnemucca, Nevada—and I've left her on cruise control, and she shifted appropriately (never did before) and stayed cool at 204-206 while climbing hills—not as steep as I-80 to Parley's Summit but close. I even took her up—inadvertently—to Angel's Lake campground right off Wells, NV and the hill was insane and the road very twisty. I took it slow and easy and made it all way up. My reward was a stunning view.

Then there was a coolant leak. Ugh. She was leaking. A lot. Upon closer look, the bottom box with hose attached—the clamp was not as tight as it should have been. So, I tightened that up and she was all good.

Whew.

Still in awe of my "new" Discovery. She now has power. Pep. And keeps cool easily. I wish I had done this much sooner.

The final reply came once again from Bruce Plumb:

Marvin,

That is great news. And I am so glad there are Josés left in the diesel repair business! Make sure and publish his contact info so others can thank him and take advantage of his expertise when in the area.

BTW, after my new engine (CAT) last fall, I had to tighten coolant clamps twice. The last time was on our way home from Yuma with 4,000 miles into the new engine! Mrs. Plumb removed the stuff under the bed, I removed the cover and tightened the clamp. Pretty easy. Could have been worse. Life is not perfect.

I love *Chicago*. Although the pain I went through wasn't something I would recommend, the lessons, the heartbreaks, the pain and the joys of discovering new frontiers were well worth the lessons that the school of hard knocks and the journey provided us. I know that we will be fine, or better than just fine… in fact, our lives will be spectacular.

As of September 2021, my student loans were discharged and I was no longer in the ridiculous three-year monitoring period, locked in by the rules of the Total and Permanent Disability (TPD) student loan discharge program and I was not allowed to earn more than the federal poverty level for two people ($16,500 a year). I was also bound by Social Security Disability income (SSDI) limitations of $14,640 a year for 2019. And I was fearful of any financial success from publishing the book that would push me over these amounts, but not by enough to enable me to take care of student loan payments.

If I had taken a job during the three-year monitoring period, I would then be stuck with $500 to $600 monthly payments for the next thirty years, creating serious drag on any salary I could reasonably hope to earn. Going through this financial suffering seemed to be the only logical choice here before I was free to find a job that paid well.

The absurdity of TPD discharge rules keeping disabled people poor for three years is a real head-scratcher. We should be encouraging disabled people to succeed via every possible means, not keeping them down due to some warped sense of "fairness." This is especially true when considering this statement put out by Bureau of Labor Statistics: "In 2018, the employment-population ratio—the proportion of the population that is employed—was 19.1 percent among those with a disability, the U.S. Bureau of Labor Statistics reported today. In contrast, the employment-population ratio for those without a disability was 65.9 percent."

Oh, come on.

The disparity is jarring. We should move to eliminate earnings caps for disabled people receiving SSDI. Treat this as an experiment in universal basic income, and track what disabled people would do with SSDI and full-time jobs or starting their own businesses. Once they reach a certain income level, their SSDI could be taxed back in graduated levels, painlessly.

With that said, I once again must emphasize the importance of being grateful for what you have in life, even though we all know life can be incredibly unfair, harsh, and unforgiving. I continue to think of family, friends, and things I am grateful to have in my life. Together, we can continue to create a more just and equitable world where everyone has similar opportunities to make something out of themselves—a life worth living. A true definition of life, liberty, and pursuit of happiness for all people of all races, ethnicities, religions, disabilities, ages, orientations, genders, and more.

In October 2021, my life took another dramatic turn for the better when I took an online training over a weekend with Landmark Forum. The forum ran staggeringly long—thirteen and a half hours each day—on Friday, Saturday and Sunday. I registered for the forum upon advice from a fellow Deafhood facilitator, Jenny Gough, Ed.D., a Latinx Deaf woman who felt the training would unlock my potential and positively impact the further development of Deafhood courses.

I reluctantly did so, knowing fully well that I would be totally wiped out for a solid week after the forum. I had a lot of assumptions going into the training, thinking this might help me improve my effectiveness and efficiency, check off some of my goal lists.

I could not have been more wrong. Within the first few hours, my mind was blown. When Monday came after that weekend, I was flying. Literally full of energy. As if a one-ton boulder I had been carrying on my back for a long time had vanished into thin air.

I had been so tired these past few years. I struggled with a lack of energy and motivation. Yet I pressed forward, avoiding people as much as possible. I craved solitude. I avoided some of my loved ones, especially my mother, who I felt was being negative all the time because she would repeat herself over and over. I couldn't even stay at her place for more than a few hours. I just could not bear it. Even though my mother tried again and again to reconnect meaningfully with me and my children, we did not respond to that.

During the forum, I reconnected with my mother. We both cried. I was authentic with her. I told her how I felt these past few years with gentleness and generosity, and I apologized for freezing her out. For not being real with her, robbing her of any chance for growth, change, and transformation.

I now find myself contemplating so many ideas, including continuing my RV journey or even putting my beloved Chicago in storage and working for Gallaudet University in order to train the next generation of Black, Indigenous, People of Color, Deafdisabled, DeafBlind, LGBQTIA+ leaders for the Deaf and signing communities. I even began to entertain the idea of pursuing my old dream: becoming the superintendent of a Deaf school, although I am not sure if that is the best use of my time, energy, and talent.

After the forum, all I see now is possibilities.

The vision board I had hanging on my wall of my books making the New York Times and Amazon bestseller lists now took on a more meaningful slant for me, because rather than hoping a piece of paper and picture on wall would bring me satisfaction, I now realize I am the source of all that is possible.

According to Landmark (www.landmarkworldwide.com), a whopping ninety-four percent of people who enroll in the forum undergo radical transformation, and I believe that. I even asked my friend, Terri Waddell-Motter, a school psychologist working towards her doctorate in psychology, if she knew of any other approach that has brought this radical transformation in one single weekend throughout her long career. She shook her head, and said emphatically, "No. The forum blew my mind and changed my life for better. Nothing else I know of comes close."

As I bring this book to close, I reflect on what has transpired these past three and half years, I am in awe of all the growth and transformation that had taken place. To borrow from an old

MasterCard commercial: RV purchase price: $34,000. Repairs and setbacks: $80,000-plus. Growth and transformation? Priceless.

Priceless, indeed.

Ask yourself what you would have done if you were in my shoes from day one after the purchase of the Discovery. Imagine being so hungry for real and meaningful solitude, after years of being a single father to four kids, and in college for three and half years.

Would you sell the Discovery after the first repair bill? The second? Or the third? Would you disclose that the air filter was blown and that a lot of debris had gone through the turbo and the engine, leading to all the leaks?

At what point would you have said, "Enough!"?

Looking back, I find it easy to say I would have done a lot of things differently, beginning with hiring a certified RV inspector at a higher cost and maybe selling Chicago at a loss to minimize the damage to my credit—but hindsight is always 20/20. Selling Chicago at a loss would have set me back, and I possibly would have been unable to get another loan approval for a different Discovery in better condition.

At any rate, this journey has taught me a lot. I did not set out to learn the ways of being sustainable. Things like conserving water as much as possible to extend my boondocking stay. Installing and upgrading solar panels to reduce reliance on non-renewable resources. Trying to find ways to reduce my dependency on the diesel generator and liquid propane for refrigerating and heating. But I learned all these things.

Next on my to-do list: I want to upgrade the solar panels to a custom slide-out system where I could extend the 300-watt solar panels from underneath, possibly reaching 3,000 watts total. This, along with expanded LiFePo4 battery capacity, could easily power two far more energy-efficient mini-split air conditioning systems at any time.

These changes would help minimize the use of generators and liquid propane fuel, making the Chicago off-grid and renewable. I find that I use about six to twelve dollars in diesel fuel each day running the generator for several hours each day when in the rainy Pacific Northwest, but nearly none when I am in a sunny desert area. Additional solar panels would produce necessary energy for the entire RV and charge the batteries even when skies are gray.

I learned those things because I took a dive into the deep end of the pool. This journey also renewed my interest in building an ASL and signing ecovillage for Deaf and hearing peoples of all stripes. One day soon, perhaps.

I've also started to think about the possibility of buying several parcels of land out in the west to serve as elegant, secluded RV resorts rented out through HipCamp whenever I am elsewhere.

And, thanks to RVing with Andrew Steele on YouTube, I have begun to dream of a custom-built Newell Coach designed for completely off-grid boondocking. These coaches go for over two million dollars (I can dream, right?). But oh, man, they are so well designed and built. The tallest ceilings of any diesel motorcoach in the industry. A fully accessible coach with visual and tactile alarms everywhere, a generator-free RV power system that runs completely off solar, and gigantic lithium batteries.

I would name this coach *Nauvoo* in honor of our beloved cat who passed in September 2021 after nineteen and half years of companionship, patience, and unconditional love. I would love to keep both coaches for my family and friends' use. It is good to have goals and dreams, yet material possessions still take a back seat to my dream of making a difference by writing as many books as I need to in my lifetime. I am so incredibly grateful for the Discovery that has made all this possible. Yes, indeed, anything is truly possible.

ABOUT THE AUTHOR

Marvin, shown here signing "Deaf school", gives a short talk in Sacramento, California. September 2014. Photo credit: John Feagans.

M arvin T. Miller has taught over 1,500 hours of Deafhood classes, which began during his term as president of the Indiana Association of the Deaf in January 2011. A dynamic and powerful presenter, Marvin currently teaches Deafhood 101 and 201 classes as well as Deafhood and Allies workshops all over the country. He holds a bachelor's degree in Deaf studies, and a master's degree in sign language education from Gallaudet University.

A founding member of the Deafhood Foundation, Marvin's prior accomplishments include launching several monthly newspapers of, for, and by the Deaf and signing community, including *The Deaf Michigander* and *DeafNation*; he later helped launch *SIGNews* with Communication Services for the Deaf.

Marvin has also worked in media and video relay service and he has consulted with organizations on business development. He devotes time to thinking about how to create a better future for the Deaf and ASL community, particularly in light of existential threats to our world. This is more concerning given the high likelihood that Deaf and disabled people are typically lower on the priority list for essential, life-saving services in the face of disasters and upheavals. He considers such heavy topics necessary if we are to figure out how to live in balance with Earth and become better stewards of finite resources.

Marvin continues to live in his 2001 Fleetwood Discovery, traveling North America, and his four Deaf children visit him whenever possible. He is currently hard at work on his next novel, *Surdocide*, a work of fiction about the government's attempt to "cure" Deaf people. Visit Marvin's website at www.sirdeafhood.com.